THE ROAD TO JUBILEE

FROM MEDICAL MYSTERY TO MIRACLE
and the Joy In Between

Melissa Keaster

PHOENIX61

Printed in the United States of America

First printing, 2017

ISBN 978-0-9988493-2-4

Phoenix 61 Publications
Farmerville, Louisiana

www.phoenix61publications.com

To Superman, my rock;

To Micah and Sara,
my reasons to fight;

To Mom and Dad,
who weathered the storm with us;

To Debbie, Nona, and Honey,
who kept us from capsizing;

To Carolyne,
who went above and beyond every duty, oath,
and expectation to keep me alive;

To my "Weirdos,"
the Ruston prayer group,
who held me up with their faith when mine was tired;

To "Jonathan"—
I would do it again;

To Jesus—
every word, every breath, every moment
is yours.

Soli Deo gloria.

Some diseases are a death sentence,
some are a life sentence.
Which is easier to bear—
a small cell or the chair,
a cage or a casket?
No one knows and both are hard
on the sick one and the watchers.
Some of us die in here,
but I believe there is a key
for me, an early release,
or so I've been told
by the Prison Warden
who is kind and good and wise and hard.
The door will open
when the cell has done its work
and the bars have made me free,
or so I believe.
But all I see
are steel and concrete;
spare walls and a lonely lock
mock my faith.
I smell sky and pine.
Sun shafts through the window.
Voices chuckle and cluck,
a murmur through stone,
a reminder of what I'm missing,
a promise of what's to come.

—Melissa Keaster

5

1

Death by Exfoliation

The hum of the baby swing and whispers from the bathroom pipes reminded me I wasn't entirely alone. At best, I had twenty minutes before Sara would wake wailing again from hunger or pain I was powerless to relieve. What to do? My belly fluttered at the prospect of twenty minutes without a fussy baby in my arms or strapped to my chest. It was nothing short of mythical—a unicorn moment.

Late-morning sun streamed through the windows of the french doors, slicing through the dark in thin blades of light. Specks of dust danced and glittered in the rays within arm's reach of the baby's swing. Yet the house on Bear Creek Road always felt dark, no matter how many lights shone within. Some days, the darkness breathed—like a living, devouring entity dwelling inside our home.

Weeks had passed since I'd left these walls for anything more amusing than a trip to the pediatrician or the hospital. I couldn't remember the last time the sun had forced its way through the gray of January and sought me out. Closing my eyes, I stepped inside the largest beam, so that it centered on my chest, and absorbed its warmth.

"Shower or nap?" I muttered to myself. As a young mother of a toddler and a colicky infant battling acute illness, both were a luxury, the choice a constant conundrum. Everyone advised young mothers to nap when the baby napped, but after three days of my wearing the same pajamas, a shower smelled important too.

Indecision gnawed at my twenty minutes. If I didn't hurry, a bleak history would reprise—I would accomplish nothing and then grump about it for the rest of the day. The house was quiet. Fifteen minutes of unconsciousness might refresh me or end in a whopping headache and regret. The outcome was impossible to predict.

The plumbing gasped. Maybe it was a sign. "Shower then."

Sara sighed in her sleep, cuing me to move. The cool floor clicked beneath my postpartum weight with every step down the dim hall. As I rounded the corner to my bedroom, the pipe-whispers crescendoed and then quieted behind my closed door. I untied my robe and peeled off my shirt, stained and starched with dried breast milk and spit-up, and caught my reflection in the mirror. Despite the dark circles lining my eyes and pale skin that had forgotten the sun, my appearance wasn't half as haggard as I felt. Even my thick, wavy brown locks were behaving—probably because I hadn't washed them in a week. Looking at me, no one would guess how hard the last two months had been. Not that I had seen anyone who might guess.

A white plastic bottle drew my attention while I waited for the water to warm. Someone had given me a tube of facial mask for Christmas. Despite my good intentions, it had sat on the bathroom counter since the night I'd brought it home. Pampering was a nice thought, one I often ignored. I did well to clip my nails, with or without children.

I scanned the ingredients for known allergens until wisps of steam drifted out of the shower. The list appeared benign.

The sound of running water drowned out the murmurs of the plumbing. It wouldn't, however, mask Sara's screams if she woke. Peace had been absent in our home for so long that every sense stayed on high alert, ready for the next emergency. "Relax," I told myself and tried to obey.

Hot water kneaded my tense shoulders. I closed my eyes as the smells of sour milk and body odor washed down the drain. Suddenly, the flow ebbed. I stepped out of the stream and waited. Two seconds later, scalding-hot water surged with the restoration of pressure. My toes stung for a moment, and then the water returned to the desired temperature.

A noise, real or imagined, sounded from somewhere in the house. My heart skittered. Certain I'd heard a whimper, I turned down the water to listen. Nothing. I'd hear something before long though. Sara rarely napped, and when she woke, her screams would rise to a sanity-shattering decibel in less than ten seconds. With a resigned sigh, I turned off the water and reached for my towel.

The house was still relatively quiet when I was dry and dressed. I hastily dismissed the idea of lying down. At this point, any attempt to nap would likely turn me into a grouch, and I'd done so well that day. I squeezed a glob of viscous gray cream onto my palm and caked it on my face and neck. Somehow, wearing that mask made me feel the way I imagined people without children or real problems must feel. I glimpsed a life outside of sleepless nights, round-the-clock breathing treatments, hourly feedings, and chronic ear infections.

An unexpected tingle settled into my skin. My fingers brushed the mask, which had begun to dry and harden. The tingle likely meant the active ingredient was working on my postpartum blemishes, which could only be a good thing.

One day, my hormones would level out again. My afternoons and evenings wouldn't consist of long bouts of wailing I had little power to soothe. I might sleep again, which would surely slow the landslide of my own disintegrating health and growing list of allergies. But I didn't have time to worry about myself. I had to keep Sara out of the hospital.

The tingling sensation penetrated deeper, warming the skin underneath the mask. The instructions suggested leaving the mask on for a full ten minutes, so I decided to wait. I'd taught myself to think in terms of "ten more minutes" so thoroughly that I believed I could survive *anything* for ten minutes.

Heat mounted, and the tingle transformed into an itching flame. My skin began to stretch and swell. With shaking hands, I grasped the sink faucet, turned on the water, and scrubbed. The mask washed down the sink, but my skin continued to burn.

I doused my face and neck in cold water. *Ten more minutes, and I'll be fine.* The medicine cabinet held nothing useful except for a bottle of calming lotion. My skin cooled as I rubbed in the cream, but the burning resumed, intensifying. I read the facial mask ingredients again, pausing at the word "sulfur." I wondered. My parents were both allergic to antibiotics containing sulfa, and my list of allergens was more than twice as long as theirs. Could it be the same thing?

Antihistamines weren't difficult to find. Since my first series of anaphylactic reactions to various foods seven years ago, I'd stockpiled and stored them in my purse, in the kitchen, and in both bathrooms. Inhalers and epinephrine were also available should the need arise. Sometimes it did. I located the bottle of Benadryl capsules in the kitchen, swallowed two, and plopped into the recliner next to the baby swing. By some miracle, Sara still slept.

What an idiot—I should have napped.

I swallowed. My tongue felt wrong in my mouth—too big—and my chest felt tight. I attempted a deep breath and wheezed instead. Lovely. The last time this happened, I'd had to go to the emergency room. One visit had taught me to avoid the trip whenever possible. No one there would take me seriously as long as I could stand and speak. Besides, I had no one but a sick infant to haul my ailing butt to the hospital, and I refused to call an ambulance. So no Epi.

My aunt. A nurse for a number of years, she'd know whether another 50 mg of Benadryl would be safe to take. I dialed her number. She answered on the second ring, her greeting kind and poised for action. She'd received a lot of calls from me recently, most of which concerned Sara.

"Hey," I said, my throat tight and scratchy. "I think I'm having a reaction to a facial mask."

After a brief silence, she said, "A facial mask?"

I told her what had happened, what I'd taken, and how much.

"That's crazy, girl. I'm so sorry," she said. I could hear her frown. "But a hundred milligrams won't hurt you."

I swallowed two more capsules as she added, "You'll just be groggy for the rest of the day."

"I'll manage," I told her. Grogginess was an irritation; breathing was a necessity. "Thanks."

"You're welcome. I'm praying for you. Let me know if you need anything else."

"Will do," I said and hung up.

Drowsiness weighted my limbs. My thoughts drifted. Where was the joke in this reaction? There was one hidden somewhere. I simply had to find it.

Turning the strange and scary parts of life into laughter was an art form that I'd developed over time. I'd been honing my skills for years now, joking about "glutenous dooms" and drinking straight out of a Benadryl bottle. I knew how to find the humor in allergy shots gone wrong and waiters who didn't understand food allergies. But this wasn't funny. Yet. I was alone with my baby. She needed me.

"God," I rasped. It was good to hear my voice. If I could speak, I could breathe. "I need you."

The prayer fell from my lips often these days. The truth of it ached in my soul. I knew in the center of my being that my survival hinged on my connection to God. I was on some kind of journey. A dangerous one. If I didn't cling to my Creator with all my might, I wasn't going to make it.

Ten more minutes.

Breathing became easier work. I was almost asleep when Sara woke, hungry again.

* * *

Sara fussed and fidgeted with the breathing mask. "I was born with an iron will too, you know," I told her and planted a kiss on top of her downy head. "And I've been exercising it for twenty-seven years. You won't win." The vapor rising from the machine thinned. I flipped the switch and set the equipment aside.

I wondered how long we'd be doing this—surviving a case of colic from hell along with an endless succession of viruses and ear infections. Antibiotics could be helpful, but I didn't want my daughter living on them.

The door opened and shut. Rapid, light footsteps pattered through the galley kitchen. Micah rounded the corner wearing a grin and dashed toward his train table in the center of the living room. A heavier, longer stride followed.

Brandon cocked his head and studied me. His dark-brown eyes twinkled into mine. "Doo-doo brown," he described them, but I thought of them more like coffee or chocolate—soft, rich, and sweet. "Death by exfoliation," he said. "You know I'll never let you live this one down, right?"

I snorted, lifting my head from the back of the recliner to meet his lips with mine. I'd known there was a joke to be found somewhere. Trust him to discover it.

"You look okay," he said.

He was right. I'd inspected my face in the mirror on my last trip to the bathroom. Only a few short hours ago, my skin had turned pink and felt like I'd splashed it with acid. It looked almost normal now. The main evidence I'd been sick was the antihistamine-induced stupor that hung about my head like a cloud. "I feel like death."

"What's for dinner?" He pretended aloofness as he raced a train car alongside Micah's.

"Monster cookies. Or cereal." I was only half joking. It was nothing to be proud of, but those two foods had kept me alive the last couple of months.

The train noises paused. I reached my arm toward Micah, who'd piqued at the word "cookies."

"Come see me, Bubs."

He obeyed, a train car in each dimpled hand, and leaned his head into my shoulder before returning to the table.

"I'll figure something out," Brandon said in mock exasperation, his train car jumping a gap in the track.

It was nice to see him joking and enjoying his son. In some ways, I was glad life had gone sideways. After we'd moved into the house two years ago, I'd lost him to a yearlong bout of depression. He'd functioned. He'd gone to work, paid the bills, and spent time with Micah. We'd watched television together in the evenings, but he was gone. Hollow. Nothing excited him. No matter how hard I'd tried, I couldn't reach him—until I needed him. Lately, he'd helped me at home as much as he could, even sacrificing precious hunting days from time to time so that I could catch a nap.

"Why don't you go to bed for a bit?" he suggested.

Sara was content at the moment, but the hour of blood drew near.

"She'll be fine with me for a little while," he said, knowing my thoughts.

I heaved her up to him with a grunt. She'd eaten almost hourly since she was a week old, and it showed. At only six weeks, she filled out clothing meant for a six-month-old and would need the next size soon. Scrumptious rolls of fat accentuated her arms and thighs. With cherubic cheeks, plump pink lips, and her daddy's big brown eyes, she couldn't have been more beautiful had she tried—even without the strawberry-blond down of her head that glinted like copper in the lamplight.

Gosh, I loved her. If I wasn't so tired and scared, I might be able to feel it more. But these days, love was all action. It looked like pacing the hall, changing diapers, cleaning spit-up, and doing little more than offering my breasts upon demand. Bless her—she'd drunk my feelings dry.

Brandon extended his free arm and helped me drag myself out of the recliner. The air felt so heavy.

Giving Brandon another kiss, I made my way to bed. The pipes in the hall bathroom hissed and clicked as I passed. This house was so weird.

I closed the bedroom door and turned the box fan on high to drown out the noise that was sure to come. A shrill cry rose above the steady hum.

2

Docola

Somewhere far away, my baby cried for me. The cries grew louder. Footsteps. Wails. A door squeaked. Hysterics.

"Babe, I've done all I can. She's asking for you."

Mechanically, before I comprehended what I was doing, I lifted my shirt and took Sara from him. Tiny arms flailed in my face, searching. Her body was stiff, arched, and hot from crying. After a couple of poorly aimed smacks, she found what she was looking for and relaxed beside me. I rested in the dark to the sound of her grunts and swallows, wondering how long I could live like this—lonely yet always needed, on little sleep, and with these crazy allergies. If I met some unfortunate doom, how would my children describe my death? I snickered. "Death by exfoliation" was a good one. It would make a funny blog post too—if I found time to write one.

When Sara finished eating, I sat up and draped her over my shoulder, groaning. How could I feel so heavy and impossibly empty at the same time? Somehow, I managed to stand without falling or dropping the baby. It was risky to burp her without a cloth, so I grabbed one from her room on the way down the hall.

Sara began fussing again before I made it to the kitchen. I ate at the table with Brandon and Micah, Sara writhing in my arms, my mind dull and listless. Brandon and Micah spoke. I heard them but couldn't absorb the words. It was an effort to bring the fork from my plate to my mouth. A long night of short naps between breathing treatments and feedings lay ahead. If I didn't eat now, I'd need to later.

After dinner, I strapped the infant sling around my back and settled Sara inside. The straps cut into my shoulders and the weight pulled on my lower back, but a sling was the only way to get things done and not go mad from the screaming. Brandon left to bathe Micah, and I cleared the table and washed the dishes. The temptation to feel sorry for myself closed in, but I couldn't muster the energy to adequately indulge. Even sin required a certain level of commitment.

Sara rested her head against my chest as if she empathized with my exhaustion. She'd probably tired herself out with crying. Warm now, with gentle pressure against her aching belly, she relaxed. Maybe I could do the same.

Tired as I was, I softly sang the hymn that had become my lifeline over the past few weeks. "Be still my soul, the Lord is on your side…" I'd sung the words as I'd paced the halls with Sara screaming in my arms, during hourly feedings throughout long nights, while I administered 3:00 a.m. breathing treatments, and as I'd cleaned up vomited breast milk that had soaked my face, hair, clothes, and bedsheets. The song had become a part of me. Part of us both. As I leaned my soul on its promise, something tight inside of me relaxed and opened to the comfort I would need to face the night ahead.

Brandon appeared and caressed the top of Sara's head. "I'm gonna jump in the shower. I'll be out in five minutes, and then you can put the boy to bed."

"Sounds good." The moment I released Sara from the sling, she began to fuss and root for my breast. "No way. You can't be hungry again," I sang at her in my high-pitched mommy voice. But of course she was. Every hour, on the hour, all day long. When she was securely attached, I rested the back of my head on the couch and closed my eyes, deciding that sleep deprivation would likely kill me before an allergic reaction did.

"Mama?" Micah rounded the corner into the living room, dressed in footed pajamas, his auburn locks damp against his brow.

"Hey, Bubs." I lifted my head to smile in greeting, but he wasn't looking at me. He focused on something in front of him above his head. "Whatcha doin'?" I asked.

"Playin'." He pointed at something I couldn't see. "Playin' wiff my fwiend."

My stomach clenched like a fist prepared to strike. The reaction didn't make sense. Imaginary friends were a normal part of childhood development. *Chill, Mama.* This was normal. "What's your friend's name?" I asked, keeping my tone light and interested.

"Docola."

Cold swept through my bones as if I'd stepped outside into the January air. "Docola." I didn't like the way the name felt in my mouth. *Don't freak out. Be cool.* If Micah sensed my discomfort, the conversation was over. "And what does Docola...look like?"

"He a monstah."

My brow rose without permission, but Micah didn't notice. He continued to stare up at nothing. "He white and blue wiff bwown hair and big wings. He big and stwong. He

18

play wiff me and watch Mickey Mouse."

"Uh-huh." I took a deep, steadying breath. "And where is Docola now?"

Micah cocked his head. "On da ceiling."

I scowled in the direction of the unseen thing. Nothing. I didn't like the way this "nothing" felt, but Docola was probably just a phase. With any luck, the invisible monster would soon be forgotten. Another question came to mind. "Have you played with Docola before tonight?"

"Yeah," he said, nodding. "We play. We play twains."

His focus shifted toward his train table, and Docola was no longer important. Maybe Micah would forget him, and Docola would become nothing more than a one-haunt wonder.

House shoes scuffled down the hall as Sara finished her meal. Brandon scooped Micah into his arms and planted scruffy kisses on soft, round cheeks until Micah was breathless with laughter. "Mama, I think this boy is ready for bed."

"Perfect timing. I am too. It would be great if you could take care of Sara's breathing treatment while I'm with him." He and I would discuss Docola later.

Micah galloped out of the room and down the hall. He waited for me to sit in the glider Brandon had bought for me not long before Micah was born. It gave a sigh as I sat and a familiar squeak as I pulled Micah into my arms. Micah leaned his head against my chest. He'd always been thick and rather solid for a small guy. Now, at almost three years old, he filled my lap and was all I could carry.

"You know that Mama loves you, right?" I asked him as the chair settled into a rocking squeak-creak rhythm.

"Mmm-hmm." His little head nodded.

My heart squeezed, aching for him to know the force of my affection. Too often, he told me what he knew I wanted to hear. Before Sara, it had been just the two of us with little to frustrate our connection. For the past few weeks, Sara had taken up much of my time, patience, and lap. Exhausted and afraid, I often snapped and said stupid words I didn't mean in a tone that shocked us both. Images of his stunned pale face and wide eyes after these episodes flashed through my mind, stinging my whole being. I apologized frequently, but I couldn't call back the words or heal the bruises they inflicted. The possibility that he might think I loved Sara more than him stabbed me through the chest.

What if Docola was Micah's answer to his loneliness? What if Docola was my fault? I squeezed my eyes shut and willed my mind to change course.

I reached for the collection of illustrated nursery rhymes and put it back. My head ached with exhaustion at the mere thought of reading. The day had been hard, and another night of round-the-clock breathing treatments felt impossible.

My mind searched for a song. "Jesus Loves Me" was all I could recall. I sang it over him and prayed for peaceful, uninterrupted sleep. Nightmares and anxiety attacks tormented him often these days, sometimes in response to Sara's midnight wails, sometimes unexplained. Fear, illusory yet always present, plagued us all.

Brandon and I had joked early on that the house was haunted. From the beginning, the pipes had muttered creepy, unintelligible nothings even when no water was running. The water pressure and temperature mysteriously fluctuated, scalding the willies out of whichever unfortunate soul happened to be in the shower. Toys came to life and sounded off without being turned on. Lights flickered. Switches flipped. Items disappeared.

For months, I'd scolded myself for being scatterbrained. I had griped at Brandon for moving my things and had once interrogated Micah about the disappearance of a necklace. It wasn't until guests—including my mother, who had seemingly misplaced her keys only to find them somewhere she was certain she hadn't put them—commented on the phenomenon that I'd dropped all accusations and had decided we lived in a very strange house indeed. I usually made light of the house's idiosyncrasies, but tonight I didn't feel like laughing.

When Micah stilled and grew heavy in my arms, I kissed his soft brow and carried him to bed. "Good night, Bubs. Mama loves you, and God loves you even more." If I died during the night, those would be the two truths I wanted rooted deep in his soul.

I collected Sara from Brandon. "We're off to bed."

Brandon's shoulders sagged. "Do you think it will always be like this?"

"Sometimes I wonder. I love you."

"Good night."

"Night," I said. In a zombie-like stupor, I carried Sara to her room. Our room. After two weeks of no more than three hours of interrupted sleep per night, I had capitulated against all professional advice, and we'd begun co-sleeping in the double bed in her nursery. Brandon, who held the lives of hundreds of pharmacy patients in his hands, continued to sleep in the master bedroom. We were all doing our best to survive.

Sara and I were settled and ready for sleep when my fingers detected moisture on her backside. My jaw clamped shut on the angry word that came to mind. Standing once more, I unsnapped the buttons of Sara's cloth diaper. My compassion stirred at the sight of her rash. Poor baby. I layered on the diaper rash cream, which wasn't doing its only job, and tried not to cry.

The midnight alarm woke me. The haze in my mind cleared enough for me to remember where I was. I didn't recall getting back into bed after the diaper change. My heart sped. Sara lay next to me, open mouthed, her chest softly rising and falling. Thank God.

I'd almost drifted back to sleep when I remembered Sara needed another breathing treatment. That was why the alarm had sounded. The reason I had to get up—now—and two more times after that. Going back to sleep wasn't an option. I had to keep my baby out of the hospital, and no one was going to do it for me.

With a groan, I rolled out of bed, cradling Sara in my arms. It would be over in ten minutes.

3

Silver Sulfadiazine

Sweat gathered on my brow and between my shoulders. I strapped the kids into their car seats, huffing clouds of steam into the midwinter air. We were running late, as we always seemed to be, and I was questioning why people went anywhere before their children were old enough to ride in booster seats. I talked myself through my mental checklist. "Bellies are full. Backsides—clean and dry. For the moment. The diaper bag—packed..." Diapers, wipes, nursing cover, pacifiers, burp cloths, Micah's cup, extra clothes, checkbook, board books. I hoped I was prepared. This excursion would take an ill-favored turn if I had to stop by Walmart.

I set the Mickey Mouse Clubhouse playlist to shuffle on my iPod and drove half an hour to the pediatrician's office. I'd been administering breathing treatments every three hours for a week. I prayed our nurse practitioner would have mercy and tell me that Sara had improved. The alternative was the hospital—at least for one of us—and no one wanted that. The blisters Sara had developed on her backside from all the antibiotic-induced diarrhea concerned me as well. Though I applied cream with each diaper change, they looked worse.

The receptionists greeted me with sympathetic smiles as we walked in the door. As a family, we had really leveled up.

These ladies rarely smiled at anyone. Between well checks, a drawn-out cold, ear infections, and RSV, we'd visited at least once a week. They probably had our faces, names, and insurance policy numbers memorized by now.

Penny, my favorite nurse, called out Sara's name. Penny reached for Sara with experienced hands and placed her on the infant scale. "Well, she hasn't lost any weight," she said, her tone chipper.

God bless her—she wanted to be sure I left with at least one piece of good news. "I can't imagine how she would manage that," I said. "She's still eating every hour."

Penny frowned. "My word. Every hour? Even at night?"

Lord, help. Why did I always answer honestly? "Maybe every two hours at night."

"How do you get anything done?"

"I don't." Somehow, I managed to keep everyone fed and alive, and we never ran out of clean laundry. I showered, not daily but often enough. Trips to the restroom were family affairs. If one went, we all went, but Micah and I rarely wet ourselves. Other than tending to everyone's basic needs, I *didn't* get anything done. I thought about bragging that I had left the house wearing a bra—a small miracle as far as I was concerned—but I wasn't sure my relationship with Penny had arrived at that degree of disclosure.

"You may want to try to stretch those feedings out. She should be fine eating every three hours now," Penny said. It was hard to tell whether sympathy or disapproval tightened her smile. "Michelle will be with you shortly." The door clicked shut.

While I was sure Penny was right, it would be interesting to see someone try to stretch out Sara's feedings. I lacked the gall. Her shrill protests could curdle blood into butter.

Sara was attached to my breast, and Micah was listening to me read our collection of Curious George board books for a second time when the nurse practitioner came in. Despite the fact that it was January and the height of flu season, she smiled brightly and fussed over how much Micah had grown since last week.

Her observant blue eyes searched mine before they ever reached Sara. Every visit, she checked on me. Maybe the dark circles concerned her, or the fact that I was losing weight faster than Sara was gaining. "How are you doing, Mama?" she asked lightly, waiting for Sara to finish.

I loved how everyone used an eggshell tone with me, as though I might crack at any moment. Chances were good that they knew something I didn't, but in true Scarlett O'Hara fashion, I would worry about that tomorrow.

I smiled, hoping to communicate that my sanity was still intact. "Surviving, and hoping for some good news. No pressure or anything."

"We'll see what we can do," she said.

Sara let go, content. Michelle pulled out her stethoscope and began the exam. I studied her facial expressions and body language as she checked Sara's breathing, her ears, the rash.

Her brow smoothed, and her mouth relaxed into a hopeful smile. "She's better."

I released a long breath I didn't know I'd been holding.

"She still needs breathing treatments twice a day for another four weeks, but she's going to be fine. Good job, Mama."

Tears stung my eyes. I could have kissed her.

"Finish out the antibiotic for the ear. I'll prescribe a cream for the rash. Poor baby's burned down there pretty good, bless her heart."

Gratitude swept over me like a spring breeze. "Praise God," I said low on my breath.

No more 3:00 a.m. alarms. I felt a disproportional giddiness over the news. I'd still wake to feed and change her. The colic hadn't gone away. But as the weight of this one task lifted, light and warmth flooded my insides, and I didn't feel quite so tired anymore.

"Maybe we'll see less of you now," Michelle said as she held the door open for me.

"No offense, but that'd be nice," I said.

"Sticker?" Micah asked.

"Of course!" Michelle said. She bent down to eye level and tapped him on the nose. "You are the *best*-behaved two-year-old boy I know."

Her words weren't flattery. He probably was. Micah collected his sticker. I paid for what I hoped would be the last "sick" visit of the season, and we left.

Sara fussed as I strapped her back into her seat. She quieted when I turned on "Hot Dog," her favorite song from Mickey Mouse Clubhouse. I took a deep breath and let the tears go. My baby wasn't going to the hospital. She was better. We were going to get her well, and life would be normal again.

My cell phone rang. "Hi, babe," I said through a veil of mucous and tears. "She's better. We get to do only two treatments a day. She's going to be okay."

After a pause, Brandon said, "That's great."

He didn't sound as excited as I thought he should be. "What's up?"

"You know that diaper rash cream Michelle prescribed?"

Wow, they sent that fax fast. "Yeah?"

"It's good stuff—great stuff. Exactly what you want for

burns."

"Uh-huh," I said, impatient for him to get to the point.

"There's just one problem."

"I assumed so."

"It has sulfa in it."

Of course it did.

"I can go ahead and fill it," he said, "but you will want to wear gloves when you apply it."

"Good idea. Thank you." He always thought of a solution, even if he presented the problem with a dramatic flair.

"That's why they call me 'Superman,'" he said.

By "they," he meant me. The guy never stopped anticipating problems and making provisions for them. "Probably so."

"Want me to pick up some disposable diapers?" he asked.

"No thanks. I got it," I told him.

Arriving home was almost as chaotic as leaving. Sara screamed. Micah covered his ears and cried. Once they were both inside, I discovered Sara had a mess in her diaper. Micah needed to pee but didn't want to be alone. Everyone was hungry. I felt weak and shaky. I tried to remember what I had eaten for breakfast but couldn't remember eating at all. In fact, I didn't remember feeding anyone, except for Sara.

"Micah, did Mama forget to feed you breakfast?" I braced myself for the answer.

He stared at me blankly while he absorbed my question. "I ate wiff Daddy."

Knowing he had been fed comforted me a little, but it was unlike me to forget a meal.

After feeding both children and myself, I pulled out the

washable cloth diaper liners I had bought several months ago per the suggestion of a friend who had cloth diapered her toddler almost exclusively. The inexpensive liners would protect our pricey cloth diapers from being ruined by the cream.

Brandon handed me the cream and a box of disposable gloves when he arrived home that evening. "May the force be with you."

"Thanks." I patted Sara's back and said to her, "Let's get rid of that rash."

Over the next couple of days, we settled into a new routine free of nighttime breathing treatments. With the weight of keeping Sara out of the hospital lifted, colic, antibiotics, and twice-daily breathing treatments didn't seem like such a big deal. The added sleep made mornings cozy and enjoyable again. I even pulled my Bible back out.

One morning, Sara stared wide eyed at the lights that blinked to the music of her swing. Micah sang along, providing a soundtrack for his trains as he pushed them around the table. The washing machine stopped. I looked up from the passage I was memorizing in Ephesians.

"Time to hang the diapers!" I sang at Sara. She grinned in reply.

Keeping watch over Sara from the utility room, I hung all the diaper shells to dry and reached for the tangle of liners and inserts. As I tossed them into the dryer, an odd feeling swept over me. I ignored it. A hot feeling filled my throat. When I swallowed, the tissue felt tight. Sara began to fuss.

My mind raced. This felt like an allergic reaction, but how? It shouldn't be possible. What had I eaten?

A flash of heat rose from beneath my skin, and my chest tightened as though it meant to prove me wrong. Maybe I had snapped under the pressure of everything. Maybe I had gone a little crazy and turned into a hypochondriac. This couldn't be real.

A dry cough barked from my throat. I could breathe, but something that should be easy and natural felt like work. Dizzy, I stumbled into the kitchen in search of the Benadryl. I managed to swallow two capsules. An inhaler sat beside the bottle. I took two slow drags and then returned to the recliner.

"Micah," I said. "Mommy doesn't feel good. Will you turn the music back on for Sara, please?"

"Okay, Mama," he said happily.

Lord Jesus, please keep me conscious for these kids.

I sent a text to Brandon, asking him not to worry but alerting him that I was having another severe reaction. My second within a week. Usually, they didn't come so close together.

A few minutes later, the tightness in my chest had gone, and I was able to think more clearly. I hadn't eaten anything to cause such a reaction. I remembered my response to the facial mask, the fact the diaper rash cream contained sulfa. In theory, creams didn't completely rinse away from cloth in the wash. That's why I'd placed liners between the treated area and the diaper shell. Still, most of it should have washed away. My body shouldn't have reacted so quickly or so violently. Allergies didn't work like this. This was unnatural.

A thought struck me hard and true. This could take me out. I could actually die. In my twenties. I may not have long with these precious babies I'd birthed and was just getting to know.

The whispers of the pipes said nothing to console me.

4

Concerning Death and Dreams

Sweet sighs and sucking sounds underscored the quiet dark of a brand-new morning. Through the window, I watched the black sky brighten to gray, revealing the silhouettes of naked oaks. Contentment warmed my insides despite the cool air seeping in from outside. Peace often evaded me in the evening hours when everyone was tired and hungry and Sara was screaming. I couldn't seem to break through the chaos to reach it. But here in the dark, feeding my baby from my own body, peace was easy to access.

Sara stopped eating and grew still. "Now, now," I said. "You know you need to burp."

As I lifted her toward my shoulder, a full feeding's worth of regurgitated milk arced out of her mouth and into my face. She spewed again, over my shoulder this time, dousing the wall and my pillow. I sat still a moment, eyes closed, braced for another round of ammunition. Spit-up dripped from my face and hair. The sheets were soaked.

Hesitant, I opened one eye. "Your ear is infected again, isn't it?"

Sara looked at me with her large, watery eyes—a portrait of innocence—but I knew. Projectile vomit was Sara's tell. I hated it—for us both. Another round of antibiotics would do nothing good for her diaper rash, which was just now beginning to heal. Brandon and I had decided that the best diaper burn remedy in the world wasn't worth my life, and improvement came slowly when we used regular diaper rash creams.

"You be quiet while I change the sheets," I told her and lowered her into her crib. I peeled away my white cotton T-shirt, gathered the soiled sheets around it, and walked cold and naked through the house to the washing machine. If it wasn't one thing, it was another.

Sara fussed while I dressed and replaced the sheets. Praying she hadn't woken Brandon or Micah, I took her back to bed. Worry nipped at the edges of my mind as I drifted back to sleep.

* * *

I was running from something, something that hunted me. Whenever I reached a place to rest, it found me, and I had to run again. Two men who looked like characters from a television show I watched accompanied me. They led me to a safe house. One opened the door for me and let me pass. "It won't find us here," he said.

The house held minimal furniture. Large open windows invited in fresh air and light that reflected off the bare white walls. Gauzy curtains shifted in the breeze. The home was spare but lovely. I made my way into the bedroom and changed into white flowing pants and a white button-down sleeveless shirt. Red satin slip-ons completed the outfit. There was no need for a mirror. I knew I looked beautiful.

Dressed, I opened the bedroom door. The men—brothers—spoke in hushed tones in the living room. A glint of gold caught my eye. A pair of small gold earrings lay on the dresser. As I slid them into my earlobes, movement outside the front window drew my attention. Someone passed by. Another figure followed and froze, as did I.

The creature stood tall and upright, as if human, but had the head and upper body of a bison. He wore black clothing and radiated all things terrible. My eyes locked on to where his eyes would've been, except that he had none. The creature snorted, seeming to stare back. He smelled me. Abandoning the frame of the window, he strode toward the front door. He was coming for me.

The brothers yelled. One braced the door. A glance at the other told me there was no way out. The Beast kicked the door off its hinges and flung the first brother aside. Slow footsteps thundered forward, rattling the rafters above. The other brother stepped between the Beast and me. The man's face suddenly looked like Brandon's. "Don't be afraid," he said. "I'll protect you."

I knew he would try; I just didn't believe he *could*.

With a swing of his arm, the Beast threw Brandon aside. I backed away, stumbled, and fell over my iron feet. The massive creature towered over me, dragging in the scent of my fear on a long breath. Something like a laugh rumbled in its chest. He slowed his approach, his feet stepping lighter this time, savoring the intimidation. I was trapped and helpless—we both knew it. His massive fist raised above his head. It wouldn't take much to kill me. I closed my eyes and prepared for the end.

The blow didn't fall.

A frustrated grunt caused me to open my eyes. A blue force field pulsated in the air between us, blocking the Beast's deadly blows. The Beast paused, peering at me over the otherworldly light of the force field. The cruel look sank into my heart like an arrow with its unspoken message: "You escaped this time, but I'll be back. When I find you again, you're dead." The Beast turned and left without another glance in my direction.

When he was out of sight, I began stuffing my belongings into a duffel bag. I didn't wait for my protectors. I couldn't. That thing would come for me again. I fled out the door into an open field with no particular destination in mind. A cloud of mist shrouded the horizon. Tall shadows hid within it. Was that a tree line in the distance?

Grass swished behind me at the steady pace of a slow run. The brother who had tried to bar the door ran past me and stood in my path. "Stay," he said, out of breath. "We'll find a way to protect you."

"No one can protect me," I said and brushed past him into the unknown.

"What about the force field?"

Something tugged at my breast, and the scene blanked. Sara wriggled in my arms. The bright, patterned curtains of the nursery came into focus. Sunlight streamed between them into the room. As the frenzied rhythm of my heart slowed, a shadow settled into my chest.

Death was coming, and it wouldn't give up until it got me.

* * *

It had only been a dream, but I couldn't shake the sense of being hunted. It followed me to the car, on the drive into town, to the pediatrician's office. It didn't leave when the nurse practitioner said Sara's ear was bad again or when the nurse administered the antibiotic shot. Sara's screams reminded me of everything at stake. How many days did I have with my little ones before the end came?

We arrived home, and I settled Micah down for a nap. "I love you, Bubs," I said, the words hot in my throat. He was so young. Would he remember when he was a man that his mama had loved him?

After feeding Sara, I pulled out my journal and asked the Lord to reveal the meaning of the dream. The pen danced across the page, leaving a trail of revelation.

My beauty in the dream represented my stage of life—years of vitality and the height of my attractiveness. The safe house served as a hideaway, but the blank walls spoke of emptiness. It wasn't a real home. My two protectors represented Benadryl and epinephrine, oddly enough. The one who had morphed into Brandon was epinephrine. These protectors could not rescue me from the Beast, who was Death. Death pursued me. It wouldn't stop. It would smell me out again and again.

But the blue force field had stood in its way, covering me like a shield. The blue shield was God. God turned death away because he and no one else decided the number of my days. A promise came to mind—"He knows the days of the upright, and their inheritance shall be forever" (Psalm 37:18). A tear splattered onto the black gel ink, which streaked down the page.

God could turn away death or send it at his will. Every force on earth answered to him. I wasn't privy to my life's determined length. Each breath was a gift from the Lord, and I was likelier to die in a car crash than from anaphylaxis. My life wouldn't be shorter simply because I was weaker than the next person. I was weak because God wanted to show me that his grace was sufficient for me. His strength would be made perfect in my weakness. I could boast gladly in my infirmities, knowing that Christ's power would rest on me.

Of course, there remained the possibility that I could die, and soon. From a reaction. From an accident. And what of it? Should I only accept good from God and not adversity? I was called according to his purpose, which meant all things worked together for my good. If God's word was true, it must also be true that for me, a Christian, death was good. Death was gain, even.

To live meant fruitful labor for me—as a wife, a mother, and who knew what else. I didn't want to leave my man. We'd just gotten started. Motherhood was all I'd hoped for since my own childhood. I wanted to raise my kids and witness their lives. No matter how long I lived, I could never drink in enough of their sweet faces.

But if death came, I could depart and behold the face of my beloved Savior. Not even motherhood could compete with that.

And who knew how hard life would get? If suffering reached a particular intensity, I might greet death with a welcome mat and a hot cup of coffee. I'd been plagued by severe, life-threatening allergies for seven years now. For seven years, I had declined. Everything I'd tried to stop the progression—medical doctors, medications, healthy eating, supplements, and allergy shots—had only worsened my condition. I was unraveling without the first clue of how to stop it.

But God knew, and he had promised to be a shield for me. Even unto death.

The fear and agony silenced as I absorbed the truth of who God was. The dream hadn't been given to haunt me. It was a good gift, a reminder of who was really in control of my destiny. Let the Beast find me. I wouldn't be leaving this earth until it was time. I could live my life not in fear or in hiding, but full, free, and out in the open until the blue force fields rescued me no more. I would wake from death's final blow in the arms of my Savior. That wouldn't be a bad ending.

I set the pen down and dragged in a deep breath—a gift from a Father who loved to give good gifts. I looked into my baby girl's cherubic face and whispered, "Thank you. Thank you."

For the first time in memory, I glanced around my untidy living room and felt no pressure to clean it. Nothing could separate me from God's love—not bad dreams, deadly beasts, ear infections, colic, anaphylaxis, or even a dirty house. My purpose was to know Christ and point others to his beauty.

Whatever happened, I had to lean hard into God. My medicines might not be able to save me, but God could. If I died, I died. But hell—I just might live.

5

The Fast

Michelle peered into Sara's ear canal, a frown creasing her brow. "Hmm," she said and looked into the other before fastening her gaze to mine. "Do you want the good news or the bad news first?"

"It doesn't matter," I said. February had been a long month of breathing treatments, antibiotics, and isolation. Winter-gray skies had found their way inside me and had frozen everything in apathy. The only thing I'd found to thaw the frost was worship—reading and memorizing scripture, prayer, gratitude, hymns—but the cold heaviness always returned.

"Right," Michelle said. "Well, her lungs sound great. You don't need to do any more breathing treatments."

I blinked at her, stunned. "Don't joke."

She smiled. "You're done, Mama. Good job."

An obnoxiously weighty "but" hung in the air.

"But," she said.

"There it is," I said aloud.

Michelle nodded. "Her ear is infected again."

"Of course it is."

"And she's got glue ear."

"What does that mean?" I asked.

"It means she probably needs tubes," Michelle said and pursed her lips.

"Like...surgery?" My stomach felt more acidic than usual.

"Probably. Eventually. But not yet. Sara's the youngest patient I've seen who needs it. I don't like them going in before six months."

"So what now?" I asked, something unpleasant stirring inside me. I'd thought no news could move me in my current state, but I hadn't counted on Sara needing surgery at four months old, even if it was a minor procedure.

"Today, another shot, another round of antibiotics, and a referral to an ear, nose, and throat specialist," she said. "It will take some time to get in, which is good. Maybe we can hold off for a few months."

Heat rose from my neck and gathered in my face. I willed myself not to cry. If I started, I'd never stop. I heard myself say "okay," but nothing about this was okay to me. Another shot? More antibiotics? *Surgery?* Hadn't she been through enough with colic, RSV, and chronic ear infections?

In the car, I breathed around the sobs threatening to surface and called my mom.

A gentle voice answered. "This is Melanie Chapman."

The tightly wound knot in my belly relaxed. "Hey. I'm glad I caught you."

"I'm between classes," she said. "I have a few minutes before my next one." An assistant professor at a professional school for medical laboratory scientists, Mom had long, full days. I could see her in my mind, white-blond hair, tender blue eyes, and a dimple in her right cheek, seated at her desk with stacks of books and papers and two computer monitors going, ignoring it all for my sake.

I reported what Michelle had said. "I don't know what to do. I thought she would be okay when she got over RSV."

"We can pray," Mom said.

"We've been praying."

If I sounded as short as I feared, Mom chose not to be offended. "True. You know, some mountains don't move without fasting."

The scripture she referenced flashed through my mind. I'd read it only yesterday. It had pierced me like an arrow. Rather than receiving the blow, I'd plucked it out and discarded the idea as ridiculous.

I was a nursing mother, sleep deprived and losing weight at a frightening speed. My temper was already abominably short, my body too frail. "I don't know how I would do that."

"Well, I was thinking more of myself than you when I said it," Mom said.

It would be easy to let her do it for me. Easy, but wrong. It was my baby at stake. "I think God might be showing me that I should too. I read Mark 9 yesterday and felt it then. I just get so hungry."

"Mmm...if I were you, I wouldn't fast all day. Maybe you and I could skip lunch this week and pray instead. For healing, and maybe for a delay on surgery. I don't like all these antibiotics her little body is getting."

"Me neither. I think I'm going to try that garlic oil idea this time instead." A friend had suggested a home remedy that I was finally desperate enough to try. The antibiotics obviously weren't working, and they upset her digestive system, which upset everyone.

"It's worth a shot." Mom paused. "It's time for me to teach my next class, but I'll start fasting with you today if you want. I didn't have time to pack a lunch anyway."

"Might as well." Then there would be less time to dread it. My stomach gurgled, protesting my decision. "I love you," I said. Hanging up, I couldn't believe what I'd just agreed to.

All things are possible to the one who believes.

The promise shot through me, as had the suggestion to fast.

"Okay. I believe," I said aloud. "Help my unbelief."

* * *

A bristly kiss woke me. "Hey, babe."

I groaned. The sleep that filled the absence of breathing treatments failed to satiate me. I never felt rested, not even after the morning nap I took in the brief window after Brandon woke and before he went to work each morning. My head pounded. Acid roiled in my empty stomach. I felt like microwaved death.

"I gotta head to work. Micah's eaten. He's watching Mickey Mouse." He laid Sara beside me. She was ready to eat.

I lifted my face to his but couldn't yet bear to open my eyes. "Love you, too."

He left the room, and Sara suckled until she was satisfied. I slid my glasses onto my face and sat up to burp her. The stack of books upon my bedside table came into focus. The "mount of good intentions," I called it. The book on the bottom drew my attention. I tried to slide it out with one hand, but the cover stuck to the wood. After placing Sara on her tummy, I set aside the mount to uncover the one—a book about spiritual warfare.

Having grown up in a Baptist church, I'd never given much thought to spiritual warfare. I believed in a devil and a hell and knew demons existed, but mostly, I'd ignored all that because I could. A friend had given me the book over a year ago when I'd been sick for weeks on end with allergic reactions, stomach viruses, and the flu. I hadn't been interested then, but as I pressed into this fast, I sensed that I was stepping onto an invisible battlefield against an unknown enemy.

Things weren't right. They hadn't been for some time. "For we do not wrestle against flesh and blood," I recited from my memory work in Ephesians and scooped Sara into my arms. Whatever she suffered from was likely beyond flesh and blood. I left the bedroom, the book in hand.

Several pages in, the author referenced the story of the demonized boy in Mark 9. When the disciples couldn't free him from his torment, Jesus said, "This kind can come out by nothing but prayer and fasting." The word was clear confirmation. With Sara's illness, I was dealing with something I didn't understand, and fasting was the only weapon that would defeat it.

What would it be like for Sara to be well? That one change could begin a domino effect that would benefit the entire household.

The first missed lunch hadn't been too bad. The second wasn't as easy. Hunger gnawed at my insides, but I prayed through it, remembering that Sara was worth the discomfort. Jesus had suffered far worse for me.

That night, however, Sara writhed and cried out in pain until I gave up hope of any sleep at all and sat up with her in the recliner. How would I survive the next day? Little sleep and skipped meals did not make cheerful breastfeeding mothers.

A promise from Isaiah 40 came to mind. "He gives power to the weak, and to those who have no might He increases strength. Even the youths shall faint and be weary, and the young men shall utterly fall, but those who wait on the Lord shall renew their strength; they shall mount up with wings like eagles, they shall run and not be weary, they shall walk and not faint."

An early breakfast helped, but by the afternoon, I felt jittery, queasy, and light headed. Every time I stood with Sara in my arms, my vision blacked out for a few seconds. When I talked to Mom, she suggested I drink a glass of goat milk. It sustained me until dinner.

Another rough night preceded the fourth day, and my prayers took on a more urgent tone. "Lord, help me to wait upon you," I prayed. "Help me to trust you and do good. Remind me to dwell with you, feasting on your faithfulness. You are my delight. Satisfy me with your presence, with yourself. I roll this impossible situation onto your infinitely broad shoulders. I fully believe you will act on our behalf. Help me to rest in you as I wait."

Mysteriously, in the pain and weakness, Jesus was becoming more to me, more than he'd ever been. All the while, ugly things hidden in the corners and closets of my heart came out of hiding as I grew hungrier. I resented Brandon for all the sleep he was getting. I mean, how dare he when I was barely getting three or four hours haphazardly strung together? Powerful waves of anxiety crashed over me every time Sara cried. Whenever Micah asked a question or needed something, I snapped. My Lord, he'd just turned three last month. He had burning questions. He needed things. What was wrong with me?

A voice in my head accused me. *And you call yourself a Christian? What a weakling you are. You think you need lunch to behave properly.*

By that afternoon, I felt beaten. Whatever I was fighting was winning. Thoroughly. I called Brandon and asked him to bring home dinner.

The smell of cumin and sautéed onions accompanied him into the kitchen. He'd brought chips, salsa, and fajitas—one of my favorite meals. I almost cried. Small town Tex-Mex had never tasted so good.

"Feel better?" Brandon asked after I'd taken a few bites.

I closed my eyes and nodded.

"How many more days?" he asked.

"Just tomorrow," I said. "Thank God." I was surprised I'd lasted four days and couldn't imagine going beyond five. *Lord, let it be worth it.*

* * *

Sara squirmed and fussed. I dropped back to sleep. A cry. I lifted my shirt. She attached, and I drifted. A series of short angry coughs was followed by a wail.

I woke and wished I hadn't. An iron vise wrapped around my head, weighing it down. Everything itched—my scalp, back, arms, knees, and chest. The itching penetrated beneath the skin. No amount of scratching brought relief. My stomach burned and roiled as I sat up. It hurt to swallow.

I staggered to the kitchen to retrieve Sara's anti-gas medicine and glared at the clock. 3:00 a.m. I was sick to death of seeing that hour. I administered the drops and collapsed back into bed.

A few hours later, the itching was worse. My throat was tight and scratchy, and a wheezy feeling had settled in my chest. Hunger and exhaustion revealed my worst parts. I wanted so badly to be good, but all that was coming out was anxiety and frustration. Was that all I had inside of me?

I yelled at the kids, swore at inanimate objects. Every noise, every need fretted the string holding me together. How much more could I withstand before it snapped?

Sara started screaming early that afternoon. I bounced her in the sling as I cooked, stopping periodically to pacify her with a breast. Clammy sweat beaded on my skin, and my mind raced toward an inevitable collision.

The door opened and Brandon stepped through, wrung out from a long day on his feet talking to customers, nurses, and insurance companies. He'd never looked so beautiful to me.

"Wow," he said. "I heard her from outside. Is everything all right?"

I burst into tears. "No."

Brandon wrapped me in an embrace and disappeared to change his clothes. A tear dripped off my chin into the pot of soup I stirred. Just as I began to crumble, he returned. "Give her to me," he said. Taking her, he smiled into her face. "You and I are going for a ride."

Sara's cries faded. A moment later, the four-wheeler growled to life.

I turned away from the pot and slid down to the cold tile floor, silent tears streaming down my cheeks. *How much longer, Lord?* Maybe I could handle her sickness if she didn't have colic too. Or maybe I could handle both if only I could sleep for more than three hours at a time. And what of my own symptoms? What of Micah?

The clack of wooden train meeting wooden tracks provoked a sob. I was so consumed with the smallest one. How was Micah doing? Did anyone know? How long had it been since we'd had some one-on-one time or planned an adventure? Did he know I loved him too?

I pushed myself off the floor and rounded the corner of the galley kitchen to watch him play. He smiled up at me, his eyes bright in greeting. "Hey, Mama."

I knelt beside him, teasing his hair with my fingers. "Whatcha doing?"

"Playin' twains." And he went on happily until dinner was ready, flashing little smiles my way now and again.

To keep Sara from howling through dinner, I lifted my shirt and let her eat too. Afterward, though, she fussed through cleaning the kitchen, Micah's bath time, my shower time, and television time with Brandon. No amount of bouncing, walking, or dancing soothed her. Anxiety clawed at my neck and chest. I felt like a splintered pane of glass. Is this what it was to have a nervous breakdown?

Pushed to my limit, I took her to bed. We'd been asleep less than an hour when she woke screaming and writhing in pain. To keep her from waking the house, I walked her around the bedroom, bouncing her with my breast in her mouth.

I could run away. I could pack a bag and drive until I found a clean hotel. I could sleep. I saw the whole thing like a movie in my mind.

Sara's cry rose to a higher frequency, and something inside me snapped. I couldn't take the screaming any more. I'd been listening to it every day, hours on end, for months. It had to stop. I had to make it stop. For one wild inconceivable moment, I was tempted to toss my baby out of the window, like one of those crazy parents I'd heard about in the news.

I plopped her onto the bed, swearing at her and myself, and walked away. Shame and self-loathing slammed into me with the force of a freight train. At the end of the hall, I turned and ran back to her. I fell to my knees at the bedside, sobbing. "I'm sorry. I'm sorry," I gasped. I cradled her against my chest. "I'm sorry. I'm so sorry, baby. I didn't mean it. Please forgive me. I'm so sorry."

I was a monster. "I'm sorry," I said again, and a gentle cloud of peace settled around us both. Sara's screams hushed, and the storm inside me stilled. We lay back down.

The fast was over, I realized as Sara's breaths deepened. I wasn't sure Sara had improved, but it had exposed me for what I was—a fraud who could pretend as long as she ate well enough. And for that, I was thankful. Now I knew with whom I was dealing and how much I needed to change. Docola and creepy pipes weren't the most significant problems in the house. The biggest problem was me.

The fast had also exposed God for who he was. He didn't strike me down with lightning in my sin and weakness. I had expected him to withdraw, but he hadn't. He'd drawn nearer. As I reached that realization, he gave us both the gift of sleep.

* * *

On Monday morning, I drove back to the pediatrician's office with both Micah and Sara in tow. I smiled at every sympathetic face who greeted me. I knew a secret. It breathed in my soul. I'd only come to hear the words.

Michelle peered into both ear canals and looked up at me with wide blue eyes and a slack mouth. "They're clear," she said, shrugging. "I don't know how, but they're clear. We can wait on surgery." She laughed a short, disbelieving laugh.

I closed my eyes and smiled, thankful but not at all surprised. I'd expected these words—not because I was so great at fasting, but because of the secret.

God was good, and he loved my daughter.

Something in me relaxed. Sara wasn't destined for the hospital or a surgeon's table. Colic would kill me before it killed her. Everyone would be okay.

It was finally okay to not be okay.

And I wasn't okay.

6

Allergic to Life

I did my best to ignore the dwindling list of safe foods to eat and the reactions, which grew stronger and more frequent every week, but that wasn't always possible. My eyes burned and watered constantly and ached in the sunlight. Sometimes I couldn't see straight. A permanent switch from contacts to glasses helped.

Sharp pains pierced my skull from behind my eyes, and my stomach seethed, its acid searing my throat. One positive side effect of all this misery was that my maternity jeans sagged. Before Sara turned six months old, everything but my milk-engorged breasts fit into my regular wardrobe.

"It's like someone pulled a plug and you deflated," one friend commented.

I felt thin on the inside, too, though the case of colic from hell seemed to be winding down.

In early May, the kids and I were enjoying one of the last cool spring afternoons before they were swallowed up by Louisiana summer heat. Suddenly, my blood sugar plunged. My head spun until I felt sick. These episodes had been happening since childhood. If I didn't eat quickly, I would faint.

Micah wasn't ready to abandon the sunshine and fresh air, so I bribed him with a bowl of applesauce and a promise that we would return. When he was settled, I searched the pantry and located my stash of large coconut macaroons on the bottom shelf. Perfect. Containing only coconut, egg whites, and honey, these macaroons had been a dependable snack since my allergies had first emerged. They always raised my blood sugar quickly and held it steady for several hours.

My hands shook as I tore into a package. I bit off a mouthful and chewed, waiting for relief and the jitters to stop. Instead, I felt something else.

The reaction came on fast. Fire flashed through me, trapped beneath my skin, which began to crawl. My throat swelled, chest tightened.

I sidestepped to the medicine cabinet and reached for the antihistamines. I popped two capsules, tossing them back with a gulp of water before my throat swelled any more.

Not coconut.

I didn't eat it that often, but I'd already lost so much. Would I eventually starve to death because I'd become allergic to everything?

I sent a text message to Brandon to let him know what had happened. He arrived home several hours later and dropped onto the couch, staring at the EpiPen I'd set on the table next to me. Silver tips in his dark hair glinted in the lamplight. His jaw clenched and unclenched. He knew I looked at him, but he wouldn't look back.

"You know how we used to joke that I was allergic to life?" I attempted a smile.

He didn't answer.

"We were mere children then." I hoped for a smile, even if I won it cheaply.

He leaned his head back. "It's not funny."

"No," I agreed. "But it is ironic."

He didn't respond. He wasn't the fan of irony that I was.

Pain. Pain in my joints. In every joint. How many joints did I have? Too many. Pain and heat. Heat everywhere. Pain, heat, and itching. Good Lord—the itching.

Sunlight streamed through the curtains into my eyes, a cruel greeting. Beside me, Sara's tiny chest rose and fell. She began to search for me in her sleep. I pushed myself up with a groan. My stomach churned, and I tasted bile at the back of my tongue, felt the burn of acid in my throat.

The muscles in my neck and shoulders ached, tender to the lightest touch. Nerves fired as I turned my head one way and another. I stood and gasped, surprised by the discomfort in my ankles and feet. Behind me, Sara cooed. I turned to meet her large brown eyes. They blinked back at me, oblivious to the relentless storm of sickness and pain she and I were caught up in.

We understood one another, she and I. My pain didn't keep her from needing me any more than her pain kept her from eating. We must endure. Gritting my teeth, I scooped her up and changed her diaper. Fire jolted through my arms, wrists, and fingers as I tried to smile into Sara's face. It wouldn't do to frown.

I followed the voice of Mickey Mouse into the living room, where Brandon met me. "I was on my way to wake you up," he said. "I have to go." His eyes appraised me. "You don't look good."

"I hurt everywhere, but I'll make it." What choice did I have?

He glanced at his watch. "Breakfast is in the microwave. Micah and I ate."

I nodded rather than telling him that food didn't appeal to me.

"Take it easy today, huh?" He kissed my brow, which hurt.

"Television all day it is," I replied. In truth, most days consisted of "television all day." Today, I just wouldn't feel guilty about it.

Mom arrived that afternoon, looking like a sharply dressed angel.

Micah ran to her. "Gwamma!"

Tossing her radiant hair over her shoulder, she greeted him with a wide smile and tender squeeze. She chatted with him about trains and Mickey Mouse before reaching for Sara, who surprised us both by reaching back. She usually clung to me like a barnacle.

"You look nice," I said.

"Thanks. It's new," she said, referring to her trim pants suit. I wasn't the only one who'd lost weight quickly. Considering what she'd been through with my sister Hannah and her abusive ex-husband, my twin nieces, and upheavals at church and work, I assumed she'd stressed it away. If Sara wasn't such a chunk, I might assume the same about myself.

"So," she continued. "How are you doing today?"

"It hurts. To sit here. To hold a fork. To wipe butts."

She rewarded my attempt at deadpan with a snicker.

I explained the pain was in the joints and the tissues. "I'm obviously dealing with something autoimmune."

Mom pursed her lips and nodded. "Obviously. But it's not rheumatoid arthritis. Or if it is, it isn't only that."

For a moment, I wondered if my thoughts had left a written record somewhere and Mom had found it. "That's good. I'd hate to go through what Aunt Suzonne has with rheumatoid."

Sara coughed, impatient with sitting still. Mom stood and bounced her. "It's probably not lupus, but it's not just allergies either. People with IgE-mediated allergies don't react to antigens within seconds of contact."

"It's nice to have a medical laboratory scientist as your mom when your body is acting weird." Not to mention a brilliant one with years of clinical experience.

Her brow creased in the center. "I don't know how much help I'll be. I don't know that I've heard of anything like this. It may be that your body just needs a break."

"You tell me how to manage that, and I'll try it," I said.

Mom's dimple appeared. "The semester is almost over. When it is, I'm going to make your rest one of my top priorities. You'll feel better when you get some sleep."

"Sleep won't fix this."

"Not right away, but in time."

Time. How that word had haunted me since my dream. An invisible clock hung over my head. *Tick, tick, tick.* How many ticks did I have left before I ran out?

* * *

On Monday, Brandon took the morning off from work to drive me to see Dr. Humble, a local immunologist. A new one. The one from years past had continued to administer allergy shots week after week though I suffered systemic reactions, which required various combinations of antihistamines, steroids, and epinephrine to bring them under control. I'd heard good things about this younger doctor, and I was hopeful he might help me.

I carried with me a handwritten list of my symptoms—food sensitivity; itching; hives; hot flashes; shortness of breath; tightness in my chest; fatigue; head fog; dry, itchy eyes; numbness, tingling, and pain in my hands; swelling; aches, burning, and nerve pain throughout my body; heart palpitations.

We didn't wait long. The nurse keyed in my symptoms and list of medications without comment. She asked if I was willing to be tested for allergies that day.

"Not today. I was tested several years ago. Allergy shots didn't help me then, and I'm afraid they'd be dangerous today," I said.

Her smile disappeared. "I'm not sure how Dr. Humble can help you if you aren't willing to be tested, but maybe he will have some ideas."

She led Brandon and me to a patient room. Brandon stroked my hand.

"Did the nurse seem angry to you?" I asked.

"I don't know, babe," he said.

I let the suspicion drop.

Dr. Humble entered the room and plopped onto the rolling stool we'd left empty for him. "Hello," he said without offering a smile. I reminded myself that good doctors sometimes forgot the importance of bedside manner, and a good doctor was preferable to a friendly one any day.

He glanced over the notes the nurse had written and asked when the problems began. The question didn't have a simple answer. As I gave an overview of the last seven years, he crossed his arms and bounced his leg. His eyes darted around the room, looking everywhere but at me. When I came to the most recent part of my story, he interrupted me. "The allergies and inflammation issues aren't related."

"Oh," was all I could say. They felt awfully related to me.

"We can run some blood tests if you won't do the skin test. It's more expensive—a couple of hundred dollars per test. It might show us something, but I doubt it."

Heat flashed through me, which had nothing to do with my allergies, and my head began to tingle irritably. What exactly did he mean by "but I doubt it"?

"You should avoid the foods you aren't tolerating," he continued. "Continue to carry your Benadryl, EpiPens, and inhaler at all times. I really don't think I can do anything for you except maybe refer you to a rheumatologist."

Was he serious? The air felt heavy. No one moved. They all waited for me to speak, but I had frozen.

Brandon cleared his throat. "What about the blood tests? How do those work?"

Dr. Humble addressed Brandon. "Well, we take a sample of blood and test its response to individual IgE-mediated allergens. We can test the foods that give your wife the most trouble, but I don't recommend we test her entire list. It would be very costly to you."

"Let's do that," Brandon said. "And you can go ahead and refer her to a rheumatologist."

I nodded, more to end the appointment than in agreement. I needed to get out of there before the hot feeling in my throat turned into tears. I didn't want to cry in front of this jerk-face who refused to look at me or help me and made me feel like I was imagining my symptoms.

We reached the car, and my anger fizzled into giant hot tears. Whatever I had expected to come from this appointment, what had happened wasn't it. Brandon stroked my hand again. "It's going to be all right," he said. "You'll see."

We listened to my favorite singer-songwriter, Sara Groves, sing about "a peace that flows deeper than pain" and a God who withholds no good thing, and I tried to come to terms with the fact that whatever was wrong with me was beyond the scope of a quick fix and that some doctors wouldn't even believe me when I told them what was going on.

7

Dehydration

The sun hadn't risen when the distant cries of my infant daughter reached me. A moment passed before I realized where I was. I hadn't slept a night in my own bed with Brandon for so long that it felt strange to wake up in it. My hands had fallen numb and useless while I'd slept. I wiggled my fingers and rolled out of bed gingerly. The bones in my feet and hips cracked loudly as I made my way around the foot of the bed and out of the room. The hum of the box fan covered the sound, and Brandon didn't stir.

I followed Sara's cries down the hall and found her in my mom's arms. Mom had arrived during the night to care for Sara so that I could get some uninterrupted rest. Sara stopped crying and reached for me the moment she saw me, eager for breakfast. Mom handed her to me, her dimple showing and eyes swollen from limited success with sleep—a look I'd worn since before Sara was born.

Mom disappeared into the kitchen. The scent of coffee wafted into the living room, perking my mind and soothing my soul. Sara finished eating, and Mom brought two steaming mugs. Coffee was a favorite, but I'd been drinking less as the burning in my stomach had increased. Still, a few sips couldn't hurt.

The pleasant heat and rich flavor comforted me, though I could tell within one sip that I would regret drinking very much.

Setting the mug on Micah's train table, I told Mom about the appointment with the immunologist. "He wasn't rude, exactly, but he wasn't very compassionate either. I couldn't tell whether he was frustrated that I didn't want allergy shots or he thought I was crazy." Hot moisture pricked my eyes. "Maybe I am."

"You're not crazy," Mom said, and I tried to believe her. She cocked her head in thought. "What you need is a plan."

Mom reminded me of her experience several years ago. After taking a series of herbal cleanses to improve her health, she had suffered from chronic diarrhea and severe rashes on her back. She'd had no idea what was wrong at the time, but by divine guidance, she'd stumbled upon a nutritional program that began with a fast. During the fast, she'd taken a liquid amino acids supplement. "Maybe something similar could help."

I flashed her an overly bright grin. "Oh goody. More fasting."

She chuckled. "It should help." After a pause, she continued, "I know you planned to nurse Sara for at least a year, but—"

"I know." A pang pierced my chest. I'd loved nursing both of my babies, regardless of the intense sleep deprivation. Fortunately, my milk supply was beyond what even Sara could handle, so the freezer was stocked full of packets of frozen breast milk. It should last through the summer, which would give me time to find a homemade formula recipe that she could tolerate.

Mom and I researched hypoallergenic amino acid supplements and found one with some promise before she left for work. I paid for overnight shipping so that I could start right away. I wasn't getting any better by waiting, and my bland diet of hot rice meal and goat milk wouldn't sustain me forever.

The supplement arrived on the welcome mat the next afternoon. Contemplating a few of my previous experiences, I decided to wait for Brandon to come home before trying it. The pain of hunger mounted throughout the evening. I hoped the drink would help.

* * *

Brandon peered into the canister, flared his nostrils, and grunted. He scooped a heap of powder, mixed it into a glass of water, and handed me a murky, brownish-green glass of hurl. "Bottoms up, babe."

Suspicious, I sniffed. It smelled like vitamins and grass. "You first."

He grimaced and shook his head. "Not a chance."

"Here goes nothing." I lifted the glass and gulped. The sandy texture activated my gag reflex. "Lord." I shuddered. "That's bad."

Brandon grinned. "You've had worse."

Had I? I'd ingested some gosh-awful concoctions in the name of health, but I couldn't recall anything this offensive.

"You can do it, babe." He slapped me on the back.

I glared at him. "You're enjoying this too much."

"Listen. These last few months have been hell. You owe me a laugh."

A deep breath steadied my quivering stomach. I chugged, gagging and choking, until it was half-gone.

"Look on the bright side," he said. "You only have to do this three times a day for the next week."

My ears prickled. A wave of heat flashed from my neck through my body. My tongue itched and grew in my mouth. "Crap."

Brandon's humor vanished. "What?"

I shook my head. Nothing in the list of ingredients should cause a reaction. It had to be all in my head, just as the immunologist had implied. Reactions had become so common that I expected them now. That was all. I choked down what was left in the glass, down to the gloppy, grainy dregs, and waited. The reaction leveled out.

Micah and Brandon ate their dinner at the table. Sara ate hers in the recliner. Though I wasn't eating much, she seemed content to receive nourishment from me. In fact, she'd rejected every bottle offered to her. Synthetic nipples, it seemed, offended her.

Over the next hour, the queasy heat in my belly developed into a sensation of impending doom. I jumped up, handed Sara to Brandon, and fled the room, afraid I was about to relive the teff flour incident of the year before, during which I'd puked seventeen times in a span of three hours.

Usually, I prayed to vomit quickly and be done. This time, I was afraid to. My heaves were so violent, and I was already hurting. I lay on the cold tile of the bathroom, waiting. The pipes burbled. The house creaked. The invisible clock hanging over my head ticked.

Footsteps approached. A gentle hand rubbed my back. "Are you okay?"

"No."

When the worst of the nausea passed, Brandon helped me to bed. "I called Mom," he said. "She thinks a water fast is your best option at this point. I agree."

"For how long?" I asked.

"As long as you can tolerate it."

Unspoken words weighed the atmosphere.

"And?" I prodded.

"I'm washing the rest of the bottles and thawing a few packs of milk."

"Okay."

"I'm sorry," he said. The apology covered more than the end of nursing.

I sighed. "Yeah. Me too."

* * *

My mother-in-law, Debbie, bounced Sara in the crook of her arm and paced the room. Sweat gleamed on her brow, and her mouth wore an unprecedented frown. Brandon had asked her to come. "If anyone can get Sara to take a bottle, you can," he'd told her. He wasn't wrong. Debbie was fantastic with children. She'd been caring for them her whole life. Sara was just a hard case. Nearly twelve hours had passed since her last meal, but girlfriend was *not* having that bottle.

"You need to eat, baby girl," she sang as she stuffed the nipple into Sara's mouth again. Sara arched her back and screamed until her face turned red and milk squirted from my breasts. Micah stared at the television set, covering his ears with his hands. "Yah, yah, yah," he belted over his sister's cries.

Poor guy. Poor baby. Poor Debbie.

It was hard to watch. Debbie shot me a helpless look. "Do you think she might do better if I go to another room?" she asked.

I hadn't thought of that. "I'll go. I need to pump off some of this pressure anyway."

Behind the closed door of the nursery, I relaxed as much as I could, seated in a hard, knobby rocking chair listening to my infant cry for me while I was hooked up to a machine designed to suction the milk she craved from my breasts. "Jesus, what are we going to do?"

Trust me.

The words pierced me. Since my reaction to the coconut macaroon, fear had dictated most of my decisions. I had sought for answers, a solution, a miracle. I had concocted a plan for self-healing when all I needed to do was trust him.

I heard the invitation in the command. I saw Jesus's extended hand. What I needed—more than answers, more than healing, more than food—was God. He was the Bread of Life, and he alone would be my sustenance for the next few days. I remembered the blue shield from my dream. Even now, I was covered. God was worthy of my trust.

My breasts had stopped giving milk. I turned off the machine and pulled away the shields to inspect the bottles. There was nothing unusual about the amount of liquid, but the color was wrong. My milk had always been white, opaque at the bottom and thick as cream at the top. Today, it was a translucent sea green.

Sara had calmed when I returned to the living room to show Debbie. The bottle, still full, sat on the hearth. Debbie gaped at the small bottles in my hands. "I've never seen anything like that. I'm glad you stopped nursing."

"If I'd needed convincing, this would have done it," I said. "I think I'm going to take a picture to show Brandon and then pour it out. Sara doesn't need this."

Debbie followed me into the kitchen, wiping her face with a burp cloth. "I'm so sorry, but she wouldn't take the bottle, and I have to go to work now."

I took Sara from her. "Thank you so much for trying. I appreciate you." My mother-in-law was an amazing woman but too quick to take blame.

To Sara, I said, "What am I going to do with you? You're too young to fast."

Trust me.

Okay. I took a deep breath. "Don't worry, Grammy. When she's hungry enough, she'll take it."

Six hours later, Sara took her first bottle.

My water fast hadn't gone so well. With each sip, my nausea increased until I wondered if I'd become allergic to water too. I sipped as often as I could tolerate it, worried it wouldn't be enough.

* * *

I was dying. That was the only viable explanation. I was dying, or someone had beaten me up and set me on fire.

With a groan, I rolled over and reached for my water bottle on the bedside table. The sip soothed my throat but roiled my stomach. My mouth reeked of bile. I tried to sit but soon gave up.

Time passed in waves of nausea and lapses in consciousness. The bedroom door squeaked. "Babe?"

I blinked, trying to focus on Brandon's face. "I can't move," I said.

"What do you mean you can't?"

"I just…can't."

Brandon lifted my hand to the ray of light seeping between the blackout curtains. "You need to drink," he said. "Can't." I shook my head. "It makes me sick."

He opened the bottle and held it to my lips. "One drink, and I'll leave you alone for now."

I obeyed and wished I hadn't. Curling into the fetal position, I fought the urge to vomit.

"I'm calling Mom," he said and left. Which "Mom" he meant, I didn't know.

The nausea and pain demanded my attention in turns. As one receded, the other intensified. I dozed miserably, never fully unaware. In another room, Mickey Mouse spoke in an obnoxious singsong voice, and a baby cried.

Sara. Sara took bottles now. She didn't need me anymore. If I died where I lay, she would survive.

I startled awake to find Mom standing over me. She brushed the hair away from my face. "How do you feel?" she asked.

"Like death," I rasped.

"She needs fluids," Mom said.

"That's what I thought," Brandon said, his voice strained. "I'll call Stacy."

Stacy, my doctor. Stacy, my friend.

Brandon continued. "I bet we can get them at the clinic and bypass the emergency room."

Mom perched on the bed and rested a hand on my thigh. Peace blanketed the room. I drifted.

"Come on." Brandon's voice was abrupt and too loud. "Let's go." He turned my legs toward him and placed shoes on my feet. His strong arms lifted me and half-carried me down the hall. He tucked me into the car, which was already running, and fastened my seat belt. A half-hour car ride had never been so miserable nor so long.

Brandon helped me out of the car, up the curb, and inside the clinic. Sue, my favorite nurse with the kind, glowing face, met us at the door. I attempted a smile in greeting. "Right this way," she said and led us to a large room with a medical bed at the center. She and another nurse exchanged tense whispers. I caught the phrase "dry arm," which sounded ominous. Despite years of allergy shots, steroid shots, multiple epinephrine injections, pregnancy, and childbirth, I still hated needles.

Do not be anxious.

How, God? How, with all this pain and a looming vein hunt?

The needle punctured my skin.

Pray. Give thanks.

The needle wiggled, searching.

I gritted my teeth. Brandon. Mom. Sara took the bottle. My blue shield.

The wiggling stopped. "There we go," Sue said.

Unclenching my jaw, I thanked God for good nurses. Brandon moved a chair near my head and settled into it. "You know, there are better ways to ask for help..."

A grin tugged at my mouth. "Better, maybe, but not more effective."

The door opened, and Stacy wheeled herself into the room, her expression bright and warm. Brandon moved to hug her. "How are you?"

"I think I'm having a better day than either of you," she said with a wink. It might have been true, but the wheelchair was a good indication that her health wasn't quite what she would have liked it to be today either. On her good days, she used a cane.

She'd been diagnosed with multiple sclerosis years ago, though no one would guess it based on her love for God or outlook on life. Standing firm in her faith through it all, Stacy possessed an otherworldly beauty that seemed to belong only to those who'd discovered joy in God in the dark, secret places many people knew nothing about.

Her brown eyes peered warmly into mine. "I take it things haven't improved since the last time I saw you."

"Not yet." When I'd come in a few days ago to run labs, I hadn't been this bad. "Any idea what I'm dealing with?"

She rested empty palms on her knees. "I got nothing. We'll have to wait for the lab results, but even then it may take time to figure it out. Whatever this is, it isn't straightforward."

My phone dinged. Brandon pulled it out of my purse to read the text. "It's Amy. She's going to bring a roasted pork loin out to the house—I may or may not have posted on Facebook to let people know what was happening," he said, pretending nonchalance. "You also have one from Hanna. She and Jeff talked to a couple of elders for you. She says they can come out to pray for you tonight, if you would like."

After reading the command of James 5:14 a few days ago, I'd asked my friend to arrange for prayer with the elders of our church. The timing—of both the meal and the offer of prayer—couldn't have been better. Tears sprang to my eyes. "Yes, please."

"Actually," Stacy said, "that's what I came in to do. May I?"

I smiled. "Of course."

Stacy took my free hand and asked God for everything

for which my heart ached—peace, comfort, answers, and for God to be glorified, even in my mess.

"Yes," I whispered in agreement. "Yes."

I'd loved Jesus since I was a little girl. As a young teen, I'd prayed my life would help people to see Jesus for who he really is—beautiful, glorious, and good beyond comprehension. Ten years ago, I'd gone off course, jaded by betrayal, bitterness, anger, and habitual sin I'd hidden in shame, sin that I'd failed to beat over and over and over again no matter how hard I'd tried. Motherhood had been a reawakening for me, but I was still so far from where I wanted to be, from what I knew was possible. It occurred to me that maybe this trial was necessary somehow—a path to find my way back home.

"Thank you," I said.

"You're welcome," Stacy replied, her face shining. "You know, it's times like these I'm thankful for what I've suffered. I can pass along the comfort God has given me." These were no recited platitudes. She meant every word.

She paused before wheeling out the door. "Where you are is holy ground. You're going to experience God in ways you can't outside of suffering. He isn't going to waste any of it."

"Thank you," Brandon and I said together. I wiped the tear clinging to the tip of my nose.

She smiled once more and left to attend her other patients.

Two liters of saline later, I felt much better. Much of my pain receded, as did some of the nausea. Stacy released me, sending me home with strict orders to drink and a prescription for anti-nausea medication.

* * *

Brandon called in the troops.

When we arrived home, Debbie had cleaned house and was entertaining children, zipping about like a shooting star, providing a happy light on an otherwise dismal day. Mom returned that afternoon with Dad. Nona and Papaw, my grandparents, came too, bringing food. They prayed for me and whispered among themselves.

Except for Papaw. Papaw didn't know how to whisper. "I bet she ain't slept since October. You'll see. Some rest will fix her right up." He said it with such conviction that I half-believed I would be well when I woke up the next morning.

My parents took Sara home with them, bottles and bags of breast milk in tow, and Nona and Papaw took Micah, who grinned widely when he was told of the arrangement.

Hanna and Jeff Peshoff, our friends and small group leaders from the Bridge Community Church, where we attended, arrived along with two elders we recognized but had never officially met. They came bearing Amy's roasted pork loin and two other meals cooked by ladies in the church.

Gratitude welled up in my heart and leaked from my eyes. Those meals meant one less thing for Brandon to worry about while I was so sick.

Our visitors talked with us, encouraged us, and finally prayed for us. I'd never before been anointed with oil and worried it might be an awkward experience. My fears were soon laid to rest. It was precious.

When everyone had gone, Brandon helped me into the truck and drove me into town, away from all the tall pines surrounding our home, where I could view the fullest, closest moon that would smile on our corner of the world for another seventeen years.

Brandon pulled into a grocery store parking lot and turned off the engine. A heavy pause hung in the air before he said, "When they prayed for me, I felt this weight lift off. It was physical. I don't know what it was, but I didn't even know it was there. And then I had this peace come over me."

"That's awesome, babe," I said and kissed his hand. Desiring a better look, I opened the door and leaned out. The sight displaced misery with awe.

The moon was just as it should be, everything it was made to be. Fully facing the sun, it shone gloriously in the dark sky.

"Here I am," my spirit said to God. "It's all yours—my pain, my mess, my weakness, my sin."

My prayer scared me. Light could be painful, blinding at times. It changed things, and change was hard. But in my truest parts, the parts not hidden by shame and false humility, I knew that I was meant to be more than a faint sliver in the sky. My cold, dark places cried out for the Light. I needed it, and the world needed to see a true reflection of that Light, no matter how pocked and marred I might be.

I didn't understand what was happening. I couldn't yet tell if God meant to slay me or save me. I suspected that he intended both. Like the moon, I could follow the path laid before me. I could turn myself fully to God's radiant face and take in all of him I could handle.

I could be still. I'd always wondered what "being still" was all about. As I settled into my new orbit, I would find out.

8

Of Milk and Meat

Sara sat up tall and leaned forward in her Bumbo seat. Her eyes, bright and expectant, followed the spoon from my plate to my mouth. I offered her a bite of my boiled zucchini and rice meal mash. She attacked the spoon like a bird snatching prey in flight. Her tongue thrust out and in, working the food around her mouth. Bouncing in her seat, she asked for another bite with loud, rapid breaths.

I laughed as I extended the spoon again. Giving up nursing had been a loss, but our little meals together soothed my grief and made eating baby food a happier affair.

My stomach protested, but I ate. Eating made hydration easier, and the anti-nausea medicine helped. So far, I tolerated boiled zucchini, rice meal, and goat milk. Experiments involving olive oil and avocado had not gone well, so Sara was officially eating more solid foods than me.

Even still, I grew stronger each day on the little food I took in. Within a few days, I'd gone from being bedridden to managing a little laundry, washing a few dishes, and caring for the kids, which gave me purpose and a sense of accomplishment, but I wanted to do more. My health affected more people than just myself. No one complained, but I'd become a burden others had to help carry.

I extracted Sara from the Bumbo. We peered out the windows of the french doors into the backyard, where Nona and Micah played. Nona ran. Micah chased. His grin spread from ear to ear. Laughter bubbled from his belly and exploded on the air as he dashed about in a zigzag.

Nona slowed, pretending to tire. Micah tagged her and ran in the opposite direction. Nona feigned astonishment and yelled, "I'm going to get you!"

A pang shot through my chest. I should have been the one chasing my son. It was like watching a movie I should have starred in.

Micah ran in a large circle, pumping his little arms as fast as they could go. Nona, a recent cancer survivor and in her seventies no less, followed with ease. At age twenty-eight, I ached all over. My bones smoldered. My joints creaked and popped in protest at any new or sudden movement. It had been a long time since I'd run like they ran. Even our leisurely morning walks up and down the driveway while I pushed Sara in the stroller sometimes tired me.

My eyes blurred and stung. As I wiped away the moisture, God's presence hovered on the air. *Look again.*

The scene hadn't changed. Micah and Nona continued to run on the other side of the glass. Their laughter and shouts rang clear. But now I saw the gift.

It was a wonder that the difficulty and losses of the past few months couldn't touch that moment for my son. How good and right it was that he ran outside, fully alive, like all little children should. I thanked God for a grandmother willing and healthy enough, even after a battle with breast cancer, to play chase with him. The movie that played out in front of me wasn't the one I had imagined when I had dreamed of motherhood, but it wasn't less beautiful.

Today, I would focus on what I *could* do. I could hold, cuddle, kiss, and love my children. I could read to them and listen to them babble. I could wash and fold their clothes and be content and grateful. The Lord would meet the rest of our needs as he saw fit.

* * *

When I woke on the Sunday morning of Sara's dedication at church, each individual joint and muscle competed for my exclusive attention. A hot invisible stake drove into each shoulder at the base of my neck. My skin was sensitive to touch, and the all-consuming heaviness of fatigue weighed down my aching limbs. Leaning over my morning serving of rice cereal, I said to Brandon, "I don't think we're going to make it to the dedication service this morning. It hurts to hold my spoon. I don't see how I can dress myself and the kids, much less fix my hair."

Brandon swallowed a bite of pancake and continued to work his jaw. "What if I dress the kids and fix your hair?"

I blinked at him.

He grinned, stabbing another bite of pancake with his fork. "What? You don't think I can do it?"

"I didn't say that."

"Challenge accepted." He cocked his head and studied my hair. "I'm not going to try to flat iron it, but with a little water and gel, I think I can make it look nice. What do you say?"

"Okay," I said, rising slowly from the chair. "If you are up for all of that, I'll go."

"Okay," he answered.

I dragged to the bedroom and selected my nicest dress. In a few hours, I would stand in front of hundreds of people. Even if I felt dreadful, I refused to look it. Removing my pajamas proved no easy task. My breath caught with each movement, and I had to prop myself against the bed to maintain my balance. Naked and exhausted, I trembled and almost gave up.

Brandon walked in and whistled low.

I rolled my eyes. "Nothing about this situation is sexy."

"Depends on your point of view. Mine's pretty good." He glanced from the dress laid out on the bed to my naked form. "Need some help?"

"Please."

He helped me into the dress and kept me from falling. "That wasn't nearly as fun as taking it off."

"How can you flirt at a time like this? I'm a mess."

"My mess," he said and grazed my lips with his. "I'll grab a chair and start on your hair."

Humiliated that I couldn't fix my own hair, I plopped into the chair.

"I'll do a good job. I promise," he said.

"That's not what bothers me."

"Oh, hush, and let me help you." Brandon parted my hair with the comb. "Is this right?"

"Yes," I answered, surprised.

A companionable quiet settled in the small bathroom as Brandon worked. His hands gently combed water and gel into my thick locks until waves formed. I silenced the critic that lived in my mind and received this precious expression of love my husband offered to me. How many men wanted to attend their child's dedication service so badly that they would offer to fix their wife's hair? How many women had married a man who could actually do it?

He helped me stand so that I could inspect his work. "Well?"

Our gazes met in the mirror. "Thank you," I said softly, hoping those two words expressed all I felt.

His voice turned gruff. "You're welcome."

We were late to church. He helped me out of the car, led Micah by the hand, and carried Sara inside. A pastor spoke, greeting the guests who had come for the dedication. The only empty seats were on the front row. I wasn't particularly thrilled about sitting in such a conspicuous place, but there was nothing to do about it.

Drumsticks clacked. The room darkened, and everyone stood as I sat. I had to reserve what little strength I had to stand on stage in a few moments. On the front row, the music made my sensitive flesh vibrate. My head pounded. I closed my eyes and listened.

The music faded and lapsed into a new chord progression. The worship leader spoke softly into the microphone. "We're going to try a new song this morning called 'My Hope' by Paul Baloche."

The lyrics and melody washed over me, inviting me to sing along: "I don't know where you'll take me, but I know you're always good."

My throat thickened and grew hot, choking on the words. I lifted my hands and let the tears fall. I cared only a little how it looked or what others might think.

Church was said to be a safe place for messy people, although truthfully I'd never seen many emotional displays in the churches I'd attended. Mostly, I'd seen nicely dressed people smile, small talk with a handful of acquaintances, sit through a sermon, and go home. This illness, whatever it was, had broken me beyond smiles and small talk, and so I leaked what was inside—pain, fear, a small sliver of hope—and offered it all to God.

The song ended. I pulled myself together during the next song. I couldn't cry tears of anguish through what was supposed to be a happy event. Not in front of all these people.

Our pastor asked the parents dedicating their children to move to the platform. Brandon carried Sara and guided me with his free hand at the small of my back. I couldn't look at the crowd. Instead, I focused on my beautiful baby girl in her splendid white dress and promised God that I would do everything in my power to teach her to love him for as long as he let me live.

Learn from her. Depend on me.

Surprised by the words, I pondered them. Sara needed me for everything. She couldn't eat, change her diaper, or even get out of bed without me. She trusted me to meet those needs.

Whether or not I wanted to admit the truth, my experience didn't differ much from hers. My illness had complicated every task, from eating to getting out of bed. That morning, I'd asked God to help me get out of bed because I hadn't been sure I could do it on my own. If he didn't provide some help and healing, I'd have to survive on rice meal and goat milk for the rest of my life.

I needed God, but would I trust him? Really trust him— like Sara trusted me? I wanted to.

Teach me, Lord.

* * *

The scents of roasted meat and herbs permeated the kitchen. Saliva filled my mouth, which ached for something savory and delicious. If only.

I added a scoop of goat milk–based protein powder to my evening serving of rice meal and boiled vegetable mash, and then turned to the roast Hanna had brought, knife in hand. Juices ran down the sides of the tender meat where I cut it and onto the crisp vegetables at the bottom of the pan. Steam rose and danced on the air, taunting me. I set three plates on the table, one sadly different than the others, and sat down next to the high chair, where Sara waited.

Sharing meals with Sara had lost some of its novelty as my hunger had grown and patience waned. In truth, I resented the dull cycle of rice meal, vegetables, and goat milk. I wanted meat, almost to the point that the sight of live cattle made me salivate. Tonight, "Death by Roast" didn't seem such a bad way to go.

Brandon looked up at me, conveniently unaware of my internal struggle. He thought nothing of what it was like for me to watch him eat like a king while I ate like a slave. I bet he wouldn't feel so indifferent if our circumstances were suddenly reversed.

His brow drew back over his ears as he took in my expression. "What?"

"Nothing," I said and stabbed the vegetable mash with my spoon.

He didn't prod.

Shame built up the storm inside. Like the Israelites, I complained about my daily manna rather than being grateful for God's provision. God owed me nothing, and still he gave. I'd forgotten what a gift it was to even eat.

My discontent reached well beyond food. I hadn't been able to enjoy Sara's babyhood as I had Micah's, and if I didn't get better, she would be my last child. It seemed as though her entire life had spanned from one emergency to another.

Micah and I were growing apart. With all these aches and pains and on little food, I lacked the energy to go anywhere or do anything fun. Things were so easy for my friends. Did they realize what a miracle it was to feel well enough to spend a day at the park or the zoo with their kids?

I finished eating and took Sara with me into the laundry room to fold diapers for tomorrow. I shoved a liner into a shell and slammed the folded diaper onto the freezer. Sara watched me intently. Something in her wide eyes sapped me of the false strength I found in anger.

Planting a kiss on her soft forehead, I glimpsed my "Wall of Gratitude." The space between the chest freezer and the cabinets overhead featured a nest of colorful Post-it notes, each boasting of God's personal gifts to me.

Vegetables in season just as I need them.

Everything was a gift. The vegetables. Rice meal. Delivered dinners for Brandon and Micah. My doctor and friend, Stacy. My mom. Hanna Peshoff. The breath in my lungs. All of it.

Gathering Sara into my chest, I nuzzled her sweet head. Illness was a hapless thief. It could steal moments and experiences. It might one day take my life. But discontentment was the real threat. It would take everything good I left unguarded. It would grow fat on my misery, and I would waste away. Unless I had eyes to see. Unless I could learn to feast on Jesus as I ate my meager rations. If I could learn to say, "Thank you, God" before "Please, Lord," and if I could learn that Jesus is enough, I might survive this crazy disease with my soul intact.

A hot tingle settled into my lips. My tongue itched. Frowning, I raked my teeth over the itchy bumps. Surely not. My chest tightened. I swallowed the swear word on the tip of my tongue and carried Sara to Brandon. "I'm reacting. It's not bad yet, but I think I'm going to take some Benadryl to make sure it doesn't get that way."

He scowled. "What is it this time?"

I shrugged. "Probably the protein powder."

"There's nothing in it besides…" He didn't finish his sentence, but I knew how it ended. There was nothing in the powder except for goat milk and a tiny bit of natural vanilla flavoring. That tiny bit of vanilla gave me hope even as I suspected the worst. I took the Benadryl and sat in the recliner.

Brandon glanced at me from time to time, his concern palpable, but he said nothing.

"It's not the milk," I said aloud, as much to assure myself as him. To prove my theory, I rose from the chair to retrieve my nightly glass.

Goat milk cost $4.00 per quart, but without it, I wouldn't have done as well as I had. It contained several important nutrients and was easy on my sensitive stomach. Not only that, the white, creamy liquid looked pretty and inviting in a glass, which was more than I could say for my vegetable mash, no matter how I plated it. Though I longed for something as good as roast, the goat milk remained a pleasure to me.

I drank, savoring the sweet taste. Within seconds of me setting my glass in the dishwasher, all the relief Benadryl had given me vanished. Heat rushed throughout my body, and the itching returned with a vengeance. Minutes later, my belly burned and bloated. I curled my arms around my abdomen and sank to the kitchen floor.

Brandon rounded the corner and stopped. "What's wrong?"

"Goat milk is gone," I whispered. Goat milk had been my lifeline, and now it made me sick. Without it, I might literally starve to death.

Brandon paced the galley kitchen, stepping around me, the phone pressed to his ear. Grieving, I paid no attention to his words. He knelt and tipped my chin. His eyes bored into mine. "Your mom and I think we need to scrap the plan. Elimination isn't working for you. Here." He handed me the phone.

"So you reacted to the goat milk, huh?" Mom asked.

"Another hundred dollars down the drain," I said. In the last month, I'd gone through several hundred in nutritional supplements. None had worked out.

"Don't worry about that," Mom said. "Listen, why don't you just eat whatever you want? Within reason."

Her suggestion startled me into silence.

"I mean, if you're going to react anyway, why not? You can try rotating your foods and see what happens."

She had a point. A quick death by anaphylactic shock beat starving every day of the week. What did I have to lose? "I could eat meat again," I said with a stuffy sniff.

"Mm-hmm," Mom said. "I think you'll do better on a rotation diet."

The cloud of doom above my head evaporated as this most recent reaction shrank in significance. Tomorrow, I would eat meat. Thank God.

* * *

Brandon snickered from across the table as I chewed the bite of hamburger patty with my eyes closed, savoring the taste and texture. "Is it really better than rice and zucchini mash though?"

I held up a hand. "Shh...you're distracting me from the experience."

"Why don't I get this kind of response when I kiss you?"

"You don't taste like meat," I said.

"Would it help if I moisturized with bacon grease?"

I opened one eye to shoot him an arch look.

"Well?"

Micah laughed. "Mama like da burga."

I ran my fingers through Micah's thick red locks. "Yes sir! Mama like da burga. Mama also like da Daddy, so he can stop being ridiculous."

Brandon finished his dinner before mine was half-gone. "What do you want me to pull out of the freezer for tomorrow?"

Tomorrow.

My lips weren't tingling. Neither my tongue nor my throat was swelling. Even if my stomach rebelled later, this meal was worth the discomfort.

I would eat meat again tomorrow.

"Take out a chicken," I said through my next bite.

After rinsing his plate, Brandon disappeared into the laundry room. "Babe?"

I stopped chewing. Whenever he said "babe" like that, the words that followed were never good. "Yeah?"

"When you get a sec, I need your help."

Why did he always hold me in suspense like this? "What's up?"

"My guess is the freezer shorted out."

I closed my eyes again, disgust displacing euphoria. The freezer was full of important things. Like meat and breast milk.

"Take your time," he said, coming out of the little room with a chicken in hand. "Most of everything is still frozen. I'm going to see if I can get it working again. We might be able to save it all."

He worked while I finished eating, which I didn't enjoy as much in light of this new development. I depended on that supply of breast milk, and meat was expensive. Brandon made good money as a pharmacist, but the medical bills had begun to come in. The supplements I'd purchased hadn't been cheap, and I'd tried several. Sick as I was, I couldn't contribute a thing to help with my expenses.

The freezer hummed to life. "Got it working," Brandon called. "But I think it's time for a new freezer. This one was probably made in the seventies if not before. Not much damage was done, but we might not be so lucky next time."

He wasn't wrong. The General Electric Harvest Gold freezer, one of the many items we'd acquired in the estate sale, was original to the forty-year-old house.

I sighed. "Okay."

He brought out two bags of slushy breast milk and set them beside my plate. "You probably want to check these."

I stared at them unhappily.

"Go play?" Micah asked.

"Yeah, Bubs. Go play," I said.

He slid out of his seat, unaffected, and Sara cooed in her high chair. Smiling at her, I grabbed the bags. "Let's hope these are still good."

When the milk had thawed and warmed, Brandon opened a bag, sniffed, and cringed. "Nope," he said and poured the contents into the sink.

I tried the second bag and discovered spoiled breast milk smelled like any other spoiled milk. "I have some in the fridge freezer that should be okay. I'll try the rest in the morning," I said.

The following morning, I thawed and sniffed one bag after another, each one sour, all ruined. I'd pumped every morning for six months, sometimes enough for two feedings, and had squirreled it all away in little expensive bags for such a time as this. I tossed them all into a black garbage sack, which might as well have been a body bag for the way I felt about all that wasted milk, and buried them in the garbage bin outside.

What was I going to do? Sara wouldn't stop needing to eat. What we had wouldn't last more than a couple of days. With all of her digestive issues, she wouldn't tolerate a dairy-based formula. The leading ingredient in nondairy options was corn syrup solids, and that didn't sound healthful to me.

Some online research led me to a recipe for homemade formula that called for goat milk and supplemental vitamins. I asked Brandon to pick up more goat milk, some blackstrap molasses, and a bottle of prune juice, and ordered folic acid and the prescribed vitamins in liquid drop form, which arrived in two days. Sara spat out her first taste of the odd concoction but, after a couple of hesitant sucks, gulped it down.

Two days later, she slept through the night for the first time. Several more passed before I realized she hadn't had a stomachache since we'd switched to the formula. One morning, she took a two-hour nap, a monumental event that quickly became part of her daily routine.

I pondered the changes. Had my milk made Sara sick? More than one family member had suggested it. Honey, Brandon's grandmother, had insisted that the problem was something I was eating. At the time, I'd dismissed the idea. Everyone knew breast milk was the healthiest option for babies. Nature itself attested to the fact.

What if the problem hadn't been a specific food but my milk in general? Considering how sick I'd been, the hypothesis wasn't unreasonable, but now there was no way to test it. I'd dried up, and the last of the milk had been hauled off to the dump.

It was interesting. Sara and I had both lost food we loved, which had been replaced with something better. I'd lost goat milk; God had delivered meat. Sara had lost breast milk. Her health had improved, and now we both slept through the night.

What all this meant about my state of health, I didn't know. All I knew was that God was better to me than I deserved. While I sat on the floor crying over spoiled milk, he was busy taking care of my baby in such a way that would benefit everyone in the household.

I added another Post-it note to my gratitude wall—*old freezers and spoiled milk.*

9

Visitation

A man with salt-and-pepper curls sat behind the reception desk of the cozy waiting room, which was painted in a soothing shade of green. Bushy eyebrows rose over mischievous blue eyes that sparkled as he asked, "Which one a you gets to fill out this stack a papers?"

I raised my hand. "That'd be me."

"Ha! Okay, 'Me.'" He handed me a clipboard, the promised stack of papers, and a pen.

Brandon and I each took a seat in a white wicker chair. Never having seen a naturopathic doctor before, I'd brought him along to help me gauge any weird juju she might pull on me.

Asian woodwinds piped through the speakers. I filled out the paperwork, pausing at times to shake the stiffness out of my hands. The space for listing symptoms wasn't large enough. I flipped over the page and continued on the back— food, environmental, and drug allergies; sinus problems; asthma; hives; itching; rash; eczema; flushing; chronic diarrhea and constipation; acid reflux; frequent nausea; anaphylaxis; pain points along my neck, shoulders, upper back, hips, buttocks, behind the knees, and legs; arthritis pain in the hands, wrists, feet, ankles, hips, and spine; tingling and pins and needles in the feet; migraine headaches; tension headaches; sinus headaches; earaches; TMJ; stiffness, especially in the morning; insomnia; chronic fatigue.

"All right, 'Me.' I'll let the boss know you're ready to see 'er." The man winked as he took the paperwork. He stood, unfolding into a tall frame.

The wait didn't last long. A short, small-boned woman appeared from around the corner. "Melissa Keaster?" Her tone was gentle, her eyes warm and mouth reserved.

I smiled and stood in reply. She extended her hand to me. "Dr. Carolyne Yakaboski. This way," she said and led Brandon and me through a room decorated with a Zen garden into the back office. She indicated two chairs next to her desk and sat in a third.

"You have quite the list of symptoms," she said, peering down at my forms through a pair of reading glasses. "How long has this been going on?"

"A while," I said. "But it's gotten much worse since my daughter was born."

"Have you run any tests for mold in your house?" she asked.

I hadn't thought of that.

"No," Brandon said. "But we did recently have the place inspected. We're getting ready to sell."

A lovely home a few miles east of us had been placed on the market. I'd fallen in love with the quaint brick farmhouse, its antique doors and stained glass windows, and the pretty yard full of flowering dogwoods and redbuds. We had a contract on the property, contingent upon the sale of our property, which also had a contract.

"Routine home inspections won't find everything. Judging from your symptoms, you may want to order a mold test," she said.

The suggestion pricked my memory. A friend from church had recently asked about our water quality. While praying for us, she had received an impression that something about our home might have contributed to my health problems. Last weekend, Dad had called to say he felt compelled to pray over our house. "Something isn't right," he'd said.

I filed away Dr. Yakaboski's suggestion for later thought.

"Let's find out what's going on," she said, rolling forward in her chair.

In my left hand, she placed a brass rod that she'd covered in a damp paper towel. After keying in my name on the computer, she reached for my other hand and a metal probe. Using the probe, she touched various points on the palm side of my fingers. With each connection of skin to metal, the computer sang a rising note that quickly descended, indicating either a sensitivity to a particular trigger or a weakness in one of my organs. According to the machine, none of my organs worked properly, and I suffered from many sensitivities, including honey, which surprised me.

Dr. Yakaboski's serious blue eyes peered at me over her glasses. "You have a lot going on. I think we should start with a few supplements to help your organs function a bit better, and we need to begin desensitizing you to some of these foods." She recommended the book *The Food Allergy Cure*, by Ellen Cutler, and several supplements.

"Let's go over to my table," she said. "I'm certified in BEST protocol. I think it could really help you."

I glanced at Brandon, who shrugged.

"Sure," I said, not at all sure what I was in for.

When I had settled comfortably on my back, she lightly touched various pressure points on my head and along my spine. She gave me specific words and numbers to think about, told me in which direction I should look, and directed me to breathe in specific patterns. It was a little strange, but no blatant witchcraft was involved as far as I could tell.

The only time I felt any discomfort was when I repeated the mantra posted on the ceiling above my head: "I believe that I am able, willing, and worthy to be perfectly healthy, physically, spiritually, and emotionally." I tripped over the word "worthy." Was I?

When it was over, I stood slowly, feeling relaxed. My pain had receded in most places. In other places, it was gone. "Wow," I said aloud.

"It's an excellent treatment." Dr. Yakaboski was quiet but self-assured.

I studied her, wondering how much of my skepticism she felt. "Thank you," I said. "I haven't felt this good in a month."

"You're very welcome."

Before we reached the front door, the tall man called out, "Bye, 'Me'! Hope to see you again! But not too soon! Ha!"

I waved, grinning. Hope expanded in my chest. Dr. Yakaboski believed me. She had treated me with dignity and kindness. I never once sensed that she doubted my symptoms or my sanity. Even if the treatment was a little strange, even though I couldn't agree with every part of it, I had been helped.

"Thank you," I breathed to God on the ride home. Despite my concerns, my new naturopath was an answered prayer.

* * *

Light from the hall closet shone into my drowsy eyes as the bedroom door yawned open. Only darkness lay behind the blackout curtains. Brandon's chest rose and fell. The hour was either very late or very early.

I blinked away the remnants of a dream and noticed a looming figure in the doorway. It was featureless, not human or even solid. It formed the perfect silhouette of the Beast I'd seen in my dream several months ago. The creature strode into the room, its horns almost brushing the ceiling.

The air chilled and was sucked from the room. My heart skittered. *Brandon!* I tried to say his name, but my tongue stuck to the roof of my mouth.

The broad shadow moved to the foot of my bed, pausing at my feet. Every hair on my body stood on end, alert to danger but unable to fight it. My legs burned and tingled, desperate to run and escape the foul shadow, but I couldn't move. My limbs sprawled beneath the sheets, heavy and useless, refusing to obey my will. Blood roared in my ears.

Brandon didn't wake.

"Jesus!" I mouthed. No sound escaped my throat. The darkness had gagged me. *Jesus! Jesus!* I fought the paralysis, determined to say the name that would save me. "Jesus!" I barely rasped it out. "Jesus!" I said again, surfacing from whatever dark magic had held me down.

The sound of my own gasps filled my ears. Brandon shook my shoulder. "Babe," he whispered. "Babe."

My heart slowed. I swallowed. "Yeah?"

"Did you know you were talking in your sleep?"

"Yeah." I breathed deeply, but the air was still thick and heavy. "Will you pray?"

He rubbed my arm, soothing me. "Dear Heavenly Father," he said. "Bind the darkness, and bring peace to our sleep…"

As I listened, the air in the room thinned and became breathable again. Fear ebbed, and I wondered what in hell had just happened. In *my* house.

* * *

A gentle rustle and the quiet rattle of a belt buckle woke me. Light drifted in between the curtains. I rolled over to face Brandon, who was dressing for work. He met my gaze. "How did you know what to pray last night?" I asked.

He perched on the edge of the bed. "It was early this morning. I woke up a minute or so before you did. Something didn't feel right. I was anxious. I prayed the Lord's Prayer and was about to pray Psalm 23 when you started fighting in your sleep. I could tell you were trying to say something, but you couldn't."

"A demon"—the word tasted odd and foul on my tongue—"probably the one Micah saw…the one from my dream…it came into the room last night."

Brandon blanched as I told him what I'd seen, felt, and experienced. Neither of us knew what to do with this. It was outside the realm of our experience. If it had ever happened to anyone we knew, they didn't talk about it.

"I think I'm going to call Dad," I said. "He offered to pray over the house the other day. He suspected something was wrong with it. I don't know if this is what he had in mind, but maybe he can come tonight when you get home from work."

Brandon shook his head.

"What?"

"This stuff—it's not supposed to happen," he said. "Not in the United States. Not outside of Frank Peretti books."

My spine protested as I sat up. "I don't like it either. I don't want to live in a world where demons live in the bathroom pipes, hide our stuff, and pretend to be friends with our son. I don't want to deal with this. But that thing can't live here anymore."

"Okay," he said in a flat tone that let me know nothing was okay in his world. He kissed me and left.

After breakfast, I called Dad. "Hey, Issy May!" he answered brightly. "How ya feeling today?"

He listened without interruption while I told him what had happened the night before and maintained his silence after I'd finished.

"Dad?" I asked to make sure he was still on the line.

"I'm here."

"Aren't you going to tell me that it was just a bad dream or something?" Part of me hoped he would.

"I can't do that. We had something like it happen here at our house not too long ago," he said.

"What did you do?"

"The only thing I knew to do. What I'm going to do tonight when I come out your way."

I loved that I didn't even have to ask him to come. "Did it work?"

"We haven't had a problem since."

I'd never cast a demon out of my home, but I didn't think I wanted my three-year-old son, who was already disturbed by nightmares and anxiety attacks, to witness it, whatever the process would entail.

"Do you think I should ask Nona to come get Micah?"

Dad paused. "Wouldn't be a bad idea. I do pray pretty loud when I do this."

After hanging up with Dad, I called Nona, explaining again what had happened. "So…do you think I've lost it?" I asked lightly.

"No," she said. "I think you're at war. I'll come for Micah this afternoon." It was nice, if unexpected, to be so readily believed.

When Brandon, Mom, and Dad arrived at the house that evening, Nona and Micah had gone.

Dad walked through each room without saying a word. When he finished, he looked at me, at Mom, and back at me. "Why don't you two stay inside while Brandon and I pray around the outside of the house. Maybe we'll stir 'em up."

Lacking a superior plan, we agreed. Seven times, Dad circled the house, holding his Bible above his head. His voice carried through the walls and reached us inside. "I plead the blood of Jesus over this household. Brandon and Melissa belong to the Living God and are covered by the blood of Jesus. Every spirit that is not of God has to leave!" Brandon trailed behind him, his hands in his pockets and lips moving.

The whispers in the bathroom pipes grew louder with each pass. A heavy feeling settled in my abdomen, strengthening when I stood near the hall closet, where the figure had appeared the night before.

The front door opened and shut. Heavy footsteps traveled up the hall. "Well? Did you notice anything?" Dad asked and paused, cocking his head to one side. "Do y'all hear that?"

"Yeah. It's the pipes," Brandon said.

Dad moved closer to the hall closet and leaned over the coats that hung inside. "Naw, those aren't the pipes. They're whispering in the closet. Can't make out a dern thing they're saying though." He straightened, raised his Bible, and again pleaded the blood of Jesus, commanding all the unseen things to leave.

The oppressive weight in the air lifted. Mom took a deep breath and said, "Whew! That's better."

"Yeah, it's easier to breathe," Brandon agreed.

"It feels like there's more light in here too," Mom said. "This house has always felt dark."

After a final walkthrough, Dad nodded. "Much better."

I frowned up at him. "Something must have happened here. Something awful. What do you think it was?"

"I don't know," he said. "There was a lot of fear. But it's gone now."

A week passed. The "pipes" were quiet, and the lights hadn't flickered. Toys had stopped sounding off on their own. Nothing had disappeared or moved. Micah hadn't mentioned Docola, and there were no more midnight visitations from evil shadows with horns. Everything was quiet.

Brandon arrived home from work one evening and said, "The contract on our house fell through," which meant the brick farmhouse I'd dreamed of having would go to the next couple in line. We were stuck at Bear Creek. The disappointment stung, but it was survivable. After all, our house wasn't haunted anymore. And who knew whether we could have managed the mortgage of a larger place with all the medical bills piling up?

"Think we need to order that mold test Dr. Yakaboski suggested?" I asked. If we stayed, it was worth considering.

Brandon kissed me before answering. "I think we've taken care of the problem with the house."

I nodded. If only my own demons were so easily dismissed.

10

The Search

Brandon had lost his mind. "Are you crazy?"

"How can you not see that this is the perfect solution?" he rebutted.

He stood in front of the television, hands extended, eyes bulging in disbelief. The kids craned their necks to view Mickey Mouse's face, ignoring our impassioned disagreement.

"Brandon, no healthy adult wants to live with their parents after moving out," I said. "No matter how wonderful they are."

"But you won't live with them. You'll live *beside* them. In your own house."

"I would need an excellent reason to move anywhere right now." Not only were we dealing with the multifarious delights of my illness, but Sara was sick again. Our last visit to the pediatrician's office revealed another ear infection, a bad of case of what Michelle had called "glue ear," and the imminent need for surgery. Though I was saddened by the recurrence of illness after our breakthrough in the spring, I was hopeful that the tube surgery, scheduled in early August, would bring Sara's ear infection saga to an end.

"Okay." Brandon shrugged. "How about being debt-free in two years?"

I paused to consider, and he seized the opportunity my silence afforded him. "Hear me out. We can buy a trailer, live in it a couple of years, and then build. Assuming you'll like living next to your parents as much as I think you will. And if you don't, we'll move."

"Being debt-free is a pretty good reason," I conceded.

"And how about having help that lives seconds away?" His tone turned light. "It might come in handy the next time you can't breathe."

I chewed my lip. "Where is this property they've bought?"

"Crossroads. Just past the church at the flashing light."

"In other words—the middle of nowhere," I said.

"Or. If you look at it another way, the middle of everywhere," he replied. "We can be anywhere we need to go in forty-five minutes or less."

He wanted this too badly. "What's in it for you?"

The question deflated him. He plopped down beside me on the couch. "Peace of mind."

"What do you mean?"

"I mean that I worry about you. And the kids. Every day that I leave for work, I worry something might happen while I'm gone."

He turned to face the television screen, but the light reflecting off his eyes couldn't disguise the swirl of worry inside them. I reached for his hand. His fingers laced through mine.

"And also...land," he said. "I've wanted to live on a spread of land since before we were married. Now we have a way to do it."

I leaned my head on his shoulder and watched the characters on the screen gather for the finale. Sara bounced in her jumper to her favorite song, "Hot Dog!"

He was probably right about me needing help. No one knew what was wrong with me or how long it would take for my body to recover. The kids would enjoy growing up near their grandparents. Mom and Dad weren't the type to interfere or overstay. And it was true—Brandon had always wanted land.

Before we married, he'd shown me several properties and talked about buying a trailer and building later. The idea had repulsed me at the time. I'd always lived in houses. I'd wanted a house. When Nona had taken my side in the argument, he'd capitulated.

It was my turn to relent. "Okay," I said and kissed his hand.

"Okay?" He turned my chin to look me in the eye. "Just like that—you'll be the queen of my double-wide trailer?"

"Not if you sing," I threatened.

"That's not very nice."

"I'm not nice."

"No, but you are sexy." He kissed me and said, "You'll love it. You'll see."

Who knew? Maybe I would.

* * *

Weekly acupressure and allergy-clearing treatments with Dr. Yakaboski provided temporary relief from constant pain, fatigue, and depression, but they didn't seem to improve my gastrointestinal discomforts or lengthen my list of safe foods. Whatever I ate, my stomach rebelled and bloated until I curled into the fetal position, panting and sweating. Hunger, nausea, and pounding headaches wore me down whenever I tried to skip meals. After two full months of living like this, I wanted to be well.

One afternoon between treatments, Dr. Yakaboski's incisive blue eyes peered at me over her glasses. "Don't be discouraged," she said. "Natural medicine is meant to be preventative. Its purpose is to nurture your health so you don't get sick. When we apply it to a body that is already very ill, healing takes time—more time than we would like."

I flashed her a wry grin from where I lay on the exam table. "You read my mail. My mom told me weeks ago that I should brace myself for a long recovery."

Dr. Yakaboski nodded, reaching for specific pressure points along my spine. "Healing is a journey, not a sprint."

"I'm going to start a gut-healing diet soon, probably after our move," I said.

Dr. Yakaboski rattled off a string of directions. As I followed them, she said, "Healing a damaged gut can take a lifetime. Changing your diet can help, but nothing is instant. In my experience, people often need more than physical care."

I didn't ask her to elaborate. I understood enough. Natural medicine was synonymous with holistic care. As a doctor of natural medicine, Dr. Yakaboski was trained to treat the whole person. God had led me here. Maybe he knew something I didn't. Maybe I needed more than the right doctor, the right diet, and the right medication.

"Sit up slowly," she instructed.

When I had regained equilibrium, I said, "I have appointments with my husband's gastroenterologist and a rheumatologist in Shreveport soon. If they have any insight into what's going on, I'll let you know."

Dr. Yakaboski pursed her lips and paused. Then she said, "Be careful with all of that. Sometimes testing and experimenting with medications can do more harm than good."

I had no idea what she meant, but I didn't ask. The answer would probably make me uncomfortable, and I didn't want to feel any more uncomfortable than I already did.

She stepped back. "How do you feel?"

"Better." I didn't understand how deep breaths and poking sensitive points along the spine could accomplish so much, but I was thankful for any improvement, however small or temporary.

"Thank you," I said. "I'll try to be careful."

Whatever that meant.

* * *

"Your paperwork says you're allergic to soy. Is that correct?" the nurse asked.

The fluorescent lighting in the pre-op of the local gastroenterology clinic was giving me a headache. "Yes," I said, trying not to think about the IV needle she was about to plunge into my hand.

"Ooo-kay." Staring at the clipboard in front of her, she released a puff of air that lifted her blond bangs. "I'll be right back."

She traveled across the room and whispered to another nurse, who glanced at me and whispered back. My nurse disappeared behind a set of double doors.

I sighed. It was always a joy to be a problem child.

A moment later, my nurse returned, her gaze latched to mine. "Okay. We usually try to give our patients light sedation for endoscopies. Unfortunately, it contains soy. We could try fentanyl."

An unpleasant trill traveled down my spine at the word. "No thanks. I had a pretty nasty reaction to my epidural when I gave birth to my daughter last November. Fentanyl was one of the prime suspects."

I considered that day. The epidural that had triggered the reaction had failed me in the eleventh hour when I'd needed it most. I'd survived an eighteen-hour labor induced by Pitocin without any working anesthesia or plan to manage my pain. "Could we try it without?"

The nurse's eyebrows disappeared beneath her bangs. "This is a very difficult procedure to do when the patient is conscious. We'll have to give you the good stuff."

I cleared my throat. "And what's the good stuff?"

"Demerol. It's not that big of a deal, but if you have any plans for the rest of today, you'll need to cancel them."

"Not a problem. I never have plans." Not for the last six months, anyway.

"No job?" she asked, prepping my hand for the IV.

I looked away as she took out the needle. "I'm a mom. My son is three. My daughter is almost eight months."

"I remember those days." She smiled and opened a needle. "You have a lot of allergies, don't you?"

"You could say that."

She coaxed a vein with her finger. "How long have you had them?"

I thought about how to answer. "Some since childhood. Others for about eight years. Most are new."

"What do you eat?"

"Rice, meat, and vegetables, mostly. Fruit and I don't get along."

"All done," she said, taping the tube in place. "Sounds rough. I guess you're healthier for it though."

"One would think," I said.

The doctor walked in then. "Hello, Mrs. Keaster."

Liquid happiness rushed through me. I answered warmly. I briefly considered breaking out in song. Someone said the word "Valium," and my giddiness made sense. They could have amputated my arm, and I would have laughed.

The doctor spoke again. He said something about the number fifty. The room blurred and faded.

Surfacing, I heard Brandon's voice. Red light shone through my heavy eyelids, and my tongue felt strange and unhelpful. "Brandon?"

His voice continued, but I couldn't understand him. He felt far away and sounded near.

"Brandon?"

"Hold on," Brandon said.

"What did he say?"

"Hey, babe." His words were clearer now. "You've woken up and asked me that question no less than fifteen times. Every time, I give you the same answer. You pass out, you wake up, and then you ask it again. I want you to relax and sleep it off. When you're able to stay conscious for five consecutive minutes, we'll talk."

I fought for those five minutes. I wanted answers. He could know what was wrong with me. The next time I woke, I found myself in bed. A glass of water sat on the table next to me. My stomach burned as I sat up to drink. Other needs presented themselves.

I flushed the toilet, and Brandon appeared. "Want me to help you to the recliner?" he asked. "The kids are ready to see you."

"Yeah. But first—"

"Promise not to pass out halfway through my answer?"

I responded with what I imagined to be my most withering look.

He led me down the hall. "Mild gastritis."

I stopped, gaping at him. "That's all? No ulcers? Nothing?"

"Mama!" Micah grinned from the train table. In her jumper, Sara bounced at the sight of me.

Brandon lowered me into the recliner. "One polyp, which they biopsied," he said. "And he doesn't think your stomach symptoms are related to your food sensitivities or joint pain."

"But they are related," I said. "The joint pain began right after a bad food reaction."

Sara bounced and huffed until Brandon lifted her out of her jumper and placed her in my arms. "Hey, don't shoot the messenger," he said. "I'm just telling you what he said. As you requested. Many, *many* times."

Grinning into Sara's smiling face, I said in singsong, "So what does he want me to do?"

"He recommends you see a rheumatologist and switch proton-pump inhibitors."

"English, please. For the non-pharmacists in the room."

Brandon shrugged. "Try Nexium?"

I shut my eyes in frustration.

"Not again." He poked along my ribcage.

Jerking away, I slapped at his hands. "So basically, I wasted a day and hundreds of dollars to be told that I have mild gastritis and I need to take a medication my new healing diet strictly prohibits."

"You could look at it that way," Brandon said. "Or you can think of it as another step in the process of elimination."

"This whole process *is* elimination."

"It's nice to see you making jokes. Half an hour ago, I thought, 'What did he say?' were the only words I'd ever hear again."

He grinned at the flat look I slung in his direction and said, "Now—what do you want to eat? I know you're hungry."

"A big plate of barbecue."

"Leftover chicken and rice, it is!" he said and marched into the kitchen.

Beneath the clatter of dishes, vocalized train noises, and high-pitched dialogue between Mickey and Minnie, quiet words reverberated in my spirit.

Wait. Wait for me.

The voice spoke so softly I almost missed it.

Be patient. This is the process. Wait.

In truth, there wasn't anything I could do at the moment except enjoy my children, eat my lunch, and wait for the next appointment, which was weeks away.

"Okay, Lord," I whispered, nestling deeper into the recliner. "I'll wait."

* * *

It was late July when Brandon drove me to Shreveport to see a highly recommended rheumatologist. Dr. Broadwell stepped into the exam room, towering head and shoulders over Brandon. He extended his hand toward Brandon and then toward me. A tuft of white hair and wise blue eyes bespoke experience—with both medicine and people.

He asked astute questions, but not too many, and listened observantly. From time to time, his eyes captured a movement of my wrist or a shift in my posture. Lacking the general air of arrogance I'd observed among younger members of his profession, he reminded me of a well-kept, less eccentric, Southern gentleman variant of Gandalf the Grey, and so I immediately liked him.

A breath of silence concluded the interview. A well of compassion seeped through his professional veneer as he asked one final question. "You've really been through it, haven't you?"

He didn't wait for an answer. "I would like to take some x-rays and an ultrasound of your wrists so that we can see what we're dealing with. It's unlikely that your pain is related to your allergic symptoms, but I will help you in any way I can."

When he left the room, I sighed. "He doesn't believe me either."

"But he listened," Brandon said. "Give him that."

I did, actually. He'd listened with his ears, his eyes, and his heart. I hadn't come across any medical doctor with better bedside manner.

X-rays, an ultrasound, and a tender point exam filled the next two hours. At the end of testing, a nurse brought three pamphlets—one about arthritis, another about carpal tunnel syndrome, and another about fibromyalgia. Dr. Broadwell followed on her heels.

He displayed the x-rays one by one, pointing out the absence of natural curvature in my neck and my uneven hips. "Pelvic girdle and early stage carpal tunnel help to explain some of your pain. It's too early to diagnose you with fibromyalgia, though your symptoms are consistent with the condition. As for the rest, we will have to wait and see."

Answers. Names. Words that provided a plausible explanation for some of my misery. Words that proved I wasn't crazy. I almost kissed him.

"I recommend you see my personal physical therapist," he continued. "She's excellent—an expert in pelvic girdle. You may find that physical therapy helps with your other discomforts as well."

Brandon cleared his throat. "Where is she located?"

"In Bossier," Dr. Broadwell said. "I know it's a drive, but I don't know any physical therapists in the Monroe area and cannot recommend them."

"I can probably work out something with Dad," I told Brandon. Dad had just retired from his longtime teaching and coaching career.

Dr. Broadwell proceeded. "I've prescribed gabapentin to help ease your pain. You'll need to start on a very low dose."

Answers *and* a solution for pain? I hugged him. "Thank you so much," I said.

"My pleasure, my dear." He patted my back.

His paternal smile reminded me again of Gandalf, and again I almost kissed him.

11

Love, Drugs, and Hallucinations

" Answers and solutions are marvelous things, but they make for a feeble hope," I penned in my journal the morning after the appointment with Dr. Broadwell. My heart had pricked on the drive home as I realized I'd felt more relieved at the name of a condition than at the name of Jesus.

Brandon had argued that I judged myself too harshly. "You're human," he'd said.

Maybe. But I didn't want to waste a single lesson hidden in this hard place. I refused to placate conviction with platitudes concerning my humanity. I loved God, but I had sought answers more than I had sought his presence. His presence was my hope—not answers, not solutions, not medicine.

Still, I was ready to try the medicine. The hope of pain relief might be feeble, but it was real. Brandon convinced me to wait until his next day off to take my first dose. "We have no idea how you'll react," he pointed out. "If something happens, you'll want me here."

Despite my eagerness, I deferred to him. He was likely right—an obnoxious habit of his. On the night before his day off, Brandon poured a dose into a medicine cup and set it before me.

Sleep came easily and overstayed its welcome. Brandon woke me three times the next morning. Each time, I saw his face, muttered an acknowledgment, and intended to get out of bed. Intentions didn't carry me far. He and Micah were eating lunch when I staggered into the kitchen half-asleep.

"Hey there, sunshine," he greeted me. "You missed your morning dose."

"I don't think I need it," I said. My voice sounded strange to my own ears.

"Do you hurt?" he asked.

I searched my shoulders, neck, back, and hips for the pain that had become a constant companion. It wasn't there. "No. Wow. I don't feel it at all."

He nodded. "Let's try a half dose and see how you do."

For the rest of the day, I lost one battle after another against sleep. The next day was no better. "I'm not sure what's worse—pain or this," I said.

"Maybe you just need a couple of days to adjust," Brandon said. He knew I wanted it to work. He wanted it to work for me.

On the third morning, he woke me to discuss something important and stalked out of the bedroom in frustration when I failed to rouse myself.

Thirst compelled me to wake. I drank from the glass on my bedside table, tended to other immediate needs, and then padded down the hall to apologize. When I slid open the pocket door, Honey, Brandon's grandmother, smiled in greeting. Sara perched happily on her knees, watching Mickey Mouse and gumming a finger.

Startled, I asked Honey, "What are you doing here?"

Her smile faltered.

"I'm sorry," I said quickly. "I'm glad to see you. I'm just confused. Brandon didn't tell me you were coming. Where is he?"

Honey patted Sara's back. "He went to work a couple of hours ago."

He worked today?

"Hey, Mama," Micah called from the train table.

"Hey, baby," I said. "Let me call Brandon. He was trying to tell me something important before he left, and I couldn't wake up."

I dialed his work number while I refilled my glass with water. A thick haze hovered around my brain, and I hoped to wash it away. One of the pharmacy techs answered my call. "May I speak to Brandon, please?" I asked.

I drank while I waited, but the haze remained, unaffected by hydration.

"Hello?"

"Hey. When did you ask Honey to come? She surprised the ever-living daylights out of me this morning."

Silence.

"Babe?" I prompted.

His tone was soft. The words came slowly. "I asked her to come yesterday afternoon. After you asked me to. We were concerned you might still have some trouble waking up this morning."

"Oh." I didn't remember the conversation, but I trusted that it had happened. "Okay. So what were you trying to tell me that was so important this morning before you left?"

The silence lasted longer this time. "Hello?" I said.

"I didn't try to wake you. I just kissed you, like usual, but you were pretty dead to the world."

The information sank in. "I think I'm going to stop the medicine."

"That might not be a bad idea. Ask him to write you a script for something else," he said.

"I'll do that," I agreed. Preferably, something that wouldn't cause hallucinations.

* * *

The next week, Dr. Broadwell prescribed duloxetine, an antidepressant. The pain in my neck and shoulders, which had reasserted itself with a vengeance after I stopped the gabapentin, receded again. I could move more freely, and my nerves, which frequently misfired stinging sensations throughout my body, quieted. While I enjoyed pain relief without the constant drowsiness, it came at a price.

Brandon and I hadn't spent much time in the bedroom together since Sara had been born, not because I didn't want to but because it was imprudent to attempt sex with a baby in my arms or while I was asleep. When opportunities presented themselves, we seized them, knowing they wouldn't last long. Unfortunately, the new drug erased more than my pain. It also stole my desire for and delight in sexual intimacy.

"This too?" I asked the Lord. With Sara's ongoing ear infections, sleep presented a continual challenge. I rarely drank coffee anymore. I'd given up wine entirely. Chocolate was a no-go. Add orgasms to the list, and that was pretty much everything I liked.

"I thought you *wanted* us to have sex. I thought you wanted us to like it!"

While I didn't fully understand, part of me suspected I did. Several boys in my kindergarten class had regularly reached down my pants and explored with their hands—during naptime, in class, especially on movie days. Their hands had awakened in me sexual awareness and desire, which had developed into sinful patterns over time. Even in marriage, selfishness and old habits tempted me to satisfy myself, cutting Brandon out of the equation. I'd never fully mastered that area of my life.

I wanted to. I'd prayed to. I'd memorized every passage of scripture I could find on crucifying the flesh and putting sin to death. Nothing had worked. Maybe the loss was an answer to prayer.

Regardless, I wrote "pain relief" on a hot pink Post-it note and added it to the wall. My spirits lifted, as did some of my depression. Day-to-day tasks seemed possible. Sara's surgery was emotionally bearable. Discomforts didn't overwhelm me following the rides to Shreveport for physical therapy, and so I began to enjoy the little road trips with my dad.

"You may have been suffering from postpartum depression, and we didn't even know it," Mom said.

The benefits helped me make peace with the cost, which came with its own blessing. In paying the price, I learned how to give myself to my husband freely. When I didn't desire it. When I received very little satisfaction. Because I loved him. There was so much I couldn't do, but I could do this one thing.

For the first time in memory, my sexual desire fell asleep, and the vice that had held me captive for more than two decades loosened its grip.

12

Jenny Freeman

A rustle followed the squeak of the door. The fan shut off. A gentle hand pressed my shoulder lightly. "Hey, babe?"

I blinked up at Brandon. "Mmm?"

"I thought we'd try to go to church this morning. We haven't been in a while."

My eyes turned to the clock. If I got up now and went straight to the shower, we'd only be a few minutes late. But did I have it in me?

"I almost have breakfast made. Why don't you shower while I fix your rice cereal?"

It had been a while. It might be nice to see people. Brandon needed friends, especially if I didn't make it out of this crazy illness alive. "Okay," I said, sitting up slowly. How was it possible to be so tired upon waking from a full night's sleep? *Jesus, help me.*

We pulled into the parking lot only a little later than I thought we would. A couple greeted us at the door as we entered the building. I didn't recognize them. Had it been so long since I'd last attended? I counted from the baby dedication. Three months.

Brandon escorted Micah to children's church while I looked for empty seats near the back of the sanctuary. Stacy, my doctor, sat in a wheelchair in the aisle near the door we'd entered. Her face gleamed in greeting. Reaching up, she wrapped an arm around my neck. "It's so good to see you," she whispered. The warm greeting lifted my sagging spirits.

The last song before the sermon had begun when Brandon and I found two empty seats near the front of the sanctuary. Brandon held Sara as we stood and sang a song about God's faithfulness. I sang along, caught between gratitude for the faithfulness God had shown us thus far and longing to know it on the other side of this mess.

The pastor began his sermon, and Sara chimed in soon after with boisterous coos and exuberant, garbled amens. Fighting a smile, Brandon passed her to me. As I walked through the doors at the back of the sanctuary, Sara loosed her final approving thoughts on the introduction.

Sunlight streamed through the windows in the foyer, its beams splaying on the floral couches, beckoning me. Spending the service in the foyer wasn't what I had imagined when I'd agreed to attend church that morning, but I decided to enjoy my daughter and be content to spend a few hours away from the house.

With the exception of doctor's appointments, road trips with Dad to see my physical therapist, and a few short visits with Hanna Peshoff, I'd become a shut-in of sorts. New faces and a change of scenery were nice.

A young woman I didn't recognize stepped into the foyer carrying a baby girl who looked a little younger than Sara. The woman grinned and said, "I guess this is where the loud ones sit."

"So it would seem." I smiled back.

"I'm Jenny," she said. "Jenny Freeman." She lived in Houston, about five hours away, and had attended so that her mother-in-law, who she was visiting, could show off her baby granddaughter, Julia. Julia had been born in February, three months after Sara. Jenny also had a son, Matthew, who was a year or so older than Micah.

After a few minutes of polite small talk, she crossed the seating area to the couch where I sat. "I'm not wearing my glasses today, and I want to see you better," she said, peering into my face.

Her eyes were a soft blue flecked with sea green. Freckles decorated her cheeks and nose, which wrinkled when she laughed. Long brown hair, drawn into a low ponytail, rested over one shoulder. Jenny was a pretty girl, but there was something intangible about her that drew me. Maybe it was her bright smile or her refreshing honesty or her disregard for Ruston social protocol, which I'd never liked anyway.

A friend that I hadn't seen in weeks approached us. Jenny moved back to the couch opposite of me so we could talk. My friend asked about the progress of our move and about my health. I offered a brief but honest overview and said, "I'm just doing my best to cope and be content with where I am."

When my friend walked away, Jenny's smile gentled. She cocked her head to one side and asked, "What's going on with your health, if you don't mind me asking?"

Compassion radiated from her entire being. Unlike most people, she wasn't looking for a "fine" or a platitude. She wanted to *know*. Gulping down the instinct to whitewash my suffering, I gave a synopsis of what I'd been through since Sara was born. I measured the interest in her eyes so that I would know how much to tell.

Soul-baring was a minefield, and every audience was different. Some wanted details; some wanted the briefest version possible. Jenny stayed with me.

As I spoke, her shoulders began to sag. Her head bowed and brow furrowed, as if my pain were her own. Genuine empathy was an expensive character trait. I wasn't surprised when she launched into her own tale.

Three days after birthing the baby I saw in her arms, she'd learned she had advanced cancer of the esophagus that had already metastasized to the liver. She'd spent a horrific month in the hospital receiving aggressive chemotherapy treatments rather than going home to mother her newborn daughter.

We exchanged stories of our personal journeys to hell and learned tactics for walking through the flames. We agreed—the only way out was through. Only Jesus Christ and his love, mercy, and grace provided the light we needed to walk such dark, treacherous paths. "The cancer in my esophagus is gone. For now. I realize that I'm not promised tomorrow, but I have today. Today is a gift," she said, smiling at her daughter.

Unbidden tears sprang from my eyes. I rarely cried in front of people I'd just met. When I did, I always felt shame at exposing my fragility, but this was different. Jenny wept with me. We didn't cry for ourselves; we cried for one another. We grieved the pain, reveled in the victories.

An unexpected emotion bubbled to the surface of my heart as the service closed inside the sanctuary. Love. I hadn't loved so easily and freely in a long time. A long history of betrayals had seen to that.

I recognized the gift extended to us. Jenny almost hadn't come to church that morning because a recent chemotherapy treatment had left her fatigued. My own battle would have prevented my presence if not for Brandon.

We never would have met if our baby girls hadn't simultaneously joined the "amen" section. I wouldn't have shared my story had not my friend approached and asked about my health. My honest response had given Jenny the freedom to share her journey.

The gift came wrapped in a question—a question that exposed a wound. Would I let her in? Would I allow her enough proximity to hurt me? If I did, she might hurt me—badly—through no fault of her own.

A wave of shame washed over me as I realized the truth. I never would've chosen a friend in the midst of a battle with cancer. I wouldn't set myself up for that level of heartache if I could help it.

The friendly attraction drawing me toward her spirit wasn't a natural by-product of my disposition. I was reserved and slow to warm up. I had to be, for I tended to lose my whole heart to the objects of my affection—and fast. Experience had taught me that all friendships were lost sooner or later, and loss scared me more than death. I wasn't on the market for a new friend, especially not a friend who might leave me bereft.

Clearly, something larger than either of us was at work and had brought us together. "Can I get your number? Maybe we could text," I said.

A new fear stabbed my heart as she recited her number. Would she be interested in friendship with me? I was no prize, especially not now when I could do so little for anyone.

The volume of the music increased inside the sanctuary, signaling the end of our visit. People poured into the foyer. Jenny introduced me to her son and mother-in-law. I introduced her to Brandon when he came to collect me. Embracing, we said goodbye.

Questions flurried through my mind as we walked across the hot pavement toward the car. Could I do it? Was I brave enough to love her with my whole heart? Love was so risky. How did God manage it?

On the ride home, I typed out a text, pressed send, and waited with bated breath. She may have given me her number out of obligation or fear of being rude. I waited.

My phone sang a short tune. She'd replied. "It was so great to meet with you and visit this morning. God is so good! I'll be in touch!"

The decision had been made several times over with each tiny step in her direction—I would love her. I already did. Something new, exciting, and important had begun. I could feel it.

* * *

Jenny sent a text the next day. I replied, hoping I didn't sound too eager or awestruck. She seemed really cool—something I'd never been—and I didn't want to scare her off. The next day, she called.

We shared stories. I'd grown up in church. She hadn't. "I was an absolute heathen," she said with a laugh. "My friend and I partied with rock bands for years. I wasted so much time." She sighed.

"Really? Which bands?" I had to know.

"You would know Blue October. I saw on your blog bio that you like them," she said. "Actually, one of their hit songs is about my friend."

"No way." I knew it. She was *way* too cool for me.

"I wasted a lot of time too," I said. "But I didn't have as much fun as you. Instead of spending my college years pursuing God, I wasted them being bitter and pissed off at him for things he didn't do."

"So I guess we just have to make sure we don't waste today," she said. In my mind, I saw her shrug. She was much better at grace than I was.

"Speaking of rock bands," I said. "Brandon and I will be in Houston in a few weeks to see Florence and the Machine. He bought tickets for our anniversary. I'd love to see you if it works out."

"Yes!" she said. "You and Brandon have to come over for dinner before the show. I'd love to cook for you!"

How to answer delicately, without offending her? "That would be amazing, but I'm very difficult to cook for."

"I'm sure, but it can't be much more difficult than cooking for myself. I'm following this weird, super-strict whole foods diet to help my body fight the cancer."

Though our trials differed in many ways, I felt understood by her. Someone out there got it, got me, got how difficult it was to be a mother of young children fighting for your life, unsure of whether you'd win.

She asked me to believe with her for a miracle of healing. "I don't know if anyone really believes with me. That God can and will do it," she said.

"I'll believe with you. I'll believe until you're healed," I vowed.

"Let's believe for each other," she said. "If one of us gets tired, we can have faith for each other."

Over the next couple of weeks, we learned about one another—favorite colors, flowers, movies, music. We prayed, we laughed, we wept. We shared our secrets and desires and discussed our hopes for healing. "I would love to be a healing story, one that displays the Lord's power to heal," she said. "But I know that not everyone gets that story. I have already gotten a miracle in being healed of my esophageal cancer. I may not get another. Either way, I trust him."

Her words landed and stuck. Miracles did seem rare. God could easily work two miracles for the same person. He could heal us both. But would he?

Maybe God had brought us together to answer that question. Maybe we needed each other to spur one another on toward faith and good works while we waited for the miracles. I didn't know God's purposes, but I wanted to believe he was good enough to bring us both out of the fire.

Every day, I looked forward to the next call, the next text, the next shared scripture or God-inspired thought. Her words rang with truth and beauty, and she said them in such a charming and endearing manner.

I only suspected she reciprocated my feelings until one day she said, "You're like David, and I'm like Jonathan. Our souls are knit together. Every time we talk, we strengthen each other in the Lord."

Our souls were knit. Yes. That was what had happened, and all we'd done was drag ourselves to church. God had managed the rest.

I added "chance meetings" and "a friend who understands" to my Wall of Gratitude.

13

Breakdown

An unexpected cold front swept through the South the first week of September, bringing hundred-something-degree temperatures down to the sixties and seventies. Jenny, whose birthday fell on September 6, insisted it was an early birthday present from God.

"Happy birthday! Glad to be a beneficiary," I replied through text.

The sun beamed in celebration, beckoning me outdoors. The crisp breeze foreshadowed the autumn to come, and the trees applauded as it swept through their still-green tops. Before I'd closed the carport door, Micah darted around my legs and ran for the slide around back.

I hauled Sara, who at ten months stretched her eighteen-month-size clothing, and a bottle to the lounge chair in the backyard. I eased down into the chair, not wanting to drop the baby or the bottle. At Sara's last checkup, Michelle had said, "She's absolutely perfect, Mama, but she's literally off the charts for height and weight." Her size and the lazy way she held her body in my arms had become difficult for me to manage in my weakened state.

I dropped the last few inches into the lounge chair and landed with an "oof." While Sara ate, I rolled up my yoga pants and shirtsleeves, exposing my pale skin to the sunlight. I stared up at the blue sky, sparse clouds, and waving pines, mesmerized. Micah chattered and sang rhythmic melodies as he played. Sara followed every drag at the silicone nipple with a brief moan of contentment. I closed my eyes, drinking it all in.

Tires crunched the gravel at the end of the driveway. Debbie pulled up behind my car and greeted us with a wide smile that lit up her eyes. Her white hair reflected the light of the sun and blew away from her face—a face I'd come to love. She was a pretty woman with well-placed features, but a deeper beauty shone through. Today, her face appeared almost angelic as she'd come to grant me a short reprieve from the-girl-who-did-not-sleep. Sara had again begun to wake every night, sometimes for hours at a time. Sleep deprivation was exposing the worst parts of me yet again.

Debbie scooped up Sara with her own "oof," singing a merry greeting, and carried her to the swing. They grinned and laughed at each other so merrily that Micah joined them. My skin tingled in the warm light of the sun.

The tingle deepened, transforming into searing heat—a familiar sensation. Puzzled, I glanced at my legs and feet. They'd turned bright red. Panic rose in my chest. "We need to get Sara out of the sun!" I shouted to Debbie. "I'm burning!"

Debbie frowned, but she plucked Sara from the swing without question and called Micah indoors. When we were all inside, she stared at my feet, which had swelled and turned scarlet. A suspicious rash spread across my arms and legs, which now itched more than burned. "Melissa, I don't think this is a normal sunburn. How long were you outside?"

I glanced at the clock. It was 10:25 a.m. "Not more than fifteen minutes," I said and shook my head. No one burned in fifteen minutes. Not at 10:00 a.m.

No. No, no, no. Not the sun too. To lose the sun would be to lose beauty, and I had two small children who needed to be outside.

After I'd taken a dose of Benadryl and slathered aloe vera gel over my rash, Debbie led the kids back outside at my request. I called Mom, crying.

She listened to me sniff and sob throughout my explanation of what had happened and then answered calmly, "Before you jump to conclusions, you need to do a little research on the side effects of the duloxetine."

The suggestion halted the avalanche of self-pity crashing inside me. Why hadn't I thought of that? As the daughter of a scientist and the wife of a pharmacist, I should have. I thanked Mom, hung up, and pulled out my laptop.

What I read staggered me. Of the 39,138 people who'd reported side effects when taking the antidepressant, 37 of them had a photosensitivity reaction. Less than 1 in 1,000. 0.09%. Of those 37 people, only 5.5% were in my age range. I was a freaking unicorn.

The official recommendation was to discontinue the drug and report the side effect to my doctor. Further down the page I read that the photosensitivity might not go away, even after the drug was out of my system.

I swore.

That night over dinner, I asked Brandon, "What would you do if it were you?"

His brow lifted as he stared down at his plate. "If a pill kept me out of the sun and from enjoying sex?" A stream of air escaped from between his lips, making a raspberry sound.

A soft laugh blew out of my nose, but there was little heart behind it.

"Here's the thing, babe"—he took a bite, chewed, and swallowed—"I can't answer that question for you. Only you know what you're willing to live with."

Staring at the opposite wall, I said, "There's going to be pain either way, isn't there?"

"You could always try something else," he suggested.

I shook my head. "I don't think my body likes medicine. Think about it—for as long as I've been on acid reflux pills, I've only gotten worse. I had that bad reaction to my epidural during labor. Sulfa tried to kill me. And I don't seem to tolerate these pain blockers too well."

"Sounds like you know what you're going to do."

"Yeah," I said. "I just don't enjoy pain."

"That's healthy. Masochism is a sign of mental illness, you know."

Cold settled in my chest. "Do you ever wonder if I am really crazy? Like a hypochondriac or something?"

"Crazy? Maybe." He winked at me. "A hypochondriac? No."

How could he be so sure? "Will you tell me? If I ever fall off the ledge, I mean." I searched his chocolate gaze for reassurance.

He set down his fork and turned toward me. "Babe—as long as I'm around, you won't be falling off any ledges."

The promise was good enough for me. "I won't need another refill. I'm quitting tomorrow."

Brandon turned back to his plate. "Okay, but prepare yourself. Coming off an antidepressant can be a bumpy ride."

* * *

I'd stopped an antidepressant cold turkey once before when I was a teenager. The experience hadn't been too awful. All I remembered was having to leave my shift at the movie theater early one night due to dizziness. I wasn't prepared for what was about to happen.

Withdrawal of some sort set in the second day. I woke with a queasy feeling that developed into nausea so intense it was difficult to eat. By lunch, my head pounded. The following day, my head ached and swam. My vision blacked out randomly throughout the day and always when I stood up. As expected, the pain returned.

Some unknown ailment disturbed Sara's sleep more than usual, waking her multiple times throughout the night. She woke from her afternoon naps fussing. Over the course of the evening, her cries transformed into angry shrieks. While she bawled, I prepared dinner. It was as if her colic had returned, and with it, Micah's anxiety. I found him more than once hiding in his bed under a pile of blankets, fists covering his ears, his cries echoing Sara's.

After several nights of poor sleep, Sara began one of her fits. I needed to cook dinner but lacked the will to even stand at the kitchen counter. I stared at the meat I had thawed. I contemplated the pans I needed. But I couldn't make myself move. Sara's wails intensified, breaking through my stupor.

Something inside me fractured. Heat rose from my stomach to my head, and I started screaming. I bellowed once. And again. A shrill "Aaaaaaahhhhhhhh!" ripped from my throat until my voice broke.

I glimpsed Micah staring up at me, wide eyed and frozen, as I stomped out of the kitchen and into the hall, unstrapping Sara from the baby sling. The look lacked the cold-water-to-the-face effect it usually had, but it helped me regain enough self-control to ease Sara into the crib.

I shut the bedroom door behind me and closed the pocket door between the hall and the living area. Sara's wails blew through the walls, but I couldn't return to soothe her. In this state, I might hurt her.

I called Mom. "I'm not okay," I yelled, gasping through tears. Yelling was the only way to get the words out. "I'm having some kind of breakdown, and I'm scared. Mom, I'm scared I'm going to hurt myself or one of the kids. I could have hurt Sara just now. Brandon won't be here for hours, and I don't know what to do."

"Call Nona," she said, her voice steady and soft. "Ask her to come over until Brandon comes home. I will spend the night, and you will get some sleep."

Calming, I obeyed and waited for Nona to arrive. How could I behave in such a way to my children? I would die for them! How could I act like this and call myself a child of God?

I loathed myself, my damned fragility. I was so abominably weak. A single word might cause me to disintegrate. Maybe I didn't deserve to live.

A whisper washed through my spirit. *I gently lead those with young.*

That was from Isaiah 40:11.

Gently.

Nothing about my life felt gentle. A storm raged inside and around me. Everything had fallen to chaos. My words and tone certainly weren't gentle. I didn't deserve gentleness.

The voice spoke again. Gently. Tenderly. *My gentleness isn't about you or what you deserve. It's about me and who I am.*

A sob racked my chest. A holy presence drew near, hovering. Everything fell still. I opened the pocket door, walked down the hall, and cracked the nursery door.

Sara's cries stopped short when she saw me. Tenderly, I retrieved her from the crib and cradled her to my chest. "Mommy's so sorry," I whispered into her soft tuft of hair. "I'm so sorry, baby girl."

She soothed, loosing sporadic hiccups—tiny aftershocks of the ordeal. I returned to the living room to apologize to Micah. "I'm so sorry, Bubs. Mama sinned, and it hurt you. Will you please forgive me?"

He nodded, his wide brown eyes sincere. Staggered, I gathered him in my free arm. He didn't push me away, and the tears flowed. My children made forgiveness look easy, as if it were no hard thing. How did they manage it? Forgiveness had always seemed an impossible task, painful and drawn out.

Micah and Sara were small, but they carried an astounding capacity to give and receive love. Maybe that was part of what Jesus had in mind when he'd said we had to come to him like little children.

For months, I'd believed this illness had been sent to teach me something. I'd been wrong. This thing wasn't here to add to what I already knew. It was an undoing, and it wouldn't stop until every wing and facet of my life had been leveled.

I just hoped I would survive the demolition.

* * *

Two days after my breakdown, I made a grave error. Brandon whipped up gluten-free pancakes for dinner, everyone's favorite treat. Gluten-free pancakes weren't as light and fluffy as regular pancakes, but they were still pretty good. Even Brandon liked them. He served them steaming.

I slathered on a thick layer of butter, drizzled a little honey on top, and ate with enthusiasm. With only a few bites left, my stomach burned. Cramps twisted my intestines. I dashed out of my seat and down the hall to the bathroom, where I spent a good portion of the evening.

The next morning, ulcers inflamed my mouth and throat, making it uncomfortable to swallow. An allergic rash spread over my legs and chest, and my joints and muscles ached. My stomach smoldered and cramped, culminating in further urgent trips to the bathroom. All of this while sudden and violent mood swings made me question whether I'd lost myself entirely.

Recovering in bed, I realized I'd never asked God whether I should take the antidepressant. Maybe all that had transpired since my first dose was punishment. Maybe it was severe mercy.

My Bible drew my gaze. I reached for it and flipped to the Psalms. The Psalms always laid a feast for my famished soul. Several chapters in, a phrase seemed to lift from the page: "You will not leave my soul in Sheol." It was there, baby. My soul lay in the holding for the dead. But God wouldn't leave me there. Until my release, my flesh would rest in hope.

Mom and Dad arrived on Saturday to take care of me and the kids. Together, we took a communion of homemade beef broth. Since my reaction to the pancakes, broth was the only food I could tolerate, so they shared in my suffering as we proclaimed Christ's.

The communion softened my frustrations toward God. Because Christ laid down his life, I would not be abandoned to hell. Because he was broken, I would be bound up. By his stripes, I would be healed. Because he drank the cup of God's wrath, I could drink the cup of everlasting joy.

After they left that evening, I followed Mom's admonition to rest as well as I could. Rest helped, but it didn't fix me.

"Give it time," Brandon said. "Drugs like that have to work their way out. That's why doctors recommend you taper the dose."

"I'd only been taking it for two weeks," I retorted.

"Which is long enough, apparently," he said.

He didn't only chide. He also helped. The last thing he wanted to do when he clocked out after a long day at the pharmacy was to buy groceries, but he did it. He ran errands and cooked breakfast. He took the kids to church. Every spare moment he spent working at the new property, preparing the land and the used trailer we'd bought for the impending move. Everyone who knew him and the weight he carried joined me in calling him "Superman."

The only thing he asked of me was to spend a little time each day packing, but fatigue dragged at my body and drained all of my resolve. Overwhelmed, I posted several prayer requests to my blog, which I'd updated regularly since my health had taken a downward turn. The response astounded me.

Many offered prayers. Others offered help, including three friends I hadn't seen since high school. One friend, in particular, warmed my heart with her kindness and honesty. "I don't pray," she said, "but I can help."

I accepted every offer of help, something I wasn't used to doing.

She arrived on the Monday morning before the move and helped me sort through items to box and items to sell and then helped me price the things we had set aside. It may have seemed a small thing to her, but I doubted I could have begun alone. Decision-making had become one of my most difficult tasks of late. She'd lightened my load with only her presence and opinions.

On Tuesday, another friend came. She packed boxes and peeled and chopped up a butternut squash I made into soup, a task that would have been painful at best. Wrestling winter squashes was a significant chore in my fragile state, and she'd made it look easy. Another friend came on Thursday, bringing her two young boys, and helped me pack more boxes. She'd even brought plastic totes for me to borrow. Micah and her oldest hit it off and had a grand time—we found them playing in the shower with a can of shaving cream.

A parade of friends, parents, aunts, and grandparents flowed through our home. Micah asked each day in expectation, "Who we gonna see today?"

Everyone's presence refreshed us all. My loneliness was assuaged, my children had playmates, and the boxes were packed in time. On the evening before the move, I realized that God had answered every cry of my heart. With people. Some of whom I would have never thought to ask for help. Jenny cried as I told her how good God and the people in my circle had been to my family and me. I blessed them all in prayer.

The day of the move arrived and with it a small army of helpers that included family, friends, and people from our community group at church, which we hadn't been able to attend in weeks. My energy lasted just long enough to pack up what was left of the kitchen and to help put it away at the new house.

I hadn't realized how much kitchenware I owned until it didn't all fit in our tiny trailer kitchen. Nonessentials were packed into boxes and tucked away in our portable storage building outside. As soon as the task was finished, I felt myself begin to fade against my will.

I shook hands with the men who had come all the way from Ruston to help us and hugged Hanna Peshoff's neck while Mom and Nona made my bed. "Thank you," I said again and again, meaning every word.

A powerful wave of fatigue washed over me, dragging me down to some unseen place I wasn't sure I would surface from. A hand grabbed my elbow and guided me into my bedroom. Mom.

Sunlight peeked through the slits in the blinds, resting in soft patches on my navy blue duvet cover I'd bought for the queen-size bed we'd swapped with Brandon's parents for our king-size waterbed that was too large for the trailer. There was so much light and air, not like the house on Bear Creek Road. A box fan hummed a lullaby over the noise of work on the other side of the thin walls.

A sigh escaped my lips as I sank. The bed caught me, protecting me from the undertow. "Rest now." Mom's voice. I couldn't have disobeyed had I tried. My head discovered a pillow, and I closed my eyes.

I didn't deserve this—all this love.

Love has nothing to do with what you deserve. Love is a gift. You can't earn it.

The words splashed over me, warm and liquid, and I drifted away, feeling so tired I wasn't sure I would wake. No fear tainted the thought. Love had guided me to Sheol. Love would guide me home.

14

In Sickness and in Health

On the morning after we moved, Brandon and I broke in the new house by hosting worship and communion with Mom, Dad, and Debbie. I drank water in lieu of bread and grape juice. Looking into their faces, I thanked God for each one and for the others he'd sent to cure my loneliness—Nona, Honey, Hanna, high school friends, our community group, Jenny. Her daily calls and encouragement splashed each day with vibrant color.

Gratitude swelled in my chest and seeped out of my eyes. In his kindness, God was meeting all of our needs—through people, his body, his Church. Friends even blessed us with financial gifts. Micah had adjusted well to the move. Sara had begun sleeping through the night again. The antidepressant had worked its way out of my system, and I could no longer detect any lingering side effects. The new gut-healing diet I'd begun after my reaction to buttered pancakes had decreased my digestive discomfort, and my energy increased each day.

To celebrate, Brandon and I enjoyed some late-night, on-a-whim love-making. Afterward, something unusual caught my eye as I glanced at the bathroom mirror. A large red splotch appeared below my left breast along my rib cage. It was raised and warm to the touch. The left side of my face began to prickle and itch. "Babe?" I called.

Brandon ducked into the tiny bathroom and frowned when he saw my spreading rash. A cough wheezed from my chest. I struggled to pull air back into my lungs.

Well, dammit.

Brandon fetched a bottle of Benadryl and my inhalers from the kitchen without waiting for me to ask. I puffed on my inhaler and popped four capsules, one at a time. Soon, my anxiety would induce the adrenaline I needed to kick it, and I'd be okay.

Brandon waited with my EpiPen in hand, ready to strike in case I wasn't able. When my breathing eased, he dialed Mom's number and handed me the phone.

"Mom, we've hit a new low. I'm now allergic to sex," I said and explained what had happened.

In the absence of words, I almost heard the cogs turn in her brilliant mind. "You're using condoms now, right?" she asked.

"Yeah." I coughed.

The Gut and Psychology Syndrome (GAPS) diet I followed strongly advised against all medication, including hormone supplements. My weight had dropped so low that my period had stopped, so it was unlikely I would become pregnant, but Brandon didn't want to risk it. A pregnancy could result in two unnecessary deaths. The sister of Brandon's coworker had recently almost died due to an allergic reaction to her pregnancy. Not to mention the fact my condition worsened with each pregnancy and labor. Abstinence wasn't a viable option—we liked each other too much—so we'd resorted to condoms, which weren't our favorite, but they served their purpose.

"What are they made of?" she asked.

Brandon left the bed to check. He called from the bathroom. "Latex."

After a pause, Mom said, "Well, the good news is you're probably not allergic to sex."

At work the next day, Brandon solved our immediate problem and discreetly purchased a box of latex-free condoms. Meanwhile, I researched latex allergy, which promised to affect me far beyond the bedroom. Latex hid itself in many common items, including medical supplies. It was time to order a medical alert bracelet, something I'd put off, not eager to mark myself as an easy kill.

A new severe allergy changed everything—everything except our plans to see Jenny and Florence and the Machine. Brandon and I packed clothes, pots, pans, and an ice chest full of food and drove out of town on the last Friday morning in September. We'd never driven to Houston. The rural landscape featured quaint barns and farmhouses, the picturesque scenery occasionally interrupted by run-down homes settled in forests of junk and scrap metal. The speed limits were very Texan, peaking at eighty-five miles per hour.

For lunch, we ate homemade beef and broccoli soup that I'd packed in mason jars and wrapped in towels to keep warm. I savored the rich broth flavored with onion and garlic. Brandon rated it only "okay." Everything tasted good to me.

We arrived at our condo on the outskirts of Houston in time to bake the chicken thighs I'd packed with butternut squash and sliced onions. Months had passed since my last quiet evening. I tried to enjoy it, but it felt wrong somehow. My mind wandered dark streets lined with questions, the answers obscured by shadow.

What could a latex allergy steal? It would exclude me from balloons and playgrounds, certainly. I had to be careful of rubber bands, pencil erasers, bandages, and Micah's and Sara's toys. We'd already replaced several pacifiers and bottle nipples. The stuff seemed to be everywhere.

From across the room, Brandon's eyes smoldered, melting my melancholy, and he sauntered toward me. How he found me attractive when I was such a mess mystified me. I fired his favorite pointed look over my shoulder before sliding the full baking dish into the oven.

His arms wrapped around my waist as I closed the oven door. "I can bake some chicken in your oven."

I turned into him, grimacing.

"I admit, it's not my best." He pressed his soft lips against mine.

"Not even close," I mumbled against his mouth.

The gentle pressure of his hand at the small of my back reminded me I wouldn't miss every moment. Good things would come. Something good was here, right in front of me, and I wouldn't relinquish it out of fear.

His mouth pulled away from mine. He leaned his head back and closed his eyes. "Crap."

"What?" I asked.

His mouth flattened. "I forgot to pack the new condoms."

"Oh." Of course. "Doesn't that kind of defeat the purpose of an anniversary trip?"

"Or it could make it more interesting." The naughty glint in his eyes made me wary.

"What do you have in mind?" I asked.

"You'll see," he said.

After dinner, he drove me to a twenty-four-hour CVS. "You're not going to make me go inside and get them, are you?" I asked.

"Oh, no. We're doing this together. Tonight, we're *that* couple."

Lord a' mercy.

Brandon led me to the aisle where condoms were sold. There were an unreasonable number of choices. "Wanna try a warming lubricant?" he asked. Glancing at my expression, he answered his own question. "Yeah, you're probably right. That's just asking for trouble. What about sheepskin?"

Shooting daggers from my eyes, I selected a sensible-looking box labeled "latex-free" with no bells or whistles. "Come on," I said, stalking toward the register.

"You're no fun," he stage-whispered, jogging to catch up. "But I'll give you this—life with you is never boring." Winking, he took the box from my hand and pulled out his wallet.

* * *

Brandon drove me through suburban Houston, past gated neighborhoods and mansions sandwiched too close together, until we arrived at Jenny's home, which was a short drive from the location of the concert. The scents of herbs and roasted meat wafted outside as she opened the door. She laughed in greeting and threw her arms open wide. Her chemo port pressed into my chest as I returned her embrace. Answering my unasked question, she waved her hand and laughed. "I know. Ignore it. I do."

She hugged Brandon and led us inside. Drew, her husband, greeted us in the foyer with a kind smile that traveled up to his blue eyes. He shook hands with Brandon and embraced me. "I've heard a lot about you," he said.

Unsure how to respond to that comment, I asked after Matthew and Julia. "They're staying with their grandparents," Jenny said. "They love that, and I wanted to make the most of our visit."

Upon my request, she took me on a tour of the house, which Drew had designed and contracted himself with the intention to sell it. The spacious floor plan was both intelligent and modern. The design choices bespoke dauntless, artistic taste.

"It's not really me, though." One side of Jenny's mouth turned down. "I'm not really suburban Texas."

"What about you?" I asked Drew.

"Me? No. I'm a farm boy at heart," he said. "I work for my dad, and development is the job." In his jeans and with his wide smile, I could see him living happily on a ranch in west Texas, wrestling cattle, fighting off diamondback rattlers, and wearing a cowboy hat atop his mostly bald head.

"Think you'll ever move?" Brandon asked.

Drew shrugged. "Maybe. But not now."

They didn't have to explain. Houston boasted one of the best cancer hospitals in the world. Jenny's mom and his dad lived nearby. Trusted helpers weren't found in every place. Neither were good jobs. I'd learned from experience one desperately needed money and good insurance during a health crisis.

A bell dinged. Dinner was ready. Just before leaving town, I'd offered to bring something for myself to eat, but Jenny had asked so many thoughtful questions that I believed I would be able to eat without getting sick. Surely, faith wouldn't fail me now.

For me, she served oxtail that had cooked slowly all day in the Crock-Pot alongside gently boiled vegetables with fresh herbs. I'd brought my own salt, which would have felt awkward had we been with anyone else. To Brandon and Drew, she served a chuck roast, seasoned with a variety of herbs and butter.

She led us to the dining room, the walls papered in a pleasing design. The polished oak of the table reflected the light of the crystal chandelier, which might have seemed old fashioned had it not been for the edgy decor.

The oxtail meat melted in my mouth, and the vegetables were cooked to a perfect consistency. A warm nurtured sensation swept over me as we ate and talked. Every bite, every laugh embraced me in a love I didn't know I was hungry for. At times, I sensed the Spirit of Jesus feasting with us. His magic hung in the air so densely I could taste his essence—a robust wine that made the heart glad. I'd never enjoyed a dinner more than the one that night.

Too soon, it was time to leave for the concert, though I might have been tempted to miss it if I hadn't known the truth—no matter how much time we spent there, it wouldn't feel like enough. We all embraced one another as we said goodbye.

Florence and the Machine was everything I'd hoped they would be. Florence Welch sang with a small orchestra, including an ornate harp, alongside her band. An extra measure of energy allowed me to stand, sing, and dance for the one-hour set. They performed several of my favorites. Brandon grabbed my hand as soon as the last song ended and whisked me away from the crowd, which now reeked of beer and cigarette smoke.

On the ride home, I squeezed his hand. "Thank you. Thank you so much for tonight."

He raised my hand to his lips. "Thank you for eight years."

"Here's to many more," I said.

A look passed between us—a smile sobered by the realities of sickness and suffering and the possibility of less time than we'd planned, a smile full of commitment and loyalty that promised, "I'll be here for it all."

Early in our marriage, I'd spent long hours at the local university, earning my degree in music education, teaching piano lessons, and performing in operas and musicals for fun. He'd gone to work and spent a lot of time hunting and fishing with his dad on his days off. We would see each other late at night, work in a date on the weekend, and go to church together, but we'd lived largely separate lives, even after adding Micah to our family.

We couldn't afford to live that way any longer, not if we wanted to survive. For many people, the vow to remain faithful in sickness and in health was an empty phrase mindlessly droned during a wedding ceremony if said at all. Few in their twenties even considered what they were saying. That wasn't true for us.

Brandon had suffered from Crohn's disease for over a decade when we married. Only two months before our wedding, he'd gone through a bowel resection to cut several inches of scar tissue from his small intestine. When I'd agreed to marry him, I was ready to care for him and to provide for us financially, if necessary. It had never occurred to either of us that I might end up "the sick one."

The vow in Brandon's brown eyes reassured me. We might have taken a detour in the course we'd mapped for our marriage, but he wasn't going to abandon me to hell, even though he was afraid I might abandon him for heaven.

I wanted to return the reassurance. I wanted to tell him I wasn't going to die. But I hadn't been promised that. Most days, I believed unflinchingly that I would live and declare the works of the Lord, but how could I know for sure? How could I be certain that one day anaphylaxis wouldn't steal the breath of God from my lungs? The danger was real. Any moment could be my last. With one mistake, I could leave him with our two small kids to raise on his own.

* * *

Rain pelted the truck as Brandon flew down the Texas highway toward the Louisiana state line. I snapped back to awareness as Brandon passed another car and tried again to work out what was happening.

I felt like I was drowning, or what I imagined drowning would feel like. My lungs burned for air. Thought dissolved into unfocused shimmers. Like the reflection of sunlight on gentle waves. Sound dulled. Had I gone under?

"Stay with me, babe. There's no hospital for miles."

Brandon's hazy features were near. His voice was far away. Odd. I tried to reach for his hand—the one that clutched the EpiPen behind white knuckles—but my arm was too heavy to lift. I was heavy—so heavy—all over.

The windshield wipers swished the rain from the glass. I tried to count swipes. It wasn't right for our weekend to end this way. If I died, Brandon would likely surmise that this wouldn't have happened had he kept me at home and therefore the accident was his fault. I had to hold on—for him and the kids. They needed Mama to come home.

Trees, barns, junkyards zoomed backward down the highway. Raindrops streaked into horizontal lines along the passenger window. Brandon put the inhaler to my mouth. "Breathe," he commanded.

I sucked in the medicine, finishing with a wheeze, and replayed the events of the morning in my hazy mind. We'd stopped at Whole Foods. Neither of us had ever been to one, and we'd been awestruck at both the selection and astronomical pricing. I'd avoided the bins of nuts but had handled several foods in the produce section. Had I accidentally come into contact with latex?

We'd also topped off at a gas station. There, I'd purchased a coffee to go—my favorite road trip treat. Halfway through the cup, the bad feeling had pounced. Since then, it had only gotten worse. I'd taken as much Benadryl as Brandon would let me. He was afraid for me to sleep. Though sleep would have felt nice.

"What was your favorite song last night?" The words sounded strained. Choked. He'd asked the question last night.

To humor him, I searched for the song title. "Cosmic Love."

"So. When we build our house, do you want a laundry room off the master closet? Like Drew and Jenny have?"

A cough cut off my answer.

"What did you think of their kitchen?"

I tried to remember, but I was too tired.

The truck slowed. Brandon spoke again. "I'm stopping for gas. I'm also going to call your parents and ask a few people to pray." Brown eyes bored into mine. "If we have to use this EpiPen, I'm taking you straight to the hospital. You hear me? You won't get to see your kids tonight if that happens. So you better fight. Got it? Answer me."

"Yeah," I forced out.

Brandon disappeared. I wandered. I wasn't afraid to die. I was afraid to be a burden—a burden of guilt, a burden of grief, a burden of resources.

The truck door opened, and I jerked awake. "Jenny's praying. Dixie's praying. Your parents are praying. And Eddie's praying. You do your part, and we'll be fine."

Brandon told me when we crossed the state line back into Louisiana. Just a little longer. I could move my arms again when we'd passed out of Shreveport. Another puff at the inhaler eased the labor of breathing.

We arrived home. Brandon carried me from the truck to the bed. He studied me, checking my eyes, my pulse. I felt drained and hollow, but not as dull. The tension he carried released over me like a wave. "I know I said you could see the kids if you stayed alive, but your mom's going to keep them one more night. We think it's best." He kissed my forehead.

I meant to say, "Okay," but sleep overtook me.

The next morning, I planned my funeral.

15

Lord of the Sauerkraut

My phone blasted Lady Gaga's hit song "Telephone," registering a Baton Rouge number I'd seen but couldn't place. Adjusting Sara on my hip, I picked it up and answered it.

"Hello. Mrs. Keaster?" asked a rich, maternal voice.

"This is she," I said, turning down the television.

"Hi, Mrs. Keaster. This is Dr. Hall's office. She had a cancellation and can see you tomorrow if you're available."

I'd been waiting for this call. The timing wasn't convenient—I hadn't yet recovered from the weekend in Houston—but if I didn't accept the offer, I might have to wait six more weeks. More than a month had already passed since I'd scheduled the appointment.

One of the few doctors certified in functional medicine in the state of Louisiana, Dr. Hall was in high demand and came recommended by trusted friends. This time around, several family members and friends prayed with Brandon and me, seeking God's direction. It wasn't a simple decision. The drive to Baton Rouge took over four hours. Her office didn't take insurance, so the cost would be out of pocket. The tests and supplements wouldn't be cheap. But in the end, we'd all agreed God was leading me to her.

"I'll take it! Thank you!" I said. Never mind that I hadn't secured a ride or childcare. The opening was nothing short of a direct answer to many prayers, and I would've been a fool to pass it up.

My people didn't disappoint. Dad canceled his plans and volunteered to drive so that Brandon didn't have to miss work. Mom decided to take a personal day from the university, for which I was grateful. Few people could understand medical jargon as well as she did, and she was an excellent patient advocate—gentle and polite but firm.

We planned to leave early the next morning and return late the same day. Honey agreed to arrive at the house before Brandon left for work and care for the kids until he made it home after his shift. We were set.

I spent the rest of the day preparing meals for my family and beef and broccoli soup to take on the road, which I would warm the next morning and pour into mason jars. Wrapped in towels and stored in an insulated bag, the soup would be enough to eat for a late breakfast and a late lunch.

We left before dawn. "Coffee, anyone?" Dad asked, pulling into McDonald's a few miles north of I-20.

"Yes, please," Mom said from the back seat. She'd offered me the front seat because it reclined, but I had failed to find a position comfortable enough to sleep, despite my exhaustion. Everything ached and throbbed.

"No, thanks," I said, sad I had to say it. As much as I loved the stuff, coffee no longer loved me back. The day ahead would be long—nine hours in the car, several more at Dr. Hall's office—and coffee would only make it longer and more miserable.

Steam curled from the small openings in the plastic lids as the cups were passed into the car. I took one and handed it to Mom. The scent teased me, tempting me to regret my decision.

I missed coffee so much, maybe more than anything. I missed peanut butter and milk and popcorn. I missed being able to eat without my stomach burning and bloating until I looked eight months pregnant. I missed meals that didn't end in cramping, writhing, sweating, and curling into the fetal position. Food had become an enemy, but hunger was often worse. And so I ate and paid the price.

After I'd spent several hours trying to discover the least uncomfortable position, we reached the outskirts of Baton Rouge. I pulled out a jar of warm beef and broccoli soup.

"You're a stronger person than I am if you can eat something that smells like that for breakfast," Dad said, his features wrinkling in disgust.

I covered the mouth of the jar with my hand. The smell didn't bother me. I hadn't considered that it might disturb others. "I can wait and eat it outside when we get there."

"Naw," Dad said. "Go ahead and eat it. I'm just glad I don't have to. Gosh dawg!"

Grinning, I dipped my spoon into the jar. The soup was delicious, especially the sumptuous bits of softened fat mixed in with the meat.

My tastes had changed with my eating habits over the past few weeks. I looked forward to a cup of hot chicken broth every morning before a breakfast of soup or scrambled eggs. It had replaced my morning cup of coffee. Butternut squash was sweet and rich roasted in coconut oil. In years past, I'd never cared for chicken skin, unless it was fried. These days, I devoured it by the mouthful whenever I deboned the chickens I boiled for broth, along with the organs and soft ligaments. It grossed Brandon out to watch me do it.

The truth was I was starving. My weight had plummeted to below 120 pounds, a weight I'd only seen once in high school when I was flirting with an eating disorder. No matter how much I ate, I couldn't get enough. When I ate, I hurt. When I didn't eat, I hurt even more.

"Lord, please help Dr. Hall figure out what's wrong with me," I prayed aloud.

"Amen," Mom and Dad said together. "And help her to know what to do," Mom added.

Light flooded the waiting area. A receptionist with a pleasant face greeted me by name and offered me papers to fill out. By this time, I had all the answers memorized. Before long, the nurse called me back to check my weight and blood pressure and key my symptoms into the computer. She sent me into a private meeting room until Dr. Hall was able to see me.

The door opened. A woman with a round figure, cropped brown hair, and a no-nonsense atmosphere smiled at the book in my hand. "I see you're off to a good start. The GAPS diet has helped several of my patients."

Confirmation. I was in the right place.

I shook her extended hand. She and a nurse sat across the meeting table from my mom and me. Dad settled comfortably on the couch to the side.

Dr. Hall's brow lifted. "May I open us in prayer?"

I blinked at her. "Yes. Please."

She bowed her head. "Lord Jesus, I ask you to be present with us today. Give me guidance and wisdom to know what to do, and give this young woman and her family peace and healing. Amen."

After reviewing my forms, she explained specific tests she would like to run. Some required blood, while others involved urine and stool samples, which would be taken at home.

Lovely.

Mom cast a sideways glance my way and chuckled at my expression.

Dr. Hall would also test my teeth. "Weaknesses in specific teeth often correlate to particular weaknesses in the body," she explained.

She led me from room to room, showing me her testing equipment and treatment options, which included chelation and BioSet. My ears perked. BioSet was the treatment recommended in the book *The Food Allergy Cure*, which Dr. Yakaboski had recommended. Dr. Yakaboski had shown me a version of the treatment Brandon could perform on me at home—which consisted of breathing in prescribed patterns, a specific allergen in hand, while Brandon karate chopped down my spine and up again several times—but it might be nice to have a licensed practitioner perform it with the proper equipment and expertise. "I think I'd like to make an appointment for that," I said.

Dr. Hall paused, frowning. "I'm not sure you're ready for chelation or that you even need it. We need to test you for metal toxicity first. For now, I recommend lighter detoxification. Maybe colonics, if you can find someone in your area who offers it."

Mom wrote the word "colonics" on her notepad. I filed away my own mental note to research what it was at a later time.

"Not chelation," I said. I didn't even know what that would entail. "BioSet."

"Oh, yes," said Dr. Hall. "You would like our practitioner. Her name is Melisa too—with one 's.' BioSet could really help your allergy symptoms."

Dr. Hall sent me home with testing materials, lab orders, and diagnoses that included irritable bowel syndrome, fibromyalgia, and severe allergies. "For now, continue with the GAPS diet. We'll look into the right supplements when your results are in."

The receptionist scheduled an appointment with Melisa for a BioSet treatment later that month and a follow-up appointment in November, during which we would discuss test results and a treatment plan.

"Wow," Mom said, echoing my thoughts as we piled back into the car. "Just. Wow."

A weight lifted from my chest. Within a few weeks, we could get to the bottom of my condition. By November, I might even have a name for this crazy illness.

* * *

Hope, I'd found, wasn't an emotion I was allowed for long. Every time I sniffed its sweet scent, it vanished on the next breath.

Mom and Dad reached our little dirt road at bedtime. I dragged up the rickety wooden steps, working my stiff joints. The door opened, and Brandon stood inside the frame, Sara in his arms. A grin spread across her face, revealing several tiny hard-earned teeth.

"Somebody's happy to see you. We were just about to go to bed," Brandon said. He planted a kiss on my mouth and then stood aside to allow my parents and me to troop into the house. Micah abandoned the television to throw his arms around Mom's knees. "Gwamma!"

"Nice to see you too, bud," I joked.

Hanging onto Mom, he smiled up at me. "Hey, Mama! I miss you!"

I knelt and gathered him in my arms. "I missed you too, Bubs." His soft cheek squished against my lips.

After emptying my bladder, I took Sara from Brandon. "Does she need a fresh diaper?" I asked, walking back to her room.

"Yeah. I was about to change her right before I heard you pull up," Brandon called after me.

Sara was still in a disposable diaper. If I had my way, we'd always use cloth, but I preferred to keep things as simple as possible for my helpers. The diaper was soggy but not dirty, making the change easy and quick. She wore a fresh cloth diaper, and I was snapping her pajamas back together when my palms began to swell and itch.

I frowned. What in heaven's name?

Brandon's features flattened when I returned to the living room. "What's wrong?" he demanded, his voice turning sharp.

I handed Sara to Mom. "I think I'm reacting." A long wheezy cough barked from my chest.

This couldn't be happening. Or could it?

"Do diapers have latex in them?" I asked, scratching my palms.

Mom's brow creased. Brandon pulled out his phone and began typing. I left them to figure it out and went in search of a bottle of Benadryl. No one found a satisfactory answer. Whether I'd been exposed to latex or some unknown chemical, no one could guess.

Mom tucked the kids into bed while Brandon sat with me. Before leaving, she said, "Dad will come back in the morning so you can rest."

The next morning, I stared at the ceiling for nearly an hour before lugging myself to the toilet. How could I feel so heavy and hollow at the same time?

"If I have to live like this, I'd rather just go on to heaven," I told the Lord.

Dad stayed until the kids were ready for their afternoon naps. Tired of the bed, I decided to make my first batch of homemade sauerkraut, a gut-healing food full of probiotics. The GAPS diet recommended that it be eaten with every meal.

I selected a head of cabbage from the refrigerator and washed it. Bruised and wilted leaves curled back, inviting me to pluck them off for disposal. My knife bit into the leaves with a crunch. I cut away the rough core and sliced what was left into thin ribbons, trying to ignore the pain shooting through my wrists and fingers.

Pay attention.

God often spoke to me in the kitchen these days. That's where I spent most of my time, making broth, cooking meals, washing dishes. I opened up, ready to receive.

I packed the shreds of cabbage into three mason jars, sprinkled a tablespoon of sea salt into each one, and filled the jars with filtered water. At the end of the hour, the cabbage was ready to be smashed, a task that would likely be painful. My joints protested as I pressed out the juices of the cabbage.

Tiny bubbles surfaced in the bowl like silent cries. I kept pressing. Without thorough pressing, the cabbage couldn't ferment into what it was meant to be. Raw cabbage would wreak havoc upon my impaired digestive system. It had to be transformed into something new, something teeming with life and nourishment. For seven days, it would wait on my counter. Then it would be ready.

Oh.

I saw it. The cabbage was me—exposed and washed, cored and chopped, salted and smashed. Like the cabbage, I couldn't reach my full potential without this season of "smash and wait." I'd been asking, "Why me? Why me?" in self-pity when I should ask, "Why me?" in grateful awe.

Wasn't it wonderful that the Lord would think of me, poor and needy, raw and cabbage-like as I was? Wasn't it marvelous that he would take the time to pick me up, shredded by my circumstances; place me into a bowl; and carefully, lovingly press me until I became something more— something I couldn't become otherwise?

Life sucked tremendously at the moment, but God had promised to stay with me in the process and redeem it for good, good that likely went far beyond myself. He wouldn't abandon me when I broke under the pressure, so easily overwhelmed by my symptoms and the needs of the children. He was right there—in the pressing. In the waiting.

I spooned the smashed cabbage back into the jars, where it would remain until it could bring healing to my body.

Instead of bouncing back, I felt myself weaken each passing day. Every morning as I fought to stand upright, I thought, "This is the worst point in my illness," only to find a worse one later in the day. I sent out a text requesting prayer and help.

Dad returned morning after morning to help me with the children. Aunt Suzonne left her own sickbed to come and pray with me one afternoon. Jenny messaged me prayers and encouragement. God provided for every need, and still I couldn't show kindness to those I loved and who deserved it the most.

I resented Brandon's simple requests, counting them as burdens rather than opportunities to minister to the one who so selflessly cared for me. When Micah inconvenienced me, as three-year-old boys naturally do, I scalded him with my coldness. Sara wailed, clinging to my ankles while I cooked, making a difficult task seem insurmountable. Heat rose from my toes to my scalp until I yelled like a heathen woman.

One morning, a plastic cup sailed through the air and bounced against the wall before I realized I'd thrown it. Jolted by what I'd done, I ran to my room and fell on my knees at my bedside, sobbing. How was I still in this place of disgrace—screaming at my precious little children and losing my mind? How could I still be this selfish and gross? Why hadn't I changed?

Resolutions to behave better had utterly failed. Every time I slaughtered my flesh, it raised itself from the dead. Mercy! What could I do? I was so sick and horrible. Why couldn't I be good and selfless like Brandon, Dad, and Jenny? I wanted to ooze sweetness instead of filth, but how could I when I was so repugnant on the inside?

One night after weeks of this internal agony, I wailed into the bedsheets. "Change me, or take me home!" Better to be dead than continue in this living death like some depraved zombie.

It is my will that you live.

The words startled me into peace.

I am willing to make you well.

He'd been saying that for weeks. I wasn't sure what he meant until the next day when I opened my Bible to the book of Mark. In the first chapter, a leper approaches Jesus and says, "If you are willing, you can make me clean."

His words sounded like my prayers—"God, if it's your will, heal me."

Jesus, moved by compassion, reaches out and touches the man, something that would make an ordinary Jew ceremonially unclean—not to mention put him in danger of catching the virus. But Jesus was no ordinary Jew. He could touch the unclean and make it clean.

"I am willing," Jesus said. "Be clean."

The next verse read, "Immediately the leprosy left him and he was cleansed."

I am willing.

Tears gathered in my eyes and streamed down my face. "I believe you; help my unbelief." If only I could be healed with a simple touch.

Hard work.

Hard work? Hello? What had I been doing if not hard work? I'd seen Stacy, specialists, a therapist, Dr. Yakaboski, Dr. Hall. I'd driven all over the state to do it. They'd run blood tests, taken x-rays, ordered procedures, and asked me to play medication roulette, which I hadn't won once. I'd tried fasting, drinking amino acids, food rotation, and now the GAPS diet, which required five hours in the kitchen every flipping day. Five hours! That was a full-time job if you counted weekends. And I liked to eat on weekends!

I'd faced dehydration, anaphylaxis, constant pain. Death—tons of it. Death of dreams. Death of relationships. Death of identity. Not to mention the humiliation of pooping into a paper food tray—the kind concession stands used to serve nachos—and sending it off in the mail. Most days I wondered whether I was losing my mind, no matter how often Brandon assured me I wasn't crazy. Hadn't the work been hard enough already? What exactly did I have to do, Jesus?

No answer came.

I read down the page until I came to the passage in which Jesus healed Peter's mother-in-law. He went to her, took her by the hand, and helped her out of bed. That was all. Whatever ailed her vanished, and then she served Jesus and the disciples.

The account struck me. No specific words came to mind, but somehow I knew I was reading a historical account of something that would happen in my future. My season of illness wouldn't be followed by a season of rest but a season of service that would simultaneously fill and try my soul. I would learn dependence in this uncomfortable place, and God wouldn't allow me to return to my self-reliant way of living.

Jenny's face flashed through my mind. Maybe the Lord meant this word for her too! My phone rang. Jenny's number lit up the screen, and my heart leaped.

"Melissa?" The strangled way she said my name made my insides frost over.

"I'm here," I said.

"I was with the doctor today—"

The noise of the highway on her side of the line filled my ears. My lungs forgot how to work.

"He said I don't have long," she said.

The words punched me in the stomach. "How long did he give you exactly?"

A soft sigh blew through the line. "Six to ten weeks if I don't treat it. Six to nine months if I do."

The air was too thick to inhale.

"I called you first," she said. "I need you to pray for me while I tell everyone."

She needed me. "I can do that."

"Thank you."

"What will you do?" I asked. Jenny might have taken a blow today, but she wouldn't simply write her will and wait to die. That wasn't her style. She was a fighter.

"First, I'm going to get a second opinion. I don't know after that."

"Good," I said.

A garbled voice said Jenny's name and mumbled something else.

"I have to go," Jenny said. "I have a lot of people I need to call. Thank you for your prayers."

"I love you." I wanted to say so much more.

"I love you too." The sounds of interstate travel cut off.

I stared at the wall, gripping the phone in my hand. Hot drops of moisture fell from my cheeks onto my lap. My own grief and questions were forgotten. My burdens seemed light in comparison.

Overcome, I fled to my bedside and collapsed, burying my face in the navy comforter. I'd promised to pray. I couldn't help in any practical way, but I could pray. I'd pray her right out of that awful prognosis. If Jesus was willing to heal a scoundrel like me, he would certainly heal a saint like Jenny.

16

Knit

For days, I heard nothing from Jenny except for her charming voice mail message. She didn't respond to my texts and sent no emails. I didn't know what to think.

Sara's first birthday approached, so we celebrated with family over the weekend. Mom and Dad offered to host the party at their house in West Monroe, which had more than twice the square footage of our little trailer. Mom made the cake. All I had to do was bring the baby. Nona and Papaw, Debbie and Boyce, and my sister, Hannah, and her twin girls, who I hadn't seen much since my health crisis had begun, all gathered with us.

After such a hard year, it was a glorious thing to see my beautiful daughter healthy and bright eyed. She demolished her birthday cake, slathering herself in slobbery chocolate crumbs each time a cake-filled fist opened on her eager mouth. Her hand moved faster and faster until the cake was gone. Her satisfied, sugar-drunk expression made us all chuckle.

I avoided the cake and coffee and almost felt good, but Jenny's abrupt silence throbbed like a wound in my chest. Used to daily conversations and multiple texts throughout the day, I felt isolated, cut out of her suffering. I tried contacting her husband, but the number I'd written down as his wasn't serviceable.

It felt like she'd already died. If she had, would anyone tell me? Our relationship had been brief, but I loved her as fiercely as I had loved any friend. What if I didn't have an opportunity to say goodbye? What if she was gone and I had to walk this road alone again? Would I survive it?

That evening after the party, I lay in bed to recover from the excitement and unzipped my chest before the Lord. A gentle weight settled over me. I recognized his peace, but I hadn't yet learned how to stay in it. The heaviness returned when I rolled out of bed to cook dinner.

The phone rang as I diced an onion. I glanced over my shoulder to read the screen. Jenny! I dropped the knife, shaking in relief. "Hello?" I gasped.

"Hey, girl," was the response.

Hey, girl? Three days had passed since she'd shared her awful news. She'd asked me to pray and then left me to worry. How could she?

My runaway emotions wouldn't be restrained completely. "I'm glad to hear from you. I was worried."

"I'm sorry. This chemo I'm on gives me terrible brain fog, and I've been"—she paused—"a little overwhelmed. I needed some space and quiet to decide some things."

The apology sounded so frail, so tired. My anger evaporated. "What did you decide?"

"I think I'm going to get one more treatment with my current doctor, and then seek a second opinion. Until then, I'll focus on milestones—birthdays, the holidays. I want to celebrate Julia's first birthday and see her take her first steps."

How absurd was I? While Jenny was making life-and-death decisions, I'd made her silence all about me. I could've been praying instead of feeling sorry for myself.

"Let me come to Houston and take care of you for a few days. I'll cook and do laundry. I'll pray for you. It's no more than I would be doing here," I said.

"That is so sweet!" she said, sunshine and champagne returning to her voice. "What about this instead? Drew and I are taking the kids to the lake house at Toledo Bend next weekend. Do you know where that is?"

"About," I said.

"Do you think you and Brandon would be able to join us?"

"I'll have to check, but I'd love to," I said, thrilled by the prospect of spending a few uninterrupted hours with my friend.

"Melissa—" The way she said my name made me want to stuff my fingers in my ears. "I no longer believe I'm going to beat this cancer."

Something inside me kicked against the words, but I held my tongue, sensing she wanted to say more.

"I still believe that God is able to work a miracle for me." She hesitated.

Yes, and he will. I still believed even if she didn't. I would believe enough for the both of us.

"But not everyone gets that."

I couldn't argue. I'd seen a lot of death in my twenty-eight years. Hadn't I suspected the day I'd met her that she would break my heart? I pushed the thought away, too weak to carry the weight of it. I wouldn't.

I'd promised to believe with her, and I would until the end. The end hadn't come yet. Maybe God had us meet so I could pray, so I could stop it.

"I didn't know," she said. "I didn't know that Jonathan dies in battle."

The world fell still and cold around me. She'd told me she was Jonathan. I was David. And who was David without Jonathan?

* * *

The road to Toledo Bend wound through rolling hills crowned with trees dressed in green, scarlet, orange, and gold. Sunlight broke through shadow wherever the woods thinned, splashing me in warmth, until it dipped behind the hills and failed to rise again.

"Thank you for driving me down on your weekend off," I said, squeezing Brandon's hand. "I know you'd rather be hunting."

He leaned his head over and kissed me with the corner of his mouth. "How do you plan to make it up to me?"

Lord in heaven, what was I going to do with this man?

"Wow," he said. "I think I just heard your eyes roll."

"Dude." I turned my body so I could face him, shifting the bags at my feet, and leaned in. He raised one thick brow but kept his eyes on the road.

"Stop being ridiculous for half a second, and hear me. I don't know what I would do without you."

He cocked his head. "Well, right now, you'd probably be lost. This GPS is a touch shady, and you're no good with directions."

"Shut up. I'm not done," I said. "Jenny means the world to me. Thank you for driving me so I can be there for her, so I don't have to help her face this awful thing alone."

So much silence stretched between us, I began to imagine I'd moved him. I strained my eyes to see if he was crying in the dark. The car slowed and turned. Streetlights cast a blue glow on his face. No tears glistened, but his jaw brooded.

"You done now?" he asked huskily.

"I guess."

"Good, 'cause we're here."

Outside in the dark, the Freemans' lake house appeared to be a large, well-kept cabin. Brandon helped me out of the car and pulled me into his arms. "I'm glad I'm here too," he said as his mouth closed in on mine. "Between fishing and you sleeping naked, I'm sure I'll have a great time." He smacked my bottom as he passed to fetch our bags from the trunk.

"I am *not* sleeping naked."

The front door opened. I spun and found myself cocooned in Jenny's arms. No one would have guessed the news she'd been given last week. A radiant smile lit up the night around her. Her hair had grown out enough to be dyed and styled into a platinum-blond pixie cut. Her slim-legged jeans accentuated her curves.

"You look great," I said, hoping I didn't sound surprised.

"Thank you," she said, embracing Brandon, who had approached, arms loaded down with a duffel, bags of food, and our Crock-Pot from home. She led us inside. "Drew laid down with the kids earlier, and I think he fell asleep."

Brandon crossed the threshold and exhaled a soft, "Wow."

A spacious room featured a kitchen designed for utility and fellowship, a pool table, a cozy sitting area, and a dining table that could seat twelve or more comfortably. The back wall was lined with tall windows overlooking the water, which I could hear lapping against the shore in an unsteady rhythm.

"This floor plan," Brandon said. The cogs behind his eyes began to turn.

Jenny's gaze swept over the baby equipment and toys in the room. "It's perfect for hanging out and making memories."

Memories she was afraid Matthew and Julia would forget. Memories she might not be part of later.

Brandon set the Crock-Pot on the kitchen island and unpacked the bags of food. Ready to care for Jenny as I'd often wished I could, I'd packed breakfast items, a chicken, and lots of autumn vegetables to cook during our visit. I'd also brought a box of tasteless rice crackers and a jar of homemade kombucha made from a SCOBY I'd named Charles. Sometime this weekend, we were going to have the weirdest communion ever.

When Brandon finished, Jenny led us to the wing opposite the kitchen. "You'll sleep in the master bedroom. Now, it has a smell," she warned.

A robust floral scent doused me at the door, burning the back of my throat. Brandon raised his brow at me in question. I gently shook my head, hoping Jenny wouldn't see, and searched for the source of the smell. An array of soaps, candles, and elegant bottles of perfume decorated the bathroom vanity. I shut them away in the cabinet and turned to them both with a grin I hoped looked genuine. "I think if we open the window, I'll be fine to sleep in here."

For the most part, I was right. I slept well, though my eyes, sinuses, and throat were swollen when I woke.

For breakfast, Brandon made gluten-free pancakes from a mix while I blended butternut squash with eggs and spices to make crepes, which I ate topped with blueberries, almond butter, and honey. Everyone appreciated both. I hadn't eaten almond butter in eight years, so between the fellowship and the food, I transcended the mortal plane.

After Jenny and I cleared the dishes, I placed some carrots, greens, and squash at the bottom of the Crock-Pot I had brought and laid the chicken on top. Drew and Brandon left to fish from the boat that belonged to Drew's dad. Jenny and I settled in for a long visit while her children played quietly on the floor.

To our credit, we were able to talk about more than Jenny's recent news. We asked questions, talked about our kids, and shared old photos that evoked nostalgic smiles and laughter. Jenny didn't ignore her children. She threw herself into the game Matthew was playing, speaking in goofy voices and adding depth to his imagined world.

"How do you do that?" I asked. I'd never learned how to interact with someone else's imagination. Most of the time, I so inhabited my own head there was no room for anyone else.

"I don't know. Commit! Whatever it is, give yourself fully." She grinned up at me from the floor.

The guys came in for lunch and a brief respite indoors. Already, conversation about boats and fishing and house plans flowed between them. Brandon told a joke I didn't understand, and Drew laughed. For a moment, I glimpsed foreshadows of a strong bond. If everything turned out all right. That little "if" stretched as taut and thin as a tightrope, but I could see the possibilities, touch them, taste their divine sweetness.

The guys returned to the lake, and the children lay down to rest, leaving Jenny and me to contend with the enormous elephant occupying the room. Jenny must have felt as crowded as I did. "Want to sit on the porch?"

We eased into a pair of rocking chairs and, for a time, simply gazed out at the water and listened to it find its end on the shore. My heart wanted to shield itself, to fold inward like a cowardly rosebud. A bird skimmed the surface of the lake and dove, piercing its wide-open expanse, and I found my courage.

"How's your mom taking it?" I asked.

Jenny sighed. "She's scared. I think everyone's scared. Except for the kids. They don't know."

"And you? Are you scared?"

"Sometimes." The rocking chairs creaked and cracked grit against the concrete. A boat glided by, a wake opening behind it. "Years ago, before Julia was born, I saw her in a dream. She looked almost exactly like she looks now. She's special, and it hurts that I won't get to see her grow up."

She wiped away a tear. "Mostly, I'm just annoyed at the way people have started to look at me. I'm a walking reminder to all my friends that they should be thankful to be alive, and it's become this *thing*. I hate it."

A wry smile tugged at my mouth. Not many days had passed since I'd confessed to Mom how wearying it was when a friend compared her life to mine. Like her troubles didn't matter because they probably wouldn't kill her.

"Wouldn't it be nice if all this suffering would just—I don't know—point people to Jesus instead of being a measuring stick for how well or poorly life is going?" I said.

Jenny laughed. I loved her laugh. It sounded the way bubbles would sound if bubbles were music instead of pockets of air encased in a womb of glycerin.

Against the uneven rocking chair rhythm of Toledo Bend, I sang "Be Still My Soul" over my friend. My voice cracked and tears streamed down my face, but as I sang, my heart opened and received courage. Freely, I received. Freely, I sang, willing it to strike and strengthen her heart. Whether she would continue to hope for a miracle or give in, both paths required a valor that only the Holy Spirit could provide.

Matthew and Julia woke from their naps, and the four of us headed to the boat dock to view a spectacular sunset. The wind tossed and pulled at us as clouds in layers danced among the rays. It lasted and lasted, taking on different shapes and hues—one moment the sun wore a brilliant halo, the next it wore a scarlet crown. Angles of light vaulted off its brow in starbursts the lake caught in her bosom. We watched until the giant ember laid its head on a bed of distant pines, and with an indigo sigh, bid us good night.

Drew and Brandon arrived not long after sunset, hungry for dinner. The tender chicken and vegetables cooked in the rich stock warmed our insides. Drew paused between bites and said, "There's something spiritual about feeding people."

Hidden in Drew's eloquent thank-you was a revelation I hadn't considered. When I'd married Brandon, I could toast bread, make coffee, and annihilate various meats on the George Foreman grill. As my illness had developed over the years, I'd learned to cook out of necessity. If I'd never been sick, I might not have taken the time to learn. Now I knew how to cook good food well, which gave me a way to love others and minister to them. The illness had given me something to offer.

The mystery of God's ways washed over me in a wave of awe. "I agree," I said. "The meal we had at your house last month was probably the best I've ever had."

After dinner, Jenny talked about her fashion tastes, which were a quirky mixture of couture and unique thrift-store finds, and brought out a favorite jacket to represent them. The mustard yellow fabric boasted high shoulder pads and frivolous embellishments—a combination of sequins and over-the-top embroidery in golden thread. We laughed over the jacket and Drew's hatred of it. We exchanged dating stories, hunting stories, and illness stories, at which point our party masks fell off.

Drew shared his side of the story, pausing to swallow and gather his thoughts. His eyes shimmered with tears at moments and flashed in anger at others. The raw, unpracticed presentation made me wonder if we were his first audience. Through his eyes, I glimpsed Brandon's perspective of my trial. Our trial. It was hard to suffer, no doubt, but there was something rather poignant about the pain of watching a person you would die for suffer, powerless to stop it.

He went on to talk about recruiting methods of cancer hospitals, the astronomical costs of medical care, and insurance frustrations. Jenny shared how she spent the days following Julia's birth losing her hair and hurling everything she ate into the toilet when she should have been home recovering and enjoying her newborn. The late-night hours gave us all a safe place to bleed. I sensed the heart of God bleeding with us, holding us steady.

The honesty of those hours prepared our hearts for communion the next morning. Drew and Brandon watched the children and cleaned up breakfast dishes while Jenny and I found a quiet corner to cry, pray, and celebrate Christ's sacrifice. I pulled out the package of rice crackers I'd ordered for this specific moment and poured the golden-colored kombucha into small glasses. The plastic packaging rattled as

I reached for two crackers.

I led awkwardly, but our hearts were sincere. For the first time in nearly a decade, I took "the bread" and was momentarily caught off-guard by the sensation of crushing it with my teeth. A loud crunching filled the room. We smiled at one another and might have laughed, but reverence won out.

I was crushed for your iniquities so that you would only be pressed; perplexed, but not in despair; persecuted, but not forsaken.

The light of truth swallowed up our darkness. Jesus was crushed so we would never be more than pressed. He despaired so we would have hope. He was forsaken so we would always have God in our midst. He was destroyed with our sin so that we could be salvaged. Nothing could really touch us—not cancer, not anaphylaxis, not hunger, not loss, not pain, not death. His love truly conquered all.

The crunching noise dissipated. A holy weight fell around us, and tears rolled down our cheeks. Communion had never been like this before.

"I feel the sentence of death inside me, but now I feel hopeful too," Jenny said.

I knew what she meant. Something haunted us. We might not live to see another sunset like the one that lit the world on fire last night, but fear had fled at the remembrance of what Christ had accomplished. We were more than conquerors. Not even death could take us down.

When I hugged my friend goodbye that morning, I asked the Lord to let me see her alive at least one more time.

17

Dead End

The trip to Toledo Bend and back had been sweet but costly. Several days passed before I recovered enough to return to my full workload in the kitchen, making multiple meals, broths, and fermented foods every day. By the time I felt somewhat myself, it was time to return to Baton Rouge to see Dr. Hall for my follow-up, where I would hear the results from all the tests run on my blood, urine, and stools.

In the chill of a mid-November morning before dawn, Brandon led me out to my mom's warm car, carrying my bags of food and books. He tucked me inside and kissed me gently. "Call me."

He shut the door, pressed two fingers to his lips, and waved us off. He didn't like staying behind but knew he should. He would take the kids to my grandmother, who would keep them while he worked a busy Monday shift at the pharmacy during cold and flu season. He would pick them up and drive home to the dinner I had prepared the day before. I hoped to be home before they were.

The drive south was uneventful and pleasant. I always enjoyed time with my parents. We arrived at Dr. Hall's office before the scheduled time of the appointment and made ourselves comfortable in the waiting room. Used to waiting rooms at this point—and waiting in general—I'd brought a book. Before long, I heard my name.

My parents and I followed the nurse to the same meeting room as before. Within a few moments, Dr. Hall joined us, taking the single chair across the table. A file folder plopped open, and she looked me in the eye. "Well, we've found out quite a lot."

First, I learned I had a genetic mutation—the MTHFR mutation A1298C. It was a homozygous mutation, which meant I inherited it from both parents. The mutation prevented folic acid from methylating properly, which could be problematic. Essential in cellular metabolism, folic acid could only be utilized when it had methionine attached to it. Dr. Hall explained that the mutation likely contributed to my symptoms of fibromyalgia, fatigue, IBS, and brain fog. "It's a big find, and the right supplementation will help," she said.

Relief relaxed the tension in my shoulders. This was the kind of information I'd hoped for. An answer with a simple solution. Praise God.

She addressed the findings of my stool sample next. "It seems you have a bacterial infection embedded in your intestinal wall."

I tensed again, unsure of how bad the information would be.

"*Pseudomonas aeruginosa* is a common bacteria, but it shouldn't be colonizing in your intestinal wall," Dr. Hall said. "This bacteria is an opportunist. It's keeping you from growing good bacteria in your gut, and it might be preventing you from absorbing nutrition. I'm going to put you on ten days of Cipro to knock it out."

"What's Cipro?" I asked.

"An antibiotic," she answered.

Other terms like "intestinal permeability," "vitamin and mineral deficiencies," and "poor liver function" were mentioned, but my brain had taken in as much information as it could. I stared blankly at the long list of supplements I would have to remember to take. She'd prescribed twenty-four.

I thanked Dr. Hall, who stood and led us to the pharmacy at the front of the office. There, I was able to purchase everything but the Cipro. Several hundred dollars later, I left with my arms and mind full, too tired to wonder how I was going to pull off taking so many supplements via the correct pathway, dose, and frequency.

The clicks of my parents' seat belts reminded me of my own.

"Well," Mom said, her expression sober, "I'm glad they found the *Pseudomonas aeruginosa*." The Latin rolled off her tongue effortlessly. Having been a medical laboratory scientist for nearly 30 years, she knew and even taught terms such as these.

"It's a bad one, huh?" I said.

"It can be."

I contemplated piecing together a schedule for my new medicine and supplements on the ride home, but fatigue pulled at my mind and limbs. I yawned. Maybe I could sleep. I would figure out this overwhelming puzzle tomorrow.

* * *

Brandon looked over my loot and whistled.

"No kidding." I frowned at the array, annoyed yet determined. If I could manage to spend five hours a day in the kitchen preparing food for myself and my family, I could figure out this nightmare of a supplement schedule and get it done. After all, God had told me healing would require a lot of work. Difficulty shouldn't surprise me.

Brandon left for work, and I spent the morning writing out a schedule for twenty-four supplements, each calling for one to four doses per day. The theme song for Mickey Mouse Clubhouse played in the background as Micah and Sara built block towers together on the floor. After a while, Sara crawled over to my chair and pulled herself up, begging to be held. I set her plump form in my lap and gave her a supplement bottle to rattle while I worked. By lunch, the schedule lay before me, complete.

I kissed the soft strawberry-blond down of Sara's head. "You're too young to know it yet, but you have an awesome mom."

A tangible plan had brought back my spark. The task of healing felt doable again.

Days flew by, marked by steady supplement doses. I did better than I'd anticipated at keeping to a schedule. I even stayed faithful to all the cooking required by the GAPS diet. It was a lot, but somehow the demands of each invigorated me. A robust challenge had always been my bread and butter.

Thanksgiving loomed just around the corner. No one would be able to cook for me, nor did I expect them to. Not wanting to suffer or to feel anyone's pity on my favorite holiday, I sat down one evening to plan a Thanksgiving feast for myself and Brandon, who had recently become sensitive to gluten, a symptom I chalked up to the stress of balancing the world on his shoulders. I made a grocery list, packed up the kids, and spent my energy and Monday afternoon shopping for everything we needed.

Brandon left early to hunt on Thanksgiving morning and was gone when I awoke. Gratitude and joy sprang from my heart as I sang, prayed, and wept over Psalm 100. The sun shone, so I took the kids outside to enjoy it and to soak in its healing warmth. It was later in the day than I intended when I put the kids down for their naps, but I would at least have roasted chicken and vegetables to eat. The scent of herbed meat wafted from the Crock-Pot I had started that morning.

Still, there were acorn squash and bacon-wrapped green beans to roast, a casserole to throw together, and a chocolate pie to make. I started with the pie crust, which I made out of almond butter, eggs, and honey. Avocados, dates soaked in warm water, and cocoa powder blended together made a smooth and decadent chocolate filling. Next, I tackled the squash. I sliced each one in half, scooped out the seeds, and filled the hollows with coconut oil, salt, and maple syrup. The green beans were more labor intensive than I had anticipated.

Brandon came in. Observing my desperate flurry, he helped me for a few minutes before leaving again for his evening hunt. Later, Hannah came over and entertained Micah and Sara while I showered and dressed. In the end, we were only a little late to dinner at Nona's.

My aunts, uncles, and cousins peered cautiously at the food I had brought, but no one touched it. Not that I minded. Leftovers meant an easy next day in the kitchen.

I wondered at moments if they thought I was being dramatic. No one said that, of course. It was possible that my own insecurities made me feel that way. At times, my symptoms were so crazy that I felt crazy, so maybe everyone else thought I was crazy too. The feeling couldn't be helped, nor did it go away. Nevertheless, I was able to enjoy my food as much as the others seemed to enjoy theirs. I wanted for nothing, except a sense of normalcy and a hot cup of coffee.

After Thanksgiving, I began experiencing an array of unpleasant symptoms that ended the drives to Bossier for physical therapy. My fatigue intensified and was accompanied by a chronic low-grade fever. Diarrhea replaced my usual constipation problem. I assumed I had caught a virus at Nona's house Thanksgiving night. The fever and diarrhea lasted two full weeks before I considered an alternative explanation.

The Lord led me to read further in my copy of *Gut and Psychology Syndrome*. In the chapter on supplementation, Dr. Natasha Campbell-McBride warned the reader that the GAPS patient was often too sensitive for supplements beyond probiotics and hydrochloric acid. The capsules themselves could cause irritation of the gut lining. Even through the haze, my mind connected the dots.

That night, I asked Brandon to help me muscle test each prescribed supplement as Dr. Yakaboski had shown us. One by one, he placed each container in my right hand while I touched the tip of my middle finger to my thumb. He then tugged at my fingers, testing the strength of my grip. Not once did my fingers maintain contact, which indicated sensitivity. The worst offender, we discovered through muscle weakness, was not a capsule at all, but a powder supplement, which I mixed with water and drank each day.

I called Dr. Hall's office the next morning. They wanted me to taper down the dosage rather than stop it entirely. I tried that. When the diarrhea continued, I stopped taking it all together.

My constipation issues returned within a few days. The fever and pain took more time to resolve. I reverted back to stage two of the GAPS diet, drinking broths and eating simple soups, which upset my plan to splurge a little at Christmas dinner. The change also meant I had to make separate meals for my family once again.

This fresh disappointment left me lost and frail. Despair was a constant shadow, difficult to resist. At my worst moments, I took out my frustrations on the kids. I hated myself when I yelled at them. I apologized and repented—or so I thought—and then I did it again. Self-flagellation had no effect on my habit. In my better moments, I mourned, focused on the cross of my Savior. He had suffered for me so that I could suffer with him. He had become weak so that I could become strong.

After all, the kingdom of God was not eating and drinking, but righteousness and peace and joy in the Holy Spirit. All these were mine, at my disposal, at all times. Nothing could steal my joy unless I let it.

* * *

On New Year's Eve, fireworks boomed across the highway, heralding the entrance of 2013. While I was grateful for the experiences of 2012, I was not sad to see the year put to bed. It had been none too kind to my family. We celebrated with a GAPS-approved feast and a dance party in our best clothes and wore the crazy socks Jenny had sent in the mail.

January 2013, however, proved no less brutal than those of the last two years. New symptoms appeared while others became more severe. Depression, brain fog, fatigue, and heightened sensitivity to fragrances competed with the focus I tried to give God. The symptoms were hard to ignore.

The stupor in which I stumbled through my days led to several bad burns in the kitchen, one which bubbled up in a blister that tore away, leaving a chunk of raw flesh I had to nurse. Fragrances provoked my immune system into powerful systemic reactions that required large amounts of Benadryl to bring under control. The Benadryl, in turn, would elicit a debilitating rebound reaction that reminded me of my most recent bout with the flu.

Eczema made the hours I spent hand-washing dishes miserable, and there was little I could do for it. A friend recommended essential oils, but even one or two drops of the gentlest, highest-quality oil brought on anaphylactic reactions. Brandon brought home nitrile gloves, which protected the raw, itchy patches while washing dishes, and I found an online recipe for tallow bars, made of rendered deer fat, shea butter, and cocoa butter. The recipe called for a lot of steps, but the bars provided some temporary relief for my wrists and hands.

I wasn't sure what had invited these new challenges. It seemed that every time I found a way to cohabitate with this illness, it revealed a new ugly side of its personality. Holistically speaking, concern for Jenny could have caused the dip. The cancer had spread to the lymph nodes in her stomach and bowel.

Regardless, Mom's surprise birthday party was rapidly approaching, and I didn't want my health to interfere. Mom had been such a help to me over the past two years, and our family desperately needed to celebrate at every opportunity. Mom herself had given me the idea for the party and its theme.

On a recent drive to Baton Rouge, she'd asked me, "Have you given any thought to a name for the farm?"

"Not really," I'd said.

"I think we should name it Jubilee Farm." She explained that the word "jubilee," which meant something like "a trumpet blast of liberty," originated in Leviticus 25, a chapter in the Old Testament of the Bible. Every fifty years in the land of Israel, the celebration began with a blast of a ram's horn. During this year, the people rested from working the land, Israelite slaves were freed by their owners, and lost property was restored to those who had fallen on hard times.

Mom had explained that the upcoming year was going to be special. It was literally to be her Year of Jubilee. Her fiftieth birthday would fall on January 21. Sometime after that, she and Dad planned to join Brandon, my sister, and me on the property and start the farm. She saw Jubilee Farm as a place of healing—for body and soul—for our family and others God would send our way. I had readily agreed to the name for the farm and tucked away the tidbit about her birthday.

To my delight and surprise, most of the guest list I'd invited was coming, including our longtime friend and spiritual mentor from out of town, Dixie Perry, and even Jenny! The planning and execution gave me tasks to accomplish and something to look forward to, which aided me in the battle against depression and self-pity.

The day of the party arrived. I had two big jobs—make and decorate the gluten-free cake and pick up the flowers. Upon opening my eyes, I prayed for grace to push through the wall of fatigue and the perpetual haze of my mind. The children were extra needy that morning, so I was late starting the cake. When I turned out the layers, one fell to pieces.

Seconds passed while I stared in wide-eyed disbelief at the chocolate crumb mess on my counter. The shock wore off, and I freaked, swearing at myself. Nona talked me off the ledge of despair over the telephone while I cleaned up the mess and salvaged what I could. "Just bring whatever you can, and we'll fix it before the party."

I stuffed Micah and Sara into their car seats, sweating away my freshness from the shower. We were late leaving to pick up the flowers, and we were late arriving at Mom's house, but Nona, Aunt Suzonne, and Jenny swooped in, saving the cake and my sanity.

Dad delivered Mom right on time, after everyone else had gathered. She was delighted. Family, friends from work and church, Jenny, Dixie, and her husband, Robert, made the perfect crew for her. High on her joy, I might have forgotten I was sick if I could have eaten anything we'd served.

After the festivities died down a bit, I stole Jenny away to my mother's sofa so we could talk privately.

"You've lost weight," I observed as we settled.

"Yes, and I bought new clothes," she said with a bright grin. "Most of my old shirts were V-necks, which I didn't like because they exposed my chemo port. I wanted blouses that would hide it." Her countenance blossomed with radiance as she laughed. "I used to want people to pity me, but God has been too good to me for me to play the victim anymore. So I bought new clothes. I'm throwing off the sick rags!"

Jenny's words reverberated in my soul like a trumpet blast, and the Holy Spirit jabbed me with his shepherd's rod. The words were for me. We talked a while longer, and then she had to leave. "Thank you for coming and for saving the cake"—and for other things I didn't mention as we embraced.

When she was gone, I processed the sermon she'd preached. Over time, my illness had become part of my identity. It was how I was known. I was the allergy girl who ate weird food and made her own soap. Without realizing it, my sick rags had wrapped around me like ancient grave clothes, holding me captive. I was letting them say more about me than the God who was sustaining me in the trial.

Dixie and Robert sat in the chairs across from me. When I told them what Jenny had said, Dixie threw her head back, sending a smile up to heaven. "Isn't it beautiful how the Lord uses even the ugly things like illness to humble us so that we disappear and he is glorified?"

Beautiful indeed.

If illness was my identity—how I saw and presented myself to others—it was time to disappear into Jesus. The longer my illness lasted, the more convinced I became that my greatest need wasn't physical healing but inner transformation. I needed a jubilee of the soul.

That day, I resolved to let Brandon buy me some clothes that fit and to no longer use social media as a pulpit where I complained about my daily struggles. Instead, I would use it to point to the God who had been too good for me to play the victim anymore.

* * *

On the day I threw off the sick rags, my perspective began to shift. For the most part, I forgot I was suffering, though my circumstances hadn't changed for the better—and in many ways, I had worsened.

I held to the GAPS diet as well as I could, though I now had to make modifications. Some days, certain foods were okay; the next, they triggered flushing, swelling, itching, pain, and respiratory distress. I couldn't visit my sister in her new trailer across the yard because the building materials emitted toxins that made me so drunk I wished for death. I couldn't even step near her door without trouble.

One sunny day in February, I was walking outside with the kids. Hannah was doing her laundry next door. The scent of the fabric softener wafted across the yard and triggered a severe reaction that put me in bed for two days.

I now became ill every time I left home. Going out was no longer a question of whether or not I would suffer a reaction but a question of how severe the reaction would be. Driving by a pile of burning leaves on my way to the doctor one morning sent me in search of my inhaler and the Acute Rescue homeopathic drops Dr. Hall had prescribed to replace my Benadryl habit. The fumes of cleaning supplies at the grocery store had me in a chokehold before I knew what had happened.

Perfume had always been somewhat of a problem for me. Now residual amounts could trigger anaphylaxis. If someone wearing perfume hugged or held my children, they carried the smell home. The smell would attack the instant the door opened. The severity of the reaction depended on the level of exposure, but over time, I tolerated less, my reactions grew stronger, and my recovery time lengthened. Some reactions left me bedridden for days. Church, the smelliest place on earth, was no longer an option for me.

My problem demanded some uncomfortable conversations with friends and family members. Some felt oddly affronted by my request that they not wear perfume or hair spray in my presence. Anyone who valued their right to wear perfume over their relationship with me was allowed to exit my life. Brandon cheerfully blessed them on the way out. Others attempted to be conscientious but simply did not understand the extent of my sensitivities. Mistakes were made; sometimes I paid dearly. A few who witnessed my reactions firsthand made major modifications. My parents, mother-in-law, and Nona stopped wearing perfume altogether. Mom even joined me in washing her hair with vinegar and baking soda.

Despite the landslide, the pressures of motherhood seemed easier to bear. Sure—I still felt stressed from time to time, especially during those moments I was chopping vegetables with a sharp knife and trying to check food in the oven without burning the crying baby clinging to my pants leg so tightly that the pants slid off my behind and bunched at my ankles while the redheaded boy chanted the wild, rhythmic music in his head and bounced off the walls of the living room like a pinball in a machine. But most of the time, I enjoyed my children more than I ever had, even on the hard days following a bad reaction when I barely had the energy to meet their most basic needs.

Hard days became more commonplace, and more and more, I earned the title "stay-at-home mom." The only exceptions were for my own treatments and appointments. Twice a month, Dad drove me to Baton Rouge for a BioSet treatment with Melisa and a lymphatic massage by a quirky little masseuse named Babette, who I loved instantly. On Dr. Hall's recommendation, I received weekly colonics treatments from Dr. Yakaboski, which were, hands down, the weirdest thing I'd ever done—weirder than BEST and BioSet combined. Only a truly desperate person would lie down naked in a cold plastic cradle to receive a ten-gallon enema and watch their poop float down a tube and into a clear, lighted tank.

Despite my efforts to protect myself and make a little progress, I suffered daily reactions, which culminated in a severe anaphylactic episode following my morning dose of supplements that Dr. Hall had prescribed to treat my MTHFR gene. For several days, I discontinued all of them, reintroducing them slowly, one by one. None of them worked. The folic acid, the methylating powder, and the B vitamins were all rejected entirely.

Something wasn't right.

I scheduled another consult with Dr. Yakaboski following my next colonics appointment. Her small jaw set when she saw the bag full of supplements Dr. Hall had prescribed. After a moment of silence, she took an audible breath and said, "This is a lot of supplements. It would be a lot of supplements even for a healthy patient."

I handed over the papers from Dr. Hall's office, complete with test results, diagnoses, and treatment recommendations. A frown gathered on her brow as she read. The only sound was the rustle of paper as she flipped from one sheet to the next. Her blue eyes lifted, bright and sharp. "My opinion is that there are too many supplements and not enough testing. I recommend that we investigate your genetics a little further. A1298C is only the tip of the iceberg as far as genetic mutations go. You can order a DNA kit, and I will schedule a phone consult with the epigenetics specialist who interpreted my results."

She explained that the results would take several weeks to receive. In the meantime, she recommended I discontinue all supplements until we were able to form a more comprehensive picture from my test results. After offering BioSet and BEST treatments, she sent me home to rest.

Though I'd reached what appeared to be another dead end, I wouldn't be defeated. Dead ends indirectly led to the path that would bring the traveler out of the maze. I would trust the Lord.

That afternoon, I sat in the recliner at the end of the kids' naptime, feeling as if I weighed five hundred pounds and had lived a hundred years, unsure of whether I could peel myself away from the chair to lift my baby out of her crib. God's voice washed over my spirit.

My grace is sufficient for you.

I stood and made my way to Sara's room. Grinning, she reached for me. My teeth ground as I pulled her out and set her on the changing table. There was so much to do— vegetables to prep, broth to jar, and a chicken to bone. I could not do it. Again, God spoke.

My grace is sufficient for you

I readied my knife and jars.

Every joint, every tissue hurt. Holding a knife felt almost impossible. I couldn't lift the heavy pot full of broth. The muscles in my shoulders cried out with each scoop and pour of the ladle.

My grace is sufficient, my child.

As usual, Sara clung to my ankles, screaming for attention. Micah's footsteps thundered down the hall and around the living room, his rambunctious, percussive chatter providing a disquieting soundtrack.

Sufficient. I am enough. I will help you. I promise.

My tears of pain transformed into tears of praise, and I was filled with a deep sense of knowing. No matter how hard the rest of my healing journey might be, there would be enough grace—enough God—to bring me through.

18

Feeding on Faithfulness

One sunny morning in mid-March, I woke with symptoms of my kids' colds. I wasn't surprised. Every illness that entered our home these days found me. I moved slowly, pondering the devotional entry from *Jesus Calling* and Psalm 90. Around 11:00 a.m., I was ready for a light breakfast. I drank a cup of hot rich chicken broth and ate two scrambled eggs—organic pastured eggs the Lord had so sweetly provided for me the previous week—warming them only until the whites cooked. The softer the eggs, the easier they were to digest. I hoped to encourage my body to spend its energy on healing the cold rather than digesting food.

But then I noticed the coconut-based brownie I had made the day before. It really didn't have anything bad in it. Just a little coconut, some coconut oil, cocoa, eggs, and honey. It had tasted so good. Just one little bite shouldn't hurt.

Wrong. I felt the effects of my indiscretion within a few seconds, almost doubling over at the sharp pain under my sternum.

Scaling down the plans for the day, I decided to spend some time outside with Brandon and the kids. Brandon was finishing his work on the porch he had built last weekend.

Micah was "helping." I plopped down in the canvas chair with Sara in my lap, enjoying the breeze and the red haloes the sun cast about my children's heads, but intense stomach pain began to overshadow the good. Still, I wasn't quite ready to give up.

Sara climbed down from my lap to play with Micah. Brandon steadily worked—measuring, sawing, and drilling—at times casting smiles in my direction. Arms free, I leaned back and pulled up my pants and sleeves, exposing my skin to the sun. God had been incredibly good to me. The antidepressant was no longer in my system. I could now enjoy the sunshine for half an hour or more before a reaction set in. Yet an eerie feeling crept up on me.

My thoughts congealed, turning lethargic. Nausea tossed my stomach. My chest tightened, and my limbs filled with lead. An out-of-body drunken sensation settled over me. Had one bite of brownie done all this? As I considered the question, flecks of wood thrown by the saw drifted past me on the wind.

The wood was treated. Treated by chemicals. *Get inside.* I wasn't sure whether I'd heard from God or my own instincts, but the words pierced my mind, sharp and clear.

The next thing I knew, I was inside the house with the kids without a clear memory of how I'd brought them in. I turned on Mickey Mouse and fell onto the couch. I felt so strange. I tried to monitor my own breathing. My only requirement was that it must continue. My body was so heavy and wrong. My soul, not liking the weight, seemed to slip out of it and hover above the scene, as if waiting to see what would happen. I lost all sense of time. *Is this what dying is like?*

The thought of death brought me back. "Tell Daddy that I need his help," I croaked to Micah.

A moment later, a shadow stood over me, smelling like wood, sweat, and sunshine. "I need BioSet," I said. A strong arm helped me up from the couch. The movement brought on a fit of sputtering, choking, and wheezing. I hobbled into the kitchen, leaning on him for support.

"Hold on," he said, propping me against the kitchen counter. "I need a cotton swab for your saliva." His arm vanished.

My chest burned and ached. My legs buckled, and I hit the kitchen floor with a thud. Vague pain shot through my hip, shoulder, and head. All my attention locked in on the fight to breathe. Brandon returned to my side with my inhaler. Involuntary tears slipped down my cheeks as I struggled to get a puff.

My awareness faded in and out as I lay on the floor. Sara cried in the background as she always did during my reactions. Words like "hospital," "Mama is sick, baby," and "Can you come over?" reached me. I surrendered myself to whatever fate Brandon deemed necessary.

The sharp, cool taste of alcohol ran over my tongue. A floral aftertaste followed. I recognized my Acute Rescue drops. A cotton swab swiped the inside of my cheek. Brandon rolled me onto my stomach and began to tap along my spine. I was too tired to think about breathing anymore…my thoughts drifted to eggs.

My papaw had begun bringing me pastured eggs from a farmer friend of his a few weeks ago. I'd been eating eggs all along, but these farm-fresh eggs tasted better and were far richer in color than the organic eggs I'd been buying from the grocery store. I craved them at all meals and always felt better after eating one.

With Papaw in the hospital last week, I'd run out. His friend and supplier was a little odd and often drunk, so Papaw had advised me not to pick them up myself. Last Thursday, as I was leaving with Dad to head to Baton Rouge for appointments with Melisa and Babette, I'd packed a couple of empty egg cartons to take along.

Dad had given me a strange look when he saw me tuck them in the back seat. "Why do you have those?" he asked.

"God knows that I'm out of eggs, and I just feel like we're going to find some on our trip today," I said.

"Okay." The way he said it let me know he wasn't so sure, which was fair. We had made the trip several times at this point and had never seen anyone selling eggs along the way.

"We'll find some," I said. "You'll see."

I looked for a road sign the entire drive south and did not spot one. When we arrived at Dr. Hall's office, I forgot about the search. Melisa always shared the most fascinating information, leaving my mind in a whirl. After my BioSet treatment, we drove to Babette's new office, which was located in a bright-yellow house across town. I walked out of the room feeling almost good and found Dad paying for something he'd found in the gift shop.

A couple walked in carrying large grocery bags. Babette swept back into the lobby to greet the couple. Taking the bags from them, she asked us, "Would you like to buy some eggs? They're fresh, organic, and pastured, and they come from happy chickens!"

Dad turned to me with wide eyes and then laughed out loud. I smiled. "Yes, please. I have two empty cartons in the car." God had provided in a clever way so that his signature could be clearly seen.

As I lay on my kitchen floor, passing in and out of conscious thought, reminders of God's goodness and faithfulness undulated like waves of a placid sea. Many months ago, he had given me a promise that I would live through this hell so that I wouldn't give up halfway through. Years ago, he had led me to Brandon because he knew I needed a Superman, a man who had the fortitude to live this life without losing his mind or his love for me.

Brandon performed two rounds of BioSet treatment and lifted me to my feet. He helped me change clothes and rinse out my sinuses and ran warm water for a detox bath. When half an hour had passed, he lifted me out of the water, toweled me off, and knelt at my bedside to help me dress.

When he'd tugged my thickest pair of socks over my feet, his gaze rose to meet mine. I gently kissed his mouth and said, "Thank you."

He didn't smile. His brown pools looked into mine, intense and afraid. "You're welcome, but I'm going to need you to stop this."

"That's the plan," I said, lying down to rest on the soft bed.

Later that evening, he brought me three fresh pastured eggs laid by happy chickens, served warm and runny on a small plate, and I fed on God's faithfulness to me.

* * *

My twin nieces' indoor swimming pool birthday party, to be held at a local wellness center, rapidly approached. The smell of that particular pool surfaced from my childhood memories, provoking an uneasy feeling in my belly. I texted Hannah to apologize and tell her I needed to stay home, hoping to avoid offending her. It wouldn't be the first important party I'd missed, and my cancellations had left behind a wake of hurt feelings.

Some days, I felt so misunderstood. Regardless of whether I missed an event or attended with a request that people accommodate my needs, someone always ended up resenting me. If I mentioned that an encounter with someone had led to a bad reaction, that person usually became offended with me as well. I assumed they simply didn't believe that I was telling the truth about my condition. No other explanation made sense.

Though Hannah was disappointed, she understood. She might not understand my illness, but she believed me. Having grown up with me, she knew I didn't exaggerate ailments.

My dad's sixtieth birthday fell not long after the twins'. Dad loved parties, so Mom had planned one for him. The party would be held in Mom and Dad's home. While several guests would attend, we knew them all. Mom had asked that each one not wear perfume or cologne. Brandon would be available to drive, so I felt it would be safe enough to go.

Just before we left the house, Brandon raked a bit of gel through his spiky hair—the same gel he'd been using since our dating days. On the car ride to West Monroe, I noticed the gel had a smell, which I'd never noticed before. The scent teased and tickled my nose for a few moments, and then it began to sting my eyes. My head swam, and my signature cough barked from my chest between gasps for air.

"What's wrong?" Brandon asked, alarm sharpening the words.

"I think…that maybe…I'm reacting to your hair gel," I said apologetically. I pulled out my inhaler and puffed.

Brandon's jaw set into a hard line. Had I offended him too?

I heard the click of a button, and the windows cracked, letting in fresh air. It helped a little. Brandon called Mom to let her know I would arrive sick. My breathing improved some, but the dizziness worsened. My neck and face swelled.

Mom met us out in the driveway and helped Brandon bring me inside. Several of the guests greeted me as I walked in. I used what effort that remained to smile in return and say hello.

Dad paused his celebrations to hug me, concern etched in his brow. I hated walking in sick, casting a cloud over the event. I hated to remind him of my suffering on his night.

Mom led me to her bed while Brandon washed the gel out of his hair. His salt-and-pepper spikes dripping, he leaned over the bed to plant a kiss on my mouth. "I'm sorry I made you sick," he said.

"I'm sorry I'm such a pain in the butt," I answered.

"Pain in the Keaster," Brandon corrected. "You have to say it right."

"You don't have to stay in here with me," I said. "Go get some food. I feel tired anyway."

He kissed me again and left to do as I'd suggested. I closed my eyes and was fading into oblivion when my phone received a text. It was from Jenny. "Are you free to talk?"

I called instead of replying.

Her sunny voice greeted me over the line, brightening my black mood. We chatted about trivialities for a few moments before I told her I was hanging out in my parents' bedroom at my Dad's birthday party. She then gave me her real news. The cancer was spreading. The tumors in her liver had grown, her esophageal tumor had returned, and there were new spots on her lungs. The chemo was no longer working.

I tried to swallow the tight ball that hung in my throat.

"Still with me?" she asked.

"Yeah." As hard as I fought for that one word, there was no substance to it. Just a breath.

"I got accepted into a trial." She continued when I didn't reply. "It's all free. There's about forty of us doing it. It isn't chemo, which is nice, and I get to keep my hair this time."

We spoke of other things when I could talk again. I prayed for her, and she kept me entertained as laughter from the other room carried through the walls. Laughter that sounded to my ears like a foreign language.

The door cracked, and Dad peeked in his head. "Ready for some company?" he asked, his smile back in place.

I said goodbye to Jenny and said, "Sure!" as brightly as I could manage, pretending that I wasn't a sick woman who might have to bury her closest friend before summer.

* * *

"The pills are too large to swallow," the text read. "I've been released from the trial. I'm fine. I still believe God can send healing another way."

Her steadfast faith astounded me, but I was worried. I prayed for her as often as she crossed my mind.

The time for planting a summer vegetable garden had come. Mom and Dad came out to the property to help Brandon prepare. Brandon, between work and caring for me, had already plowed up the hard clay with his tractor and made rows. Dad had come out one day to lime the acidic soil. Today, they would hook up the irrigation, roll out the plastic weed barrier over the rows, and plant the beautiful baby plants we'd bought from Dr. Yakaboski's wise-cracking husband. With two small children and little stamina, I knew I wouldn't be much help outside, so I volunteered to make dinner for the workers; Hannah; her boyfriend, Rich; and the twins, who were a year younger than Micah.

The day was cloudy and cool, perfect for hard work outdoors. In between my own tasks, I stepped outside to view the progress. Soon, the large red field boasted rows and rows of vibrant green plants, a promise of the feast to come. At the end of the day, Brandon set up a table on the back porch, where we all gathered for hamburgers.

We celebrated the day's labor with a meal served in the cool evening air. We ate, talked, dreamed, and laughed. The kids squealed in delight as Rich teased and chased them around the open yard. Rich didn't say much, but the way he related to my nieces and anticipated Hannah's needs had me hearing wedding bells in the back of my mind. Nothing touched this moment—not my unnamed illness, not Jenny's cancer, not even the wasp that had stumbled out of its winter nest and delivered a sleepy sting to Sara's hand during dinner.

I thanked God for redheaded babies, towheaded nieces, green plants, strong backs, and the good men who had stumbled into our lives. For a night, all our trouble seemed out of reach. Only God and his goodness were real.

19

Masked

I studied the price of peanuts on the computer screen, working through the math. I'd become quite efficient at making all kinds of things I'd once bought at the grocery store. Shampoo, deodorant, lotion, kombucha, fermented vegetables, almond butter, mayonnaise, ketchup—I could make it all. Why not try to make peanut butter? The kids loved it. There had to be a way to make a cheaper, healthier version. I ordered a two-pound bag of peanuts.

The day after the shipment arrived, I placed the peanuts in jars to soak for a couple of days to make them more digestible. I hadn't been able to partake in peanut butter for a year and hoped that my recipe might work for me too. When the soaking process was finished, I rinsed the nuts and placed them on my largest cookie sheet to roast in the oven at a low temperature for the next twenty-four hours. Soon, the smell of peanuts filled the house with sweet promises of salty goodness.

The next morning, I took the peanuts out of the oven, golden and crisp. I placed half into the food processor with coconut oil, honey, and salt and turned on the motor. A strange noise alerted me that something wasn't right. Frowning, I peered inside the processor bowl. Black flecks mixed with the golden-brown butter.

I turned off the motor and opened the lid. Somehow, I had misaligned the blade with the notch in the lid. As the blade had spun, it had cut into the plastic, throwing bits into the peanut butter. All that money, time, work, and physical energy—wasted! With a frustrated sigh, I scooped the contaminated peanut butter into the trash and set the processor bowl in the sink. My ear canals began to itch as I wiped countertops, a sensation that often accompanied reactions. Suspicious, I threw the rest of the peanuts into the garbage and counted it all loss. A few drops of Acute Rescue alleviated my symptoms and allowed me to go on with my day.

The peanut episode had been forgotten when I placed a small bag of trash I'd collected from the master bathroom into the large bin in the kitchen. I pressed the bag down, making room at the top of the bin; smelled the peanuts; and remembered the wasted time and money. "Make your own peanut butter, they said." I rolled my eyes at my foolishness.

Pulling out pots and pans, I began to prep for dinner. My vision blurred as I heard tiny footsteps toddle into the kitchen. I turned. Sara's big brown eyes stared up at me. The itching returned to my ears. Sara crawled to my ankles and pulled up, whining. My throat began to swell. "Brandon," I rasped between coughs, "I think I'm having a reaction. It's bad."

He sprang from the couch where he'd sat watching television and led me to bed. I collapsed onto my pillow, struggling to breathe. A dreamy haze settled over me as Brandon's hands tapped and tugged, performing the BioSet treatment that was becoming second nature to him. The sharp floral taste of Acute Rescue spread over my tongue. My breaths came quick and shallow, but I wasn't afraid.

Brandon spoke to me. My mind couldn't make sense of what he said. I wished I could share some of the peace I felt, but I couldn't speak.

A soft beep sounded nearby. Something cool entered my mouth. Brandon spoke in my ear: "Your temperature is 94.6. If you don't take a turn in a minute, I'm taking you to the hospital."

He knelt by my side, whispering prayers over me. Silently, I prayed for him. *God, let him taste this peace. Let him know that I'm not going to die tonight.*

Again, Brandon performed BioSet on my listless body and gave me another shot of Acute Rescue. The haze lifted, as though the sun shone down on the fog in my mind. Brandon's worried features came into focus. He released a held breath and collapsed over my legs, burying his face in the sheets.

That night, he tossed all the peanut butter, bars, and candies into the trash and hauled it off to the dumpster.

* * *

A little girl stared quizzically as the kids and I passed her on our way into the grocery store. I smiled back, forgetting that she couldn't see my expression behind the double masks I wore. Following my most recent close encounter with death, I decided I needed a little extra protection when I left the house. The stakes had escalated. Now there weren't only fragrances, chemicals, and latex to contend with. There were peanut particles, which might be present in a grocery store.

Inside, some fellow customers gave us a wide berth, something I may not have noticed had I not felt so conspicuous. Most avoided eye contact, which was just as well. I slipped on my nitrile gloves and focused on my list, the kids, and the task at hand.

Double-masking offered more protection than a single mask, but the smells wafting from the cleaning aisle penetrated the layers of organic cotton. My vision swam. "You'll be fine," I whispered to myself. "Finish up, and you can take some Acute Rescue when you get to the car."

"What you say, Mama?" Micah asked.

"Nothing, baby." I patted his head.

At checkout, a woman who appeared to be in her sixties parked her cart behind mine. I tried not to breathe in too much of her perfume. "Excuse me," she said. "May I ask why you're wearing that mask?"

Few people were so audacious. Had it not been for the perfume, I might have admired her spunk. As it was, responding meant breathing, and breathing meant further exposure.

Count it all joy.

"I have a lot of allergies," I said, hoping I sounded warm but also trying to keep the conversation short.

"Oh! I thought you might have cancer. Or the flu."

No one wanted cancer, but it was a name people understood. Who knew what this lady thought I meant by "a lot of allergies"? Probably hay fever. Sneezes and itches. I snickered. "No ma'am...just allergies."

"Your children are darling," she said, changing the subject. "Where do they get the red hair?"

The customer in front of me moved forward. Unloading the items in my cart onto the belt, I tried to think of a kind one-liner, but my thoughts thickened as the reaction began to set in. "My husband's family has some redheads. We're just blessed, I guess."

Once the kids were strapped into their car seats and the groceries were stashed into the trunk, I ripped off the masks and deposited several drops of Acute Rescue under my tongue. Sending up an SOS prayer, I pulled out my inhaler and took two drags, which eased the tightness in my chest.

Sara fussed. Fumbling with the screen of my iPod, I was able to turn on "Hot Dog." My mind had cleared by the end of the song. I pulled out of the parking lot wondering how I was going to tell Brandon that I probably shouldn't grocery shop anymore and that he was going to have to do that too.

Later that week, I drove myself to a consult with Dr. Yakaboski to discuss what she had learned at a MTHFR genetic mutation conference. Based on my symptoms, she suspected I had genetic defects that extended well beyond A1298C. She handed me a testing strip with which we could test my urine sulfate level. Within a few moments, we saw that it was at the highest possible reading, which, combined with my intolerance to sulfur-based medications and supplements, indicated a cystathionine beta-synthase (CBS) defect.

This defect caused a range of metabolic problems, including an overabundance of ammonia, that affected my overall health. Because supplements hadn't worked too well for me, Dr. Yakaboski and I looked into a diet that would decrease my ammonia burden. I was less than thrilled to find that meant cutting out animal protein. Meat was often a safe food for me. Dr. Yakaboski also suggested I look into a diet low in sulfur and free-thiols.

For the next two days, I researched these diets. Unfortunately, a diet low in sulfur would eliminate several other safe foods. Eggs, broccoli, cauliflower, garlic, onions, and leafy greens all made the no-no list. It wasn't possible to eliminate all of the foods on the list. I'd starve. Much to my dismay, I compromised by eliminating garlic and eggs, at least until I had my consult with the epigenetic specialist.

It was just as well. Papaw, my fresh egg supplier, was scheduled to have a heart valve replacement the following week and might be unavailable to deliver eggs for some time. We all prayed as a family for a successful surgery with no complications and a quick recovery, but I couldn't shake the uneasy feeling in the pit of my stomach. I didn't believe Papaw would die, but neither did I feel that the surgery and recovery would be as easy as the doctor said they would be. It wasn't his first rodeo. We'd seen him go in for simple surgery before and barely make it out alive weeks later. I prayed the feeling was just a feeling and nothing more.

The doctors reported that all had gone well during the surgery, but several days later, Mom called to tell me Papaw was in severe pain and could not get relief. "He thinks he's dying," she said, "but I'm not so sure."

Mom kept me up to date. During visitation hours, the family gathered around him, singing hymns. Even in pain, Papaw lifted his hands in worship and praised the Lord. I praised God too when I heard, for I knew from experience that only God could redeem a heart so completely that it praised his name when it crossed the shadow of death. There would also be healing in the singing.

I wanted to be there with him and Nona. I wanted to sing to him too, but Mom advised me not to come. Hospitals held a myriad of triggers for someone as sensitive as me. Nona had support, and Papaw was in too much pain to appreciate a visit. So I prayed from home.

X-rays revealed two bowel obstructions, and Papaw was scheduled for a second surgery. The doctor was confident he could correct the problem laparoscopically, but in the end, they had to open him up. When both obstructions had been corrected, Papaw was sent to the ICU, sedated and on a ventilator.

The next day, I received a call from Mom after her visit with Papaw at noon. "I think it might be time for you to come. Just in case," she said.

Everything inside me felt heavy. "We'll come tonight."

Armed with two clean masks, nitrile gloves, a hymnal, and Brandon, I made my way from the parking garage to the ICU. Nona met me in the corridor a few minutes before the evening visit began. She embraced me and asked how I was doing.

"How are *you* doing?" I returned.

"Really good. The days are long, but I go home at night and get some good sleep. They won't let me in there anyway."

I smiled at her wisdom. She'd always known how to take care of herself, even in difficulty. Now, the peace of God surrounded her, a presence outside of herself, and yet coming from the inside too. It shone from her eyes. No matter what happened, she would be okay.

The door to the ICU opened. A male nurse looked me over. "Are you sick?" he asked me.

I blinked at him, unsure of how to answer his question.

He barred my way. "Why are you wearing a mask and gloves?"

Brandon stepped forward, squaring his shoulders. "They're for her."

Nona added, "She's fine. This is my granddaughter, Melissa. She's allergic to just about everything, but she isn't contagious."

The nurse's gaze traveled from Nona to my masked face, softening. He stepped back and held the door open for me. "I'm sorry. I have to be sure. No one in here can afford to catch anything."

"Thank you," I said softly, ducking my head. I appreciated that he protected his patients—my papaw—but I couldn't remember the last time my face had felt so hot with embarrassment.

Nona led us to Papaw's tiny compartment. Bible verses printed in large text on colorful paper decorated the walls. Papaw lay in bed, thin and pale, hooked up to a number of tubes and equipment. A knot lodged in my throat at the sight. Papaw had always been a strong man with the biggest personality in the room. He was a commanding presence and a hilarious storyteller. When he preached the Gospel before a congregation, he was a force. Tonight, he looked like a dying old man, but I refused to allow that to stop me.

He opened his eyes and looked into my face. I knew that look. He was halfway on the other side and entirely okay with it.

"Hey, Papaw," I said, taking his hand. Maybe I could help him like Brandon helped me.

He answered with a squeeze.

"Brandon and Melissa have come to visit you," Nona said.

I opened my hymnal and sang a few of Papaw's favorite songs. He responded with smiles. Tears. Once, he gestured for me to repeat a song. Each of us took turns reading the promises of God posted on the walls around his bed, and then we prayed. Brandon small talked about the weather and Papaw's new cook shack he had fixed up at his hunting camp, teasing that he would be expecting some fried catfish next week. Papaw took all this in, astoundingly alert for someone under sedation.

The visit was healing for me. I'd sung and said goodbye to my grandmommy a few days before she had died and my granddaddy a few days before his time. Not everyone was given such precious moments. I didn't know whether Papaw would live or die, but I was grateful for the two cotton masks that made this visit possible, wherever it fell in his story.

"Thank you," I said again to the nurse on the way out, hoping the smile reached my eyes and he could see it.

"Thank you," he said. "You have a pretty voice. The whole unit seems to perk up a bit when your family comes in."

Yes, I'm sure they did. Because when my family walked into that death-ridden place, so did the presence of the living God. For the sufferer, that made all the difference.

20

Poisoned

Papaw's condition improved rapidly. Mom reported that he was acting more and more like himself all the time, which I interpreted to mean that he was no longer a compliant patient. In fact, "patient" probably didn't describe him at all. Mr. Bossy Pants was back. The nephrologist told Nona that Papaw's kidneys might even begin working again.

Jenny, on the other hand, declined. We spoke briefly one morning. She could do little more than pant through the pain. The next time I heard from her, she was in the hospital. I braced myself for what was coming.

May arrived and with it, the anniversary of the day I had reacted to the coconut macaroon and had become so ill. I wrote a blog post in acknowledgment of the date but had no idea that I would celebrate in a more participatory way.

Late one evening, I took the kids outside to enjoy the cool spring air while my mother-in-law, Debbie, finished cleaning the house for me. Dad had come out to work in the garden, where the plants had grown and blossomed.

He called out a greeting and said, "You might not want to let the kids play too close to the garden. I just sprayed out here."

"Okay," I called back, somewhat disheartened that I wouldn't be able to partake of the vegetables when they came in.

The gardening class Dad had just completed had taught that certain plants simply couldn't thrive in Louisiana without the help of pesticides. Papaw, a longtime gardener, concurred. Though we had agreed to attempt an organic garden, Dad worried we would have no garden at all. There were too many predatory bugs in the South. He had sprayed the squash two weeks ago, news I had already grieved and accepted. Someone should be able to enjoy the garden, even if I couldn't.

Micah and Sara yipped and squealed, delighted to be outside. I breathed deeply, taking in their joy, and coughed. Micah glanced my way at the sound. When I smiled back, he returned to his work in the rock pile that would eventually become our driveway. Sara babbled at me, proudly displaying a rock in her tiny fist.

I walked over to admire it. At nearly eighteen months, she didn't say much. I rewarded every attempt at speech I could. I took the ordinary rock in my hand and coughed again. Another cough followed, and a strange feeling settled over me. Alarmed, I scooped Sara into my arms and said, "I think we better go back inside."

"What's wrong, Mama?" Micah asked, eyes wide. Sara squirmed and began to cry.

"I'm not sure, baby, but I think Mama might be getting sick."

Debbie paused mopping the floor when we walked in. "Is everything all right?"

"I'm not sure," I said. "I might need you to do the BioSet treatment on me."

By the time Debbie had collected the cotton swabs, it had become difficult to breathe. She swabbed the inside of my cheek and performed the treatment as Brandon had shown her. Sara wailed and clung to her legs. My symptoms didn't improve. She led me to bed, and all of my focus went into breathing.

"What happened?" Debbie asked, trying to comfort Sara.

"I think..." Speaking was a labor. "Maybe...I'm reacting...to the pesticide...Dad sprayed."

I heard her on the phone. When Brandon stepped through the door from work, his dark eyes were livid, live coals.

"Don't be mad," I rasped when he knelt to study my face.

"It's too late for that," he said.

"He didn't know."

No one knew. No one ever knew when I would trigger or what I would trigger to. No one understood the source or nature of this ridiculous illness. No one could anticipate my needs or prevent these reactions. But I knew my dad. The moment he heard I had reacted to the pesticide, he would begin to curse himself up one side and down the other as he'd done since I was a little girl. The last thing I wanted was for Brandon to unleash his wrath on him. Dad would do the job himself—and thoroughly.

When I woke up the next morning, everything was inflamed from the inside out. I felt my organs, my lymph nodes, and every joint and muscle in my body. The fatigue was so bad that Brandon had to help me out of bed and lead me to the recliner. Before leaving for work, he placed Sara in my lap and my phone on the table beside me.

"Mom will be here soon," he said. Then he kissed me and left.

I thought of my new friend Caroline Lunger, a girl several years younger than me who had been sick most of her life. We'd met online through a friend after I'd found her blog, *Gutsy*. She and I made quite a pair with our mysterious illnesses. Caroline was largely bedridden at the time I'd met her, but she was still fighting for her health. She loved God and believed he would heal her despite all the evidence to the contrary. Having been sick for much longer than me, she practiced a number of natural remedies I hadn't heard of—knowledge that had already proven to be helpful.

I messaged her. In as few words as possible, I explained what had happened and how I was feeling and asked for her advice. Less than an hour later, my phone pinged as it received her reply. She offered several ideas about how to relieve my body's toxic load after the exposure. I would try them all.

I gulped down a glass of activated charcoal water and almost threw it up into the sink. The charcoal didn't have much of a taste, but the texture activated my gag reflex. After that, I began to boil coffee beans on the stove.

I'd contemplated trying coffee enemas for a while now. Caroline did them every day and swore by the practice. I'd ordered the supplies two weeks ago but hadn't worked up the nerve to put them to use. Today, I felt so pitiful that I was willing to try anything that might make me feel better. And it did, though only slightly.

When I hadn't improved by the following morning, I called Dr. Yakaboski and told her what had happened. She didn't like the way I sounded and insisted I come in for a treatment. Brandon was at work. Only Nona was available to watch the kids, which meant I would have to drive myself. The idea frightened me, but I decided to try.

"Call me when you reach the parking lot," Dr. Yakaboski said and hung up.

I dressed and drove to West Monroe, arriving at Dr. Yakaboski's office without any recollection of the drive. She answered the phone within two rings, came out through a side door I'd never noticed, and led me to a room by the arm. Two women I didn't know were waiting for us. "Melissa, this is Lynette Frieden and Dr. Rose Kuplesky. Dr. Frieden is my friend and associate and will help me treat you today. Dr. Kuplesky is here to observe and assist me just in case you need anything."

What could I need?

"I also have Dr. Jess Armine on the line. He'll check behind my protocol."

I didn't understand why she wanted Dr. Armine to check behind her or the need for such a team, but I gave myself over to whatever she thought best. She'd earned my trust.

She performed BioSet, treating me for several triggers, followed by BEST. "This will pull you out of the parasympathetic state," she explained.

Dr. Frieden then did some energy work called total body modification, or TBM, treating the pesticide exposure, candida, and zinc toxicity. I didn't understand it all, but I felt better when it was done.

"How did you know to treat me for all that?" I asked.

Dr. Frieden shrugged. "I asked the universe this morning, and it told me."

I blinked at her, unsure how to answer, unsure I could accept this treatment. That's when I heard God's gentle voice. *I told her what to treat. Now relax, and let them take care of you.*

Relaxing as ordered, I kept the revelation to myself. Dr. Frieden could think what she wanted.

"If you can stay," Dr. Yakaboski said, "I'd like to give you a lymphatic drainage treatment. I'll only charge you for the hour visit. No more."

Money hadn't entered my mind, but I appreciated her generosity. "Yes. Thank you," I said.

Dr. Kuplesky wrote me a fresh prescription for EpiPens and stayed on hand until my appointment was over. It didn't occur to me until I was on my way home that she was probably there in case I crashed on the table.

* * *

Recovery was slow. I spent most of the week in bed wondering if I was dying. Honey came every morning to take care of the kids so that I could rest, give myself a coffee enema, and take a long detox bath. These home treatments brought a little relief during the day, but I always felt bad again by evening.

Mealtimes were strange and sketchy. Despite the seven months I'd spent following strict gut-healing protocol, my digestive health was declining. Old allergies reemerged; new ones developed, seemingly for no reason. I scrapped the low-sulfur diet.

Most of my recovery meals consisted of eggs, rice cereal, boiled squash, and pureed broccoli. I couldn't tolerate much else. Food rotation was also important. I might tolerate eggs at breakfast and react to them at lunch. Muscle testing everything before I put it in or on my body helped to prevent reactions that would put me back in bed. Regardless of how gentle or "safe" the meal, I experienced digestive pain after eating and grew lethargic, as all the resources of my body were expended upon digestion.

A new dinner routine developed. Once Brandon and the kids were seated and eating their meal, I proceeded to muscle test several different foods to see what my body would accept. I threw together whatever tested "safe and tolerable" that evening and sat down to eat as my family finished and left the table. The evening meal had been our only regular family time, so this small upset felt bigger than it was.

Papaw finally graduated from the ICU, earning his own hospital room, and Jenny returned home. She called one afternoon to let me know she would begin chemo again on Friday and that it might be a while before we spoke again. I dismissed her full meaning. She prayed for us with power and awe, leading our spirits in worship. The presence of God filled the room as I stretched my hands and heart to heaven from the depths of my sickbed. Tears spilled over my cheeks, and for a moment, I flew, free from suffering.

"Wow," she breathed into the phone. "That was amazing."

Moved as I was, I could only whisper, "Amen."

When we hung up, I feared it was goodbye.

All hell broke loose when the kids came home from church on Mother's Day, covered in fragrances. Not having fully recovered from the pesticide exposure, my body gave way. They were tired and wanted me, but they had to be stripped and bathed. Their cries reached me through my bedroom door. I ached to care for them, but I couldn't. Every time I came close, my head swam and throat tightened. My masks didn't help. And I didn't even receive a card on the holiday.

I felt sorry for myself until Jenny sent a text. "Thinking of you," it read. My Mother's Day was hard. Hers was impossible. The next day, she was scheduled to have a feeding tube put in because she could no longer eat at all. Who was I to complain?

21

Floxed

My DNA results came in, offering a more complete picture of what was going wrong. The specialist who had interpreted my results gave me her report the day she finished her work but told me to wait to speak with Dr. Jess Armine before I attempted treatment. When Dr. Armine heard that my results were in, he scheduled the consult even though we didn't have the results from my extensive blood tests. Having been on the phone with Dr. Yakaboski the day I'd come into the office so sick from the pesticide exposure, he was familiar with my case.

Mom drove out for the phone consult to help me take notes and ask questions. Dr. Armine greeted us both cordially in his robust New York accent. "Your Dr. Yakaboski is something else in the way she champions for you. Her compassion is inspirational. Did you know she called me from vacation to set up this consultation?"

"No," I said, touched. What a gift she was.

"Before we begin, Melissa, I want you and your mother to know that you are not the sum of your genetic abnormalities. You are not this paper or these results. You are you. Can you keep that in mind as we talk?"

"Yes." And I would try to keep my promise.

"Well, this will be a lot, so let's get started," he said. "What's happening is that all these genetic polymorphisms have turned on your negative genetic traits. Sure, you have leaky gut, but the polymorphisms are causing multisystem problems, weakening your thyroid and adrenals and preventing healing from taking place."

I wrote as fast as my aching joints allowed me. My IgE indicators didn't look that bad, which was unsurprising in a way. The finding explained why allergy testing never showed much and why the shots hadn't worked. The IgA indicators, which affected the digestive system, however, were a big problem.

The number of genetic mutations alone was overwhelming, but the way the mutations interacted with one another created seemingly insurmountable problems. My methylation-related mutations required folate while another mutation meant I couldn't process certain sources of folate, and a problem with my vitamin D receptor indicated that even with the appropriate type and level of folate, methylating would still be difficult. I desperately needed Vitamin B12, but I needed to be extremely careful about how I received it.

The methylation situation was so complicated that I really needed to treat it with food, but my body didn't make diamine oxidase enzyme. Dr. Armine explained that the naturally occurring enzyme breaks down histamine in the small intestine, which was a major contributing factor in all my food allergies. Furthermore, I likely had little if any mucous layer lining my gut. Particles of everything I ate were passing into my bloodstream, creating new problems with every meal.

"As you see, we're going to have to brake and pedal a lot to get you well," Dr. Armine said.

Even as my eyes glazed over, I saw the mess I was in. God hadn't been kidding about "hard work."

I copied down letters, numbers, and symbols for homozygous and heterozygous genetic mutations. My thoughts began to jumble in a depressing alphabet soup.

Dr. Armine paused and said, "The sheer number of presenting polymorphisms tells me you've been given a fluoroquinolone drug."

"A what?" I asked.

"Have you been prescribed Cipro or Levaquin in the last year?"

If I had, I couldn't remember. I glanced at Mom, who shrugged. "Maybe."

"Trust me. You have," he said. "Frankly, my dear, you have been floxed."

"What does that mean for me?" I asked.

"In short, you've been injured by a fluoroquinolone. For some, it means ruptured tendons. For others, it means a healthy person is suddenly bound to a wheelchair. For you, it means an A-bomb has been dropped on your mitochondria. You can't heal without a major reset."

A pause. "Still with me?" he asked.

Mom looked at me. "Yeah," I said.

"It's not as bleak as it looks, but I will say you're one of the most challenging cases I've seen in a while. So, what do you think we should do?"

"You're asking me?" I was incredulous.

"Yeah. What do you think? What should we start with first?"

Mom jumped in. "Methylation, and maybe the mitochondria. She's done everything she can for her gut."

"Bingo," said Dr. Armine. "I recommend looking into IV nutrition for your B12 and glutathione deficiencies and possibly an NAD treatment or two to reboot your mitochondria. We need to bypass the gut."

"NAD?" I asked.

"Nicotinamide adenine dinucleotide. It's a coenzyme that fuels metabolic reactions. IV therapy has helped some of my patients, but it is still experimental. Someone in your state offers it."

Mom wrote all the information down, including the name of the doctor. I was still trying to figure out if I'd even taken the drug he thought I had.

"For now, I recommend you rotate some ground flax or chia seed, marshmallow root, and slippery elm in your diet, starting with about a teaspoon and working up to two tablespoons every day. They should begin to restore the mucous lining of the gut and decrease the permeability of the intestinal wall. I'll talk to your Dr. Yakaboski about finding some safe co-enzymated B12."

The consult had come to an end, and there had been no discussion of payment. "How do I pay you?" I asked.

"About that—" I heard a smile in his voice. "I had a chat with Dr. Yakaboski. I asked her what she's been charging you for all her extra work. She acted like she didn't know what I was talking about. 'Not a thing,' she said. So I'm going to match her. Normally, I charge about $400 for an initial consult, but I feel like I'm supposed to do this one pro bono."

His kindness startled me into silence. "Thank you so very much, Dr. Armine," Mom said.

"Call me Dr. Jess," he said.

"Thank you, Dr. Jess," I echoed. "God bless you."

"You too, sweetheart. And know you'll bless me when you're feeling better."

The call ended, and I looked at Mom. "For the life of me, I can't remember ever taking that floxy drug he talked about."

"Call Brandon," she suggested as she stood to leave.

So I did. The background bustle of retail pharmacy filled my ears as I waited on the line. Computer keys softly clicked. "Here it is," he said. "That's what Dr. Hall gave you last fall for that bacteria in your gut."

The words hit me like a sucker punch in the stomach.

I spent the next few hours researching fluoroquinolone injuries and their victims. Floxies, they called themselves, and they were overall a desperate, devastating lot. Some were in wheelchairs. Some had hair falling out. Others were bedridden. Some looked like they were on death's door; others claimed they'd rather be dead than continue living as they were.

I shut my laptop and took Micah and Sara outside to distract myself. The sentence of death rang in my ears, and I didn't want to listen. The kids ran to my sister's gravel driveway to play in the rocks. Falling to my knees, I sobbed so forcefully I thought I might vomit.

Micah and Sara paused their play but only for a moment. They'd witnessed a number of meltdowns over the last few months. They were like little lion cubs—unaware they were too small and dependent to be so brave.

My God, my God, why have you forsaken me?

I was no stranger to betrayal. I knew what it felt like. In my late teens and early twenties, family, friends, and even church leaders had set traps, attacked my character, and accused me of things I hadn't done. In fact, my anaphylactic reactions had begun smack dab in the middle of those betrayals, a reality that often led me to wonder if the emotional stress had helped the progression of my symptoms along. But in all those experiences, never had I felt betrayed by God himself.

My spirit raged. *How could you? When my family cried out to you for healing, you sent me to Dr. Hall. You told us all we were supposed to go there. How could you send me to her knowing what would happen? How could you do this to me? To my family? Why?*

Bitter tears spilled onto the dirt and gravel where I knelt curled over. I cried until I was hollow. Never had I imagined I lived in a world in which God betrayed. In such a world, I was lost.

* * *

God allowed me to rage and weep. Lightning did not strike my head. The ground didn't crumble beneath my feet. For the next several days, I was spared any significant reactions. I wasn't sure where God was. Maybe he was with me; maybe he wasn't. I wasn't sure of anything anymore. But when I had quieted myself, I could hear his voice again. It lifted off the pages of my Bible and reverberated in my soul.

Be glad and rejoice in my mercy. I have considered your trouble. I have known your soul in adversities. I have not shut you up into the hand of the enemy. I have set your feet in a wide place. I have not hidden my face from you, my afflicted one. I have heard your cries.

No weapon formed against you shall prosper. I am for you. Who can be against you? I did not spare my own Son. No good thing will I withhold from you. In all these things, you will be more than a conqueror through my Son's love. You will overcome by the blood of the Lamb.

Do not fear. You are mine. I have brought you to this crucible, and I will stand with you in it. As you walk through this fire, you will not be burned.

Nothing God said told me why he'd done it. He only told me what the reason *wasn't*. It wasn't that he didn't love me. It wasn't that he'd abandoned me. Even as I camped at the gates of hell, he laid out his bedroll beside me.

I didn't understand how someone who loved me could lead me to seek help from someone who would hurt me, but I decided to accept the love. I'd known from the beginning I would die without it, and now things were worse. There were decisions to make, a mess to clean up. I wouldn't get anywhere without God. To spurn the source of my help would be foolishness.

Late at night after the kids were in bed, Brandon and I researched NAD IV treatments. We read, considered, and prayed but felt no peace.

Dr. Yakaboski kept fighting for me. One day, she drove nearly half an hour from her house to mine to teach Brandon the combination of treatments she and Dr. Frieden had performed after the pesticide exposure. The new technique was more meticulous and effective than the BioSet treatment alone. Not only did it halt anaphylaxis, but it also temporarily pulled me out of fight or flight, a state I seemed to live in.

She contacted doctors and specialists in holistic healing and located a compounding pharmacy that would encapsulate NAD for me. Unfortunately, the NAD came in blue capsules, and muscle testing showed I would not tolerate them. We tried homeopathy in the place of supplementation, but I began to react to preservative alcohol. Less intervention seemed to accomplish more, so we prayed over each specialist recommended to us.

Brandon came into the bedroom one morning to kiss me before he left for work and said, "I may be a few minutes later getting home today. Kevin Tyson is going to meet me in the parking lot after I get off. He said he feels like God said something to him about you, for me."

"Intriguing," I said. Kevin was a family friend—mostly a friend of my dad's. He lived over an hour from the store, and we hadn't seen him in two years.

I was cooking dinner and muscle testing various foods for safety when Brandon walked in. I paused. "So?"

Brandon set down his lunch box, cell phone, wallet, and keys. "Let me change my clothes first, and then we'll talk."

I'd begun reacting to the smells on Brandon's shirt when he came home from work. It had become his habit to strip down and put on fresh clothing whenever he arrived home. If his clothes were especially fragrant, he would immediately put them in the wash.

A moment later, arms wrapped around my waist. "Well?" I said.

Brandon studied my face as if trying to memorize it. "Kevin's been praying for you. He said I need to be careful who I let touch you. He was so sure the word was from God that he drove over an hour on his motorcycle to meet me at work and tell me, and then he drove straight home."

I leaned my head on Brandon's shoulder. "That's confirmation. No more doctors."

"What about Dr. Yakaboski?" he asked.

"She stays," I said, searching his expression for any sign of objection. I found none. "She's done so much. I need her. I want to try the foods Dr. Jess recommended. But I don't want to see anyone else. They either think I'm crazy, can't help, or make it worse. I'm done."

With a resigned sigh, he said, "Okay."

As I lay down in bed waiting for sleep to come, I thanked God for speaking to Kevin, who was crazy enough to make a two-hour round trip to deliver a one-sentence message in person.

* * *

The ground chia and flax seeds arrived in the mail, and I began my four-day rotation of mucilaginous fibers. To bypass my gut, I added a few drops of liquid co-enzymated B12 to my daily coffee enema and began a new regimen of homeopathics, which I first placed in hot water to boil out the preservative alcohol. For meals, I ate plain rice cereal, a few vegetables, and eggs.

The new routine wasn't easy, but I made it work. Little by little, I improved enough to expand my diet and began planning a birthday celebration. I wanted dinner and communion with family and a few close friends who had hung with us through the trial. Steak, potatoes, fresh vegetables, and artichoke salad made a nice menu, but I really wanted a birthday cake. Searching Pinterest, I found a recipe for a rice flour zucchini cake with an avocado-based dark chocolate ganache. To keep things simpler and safer, I would make it myself.

Mom and Dad hosted the dinner on June 1, two days before my birthday. The presence of God sweetened the atmosphere. Our dear friends the Davises joined my family and in-laws for the feast. Sara called me "Mama" for the first time, which was something I'd waited nineteen months to hear. The food was good; communion was better. It was uncanny how much I missed the Lord's table after taking it for granted for so many years.

Glancing around the table, I recognized a dim shadow of what we would enjoy in eternity. There was so much life in the moment I could have died that instant and known my years had been good and full and worthwhile.

The days that followed weren't so kind. When I kissed Brandon on the following night, my tongue began to itch and swell soon after. He'd just brushed his teeth, and though he'd swished and gargled to protect me from the smell of the toothpaste, the residue had been enough to trigger me. On the morning of my birthday, I forgot to muscle test my morning dose of ground flax seed, a mistake that resulted in a severe reaction. Teeter-tottering on the edge of an unseen precipice, I wasn't surprised—only heartbroken—when I reacted to the little bit of ghee I'd come to enjoy in my morning helping of rice meal. After that, everything I ate induced nausea, pain, and swelling in my throat.

A strong sense of déjà vu struck when I could no longer drink water without retching. Though I sipped through the discomfort, I couldn't stay hydrated without food. The fatigue and pain were so bad I mostly stayed in bed. Through the bedroom door, Brandon's voice rose over hushed conversations. I hated this for him. In some ways, it would be better if I were dead and he didn't have to worry about keeping me alive anymore.

Brandon never treated me like a burden, but he pulled away. The unspoken distance throbbed dully in the background. It was probably his way of coping, bracing for what he imagined to be the worst-case scenario, but he never stopped advocating for me. When most men would have run for their lives, he stayed. He put his head down and leaned in, serving, supporting. He wouldn't give me up without a fight.

Dehydration set in. Brandon spoke with Stacy, my general practitioner, who reached out to home health. We wanted to avoid the hospital, if possible. The combination of people, cleaning chemicals, and medical professionals who were unlikely to understand made for a volatile environment. But home health fell through. Out of options, Brandon tucked me into the car and drove to a nearby emergency room.

Armed with two masks, I instantly reacted to the strong orange-scented disinfectant that polluted the air. The smell triggered my barking cough and made my head swim. Brandon guided me to the exam room as quickly as he could. The nurse practitioner bustled in with a clipboard and an assistant. Her eyebrows disappeared beneath her fringe bangs as I shared my symptoms.

"Well," she said, "we'll need to do some blood work and x-rays to find out the source of this stomach pain."

Brandon calmly said, "I don't think we need the x-rays. We came for fluids only."

The nurse's head turned sharply from Brandon to me. "I highly recommend the x-rays."

"Just the fluids, please," Brandon said.

Her shoulders tense, she made notes on the clipboard in flustered strokes. "I don't know how much we'll be able to do for you without the proper tests." Each word clipped short. "Laboratory will be in soon." With a curt huff, she spun on her heel and stalked out of the room, her assistant trailing behind her.

The door didn't open for a long time. I lay back on the firm bed and shut my eyes against the fluorescent light above. Everything hurt—my joints, my muscles, my head, my stomach. The nurse practitioner's behavior baffled me. I sighed. Inexplicably, we'd somehow offended her by refusing an x-ray.

Feet shuffled past the door. A cart squeaked down the hall. With each tick of the clock, the atmosphere thickened, pressing down on my chest. Brandon shifted in his chair and sighed. Mom prayed quietly under her breath. I began to wonder if I would receive any care at all. Another cart squeaked and stopped. Someone knocked.

"Mrs. Chapman?" said a young female voice as a cart rolled inside my room.

"Nicole!" Mom said, standing to receive an embrace. "Melissa, this is a former student of mine."

A beautiful brown face smiled at me. "Hi." She extended a smooth hand, decorated with perfectly manicured nails. "I've been following your story. Your mom is very special to me."

I squeezed her hand and mustered a smile in return.

"How are you doing?" Mom asked Nicole. "How are your boys?"

Nicole pulled on gloves and gathered materials, chatting about life and her two growing boys. Her radiance and cheerful demeanor began to cut through my despair.

"I might not be an easy stick," I warned.

Nicole winked at me. "Don't worry. I had an excellent teacher." She struck a vein on her first attempt. "So what brings you in here?"

"A bad flare," I said. "I can't eat anything without a reaction, and I haven't been able to drink enough."

"Well, I'm glad I get to take care of you," she said. "You really inspire me the way you've held on to your faith through all of this. You're like that woman that Jesus healed. The one with the bleeding issue. You've got her spunky faith. God's going to heal you, and it's going to be amazing to see."

She finished collecting the blood she needed and popped off her gloves. "God bless y'all. Let me know if you need anything, Mrs. Chapman." With a brilliant smile, she left the room in much better condition than in which she'd found it.

A nurse soon walked in my room with a bag of saline and a gentle smile. "How about some fluids?" he asked.

"Yes, please," I said. Something had shifted while Nicole had been in the room. I didn't understand it, but I felt it. Things were happening.

I braced myself for the needle, knowing he might have a difficult time. I didn't have to hold my breath for long. Before I knew it, saline dripped from a line into my veins.

A half hour passed, and I didn't see anyone, which was fine with me. I'd received only half of the bag of saline when the nurse practitioner blew in and handed the lab results to Brandon. "There's nothing wrong with her that we can tell," she said. "You can go home now."

The IV was pulled out more quickly than it had been put in. Someone bandaged my arm and left the room.

"Wow," Brandon said. "They didn't give you much. You must have really ticked her off, babe."

Mom scowled at the lab results. "You think they would have at least let her finish the bag. She's clearly dehydrated."

"I could make them," Brandon said.

"No," I said. "Let's just go home. I'm tired of this place, and I feel better."

The fluids helped but didn't suffice. By the next morning, I needed more.

When I told Dr. Yakaboski what had happened in the ER, she was livid. "This kind of thing is why I left Western medicine." She paused. "If I were able to get a prescription for saline and IV supplies, could your mom start the IV?"

"Probably," I said. "If not, we'll find someone who can."

She called her nurse practitioner friend, who was able to write the prescription. Mom didn't want to start the IV, so Brandon called our friend Heather Davis, who was a nurse practitioner. She picked up the supplies and made the hour drive out to the house after work. By then, my veins had drawn up, but after two sticks and some wiggling around, she found one that would do.

Fluids helped, but I was still weakening from lack of food. Because my system wasn't tolerating much of anything, I went for the most well-rounded, easily absorbed nutrition I could find. I rolled my IV stand into the kitchen and took two eggs from the refrigerator, which I scrambled, salted, warmed in a pan, and drank. They were slimy going down, but they tasted good. The reaction was mild, and the food helped settle my stomach.

Exhausted, I returned to bed, wondering how long I could survive like this.

22

The Garden

Mom and Dad called for a prayer meeting on my behalf. "Something has to change," Mom said over the phone. "We need God to move."

They asked the Lord who should attend, and Jesus put together a fabulously eclectic group. Randy, a church elder and Brandon's friend who had prayed for us a year ago came, as did Jeff and Hanna Peshoff. The Davises, who had come to my birthday celebration, drove from Rayville, which gave Heather an opportunity to check on me and the IV. Papaw was recovering nicely, so Nona was able to attend. The Cranstons, my parents' longtime friends and neighbors, walked next door, and Tim Sharplin with his daughter Shelly, a childhood friend, surprised us with their attendance. Together, they represented seven different congregations and five different denominations of believers in Christ, not including Dixie, who prayed with us over the phone.

We arrived at Mom and Dad's a little early. Brandon helped me roll the IV stand to their bed, where I rested until everyone had gathered, and then he led me out into the living room, double-masked.

"Thank you for coming and praying with us for Melissa," Mom said. "Truly, we don't know what to do. Our eyes are on the Lord. We called you all here because God brought each of you to mind. We believe each of you has something to contribute tonight."

The men blessed me by praying with authority and power. The women pled my case before the Lord. Nona prayed the prayers of a seasoned saint who had a long history of witnessing God's faithfulness. When Randy anointed me with oil, Nona reported that she felt a physical heat. Mom's anxiety lifted. The incense of their prayers mingled with the presence of God. He was in our midst in such a way that no one could miss it.

I didn't experience heat or any immediate change, but I expected God to act. Nicole's word about the woman with the bleeding issue wouldn't leave me alone. I studied the accounts of her in the Gospels. The woman had suffered from a debilitating, socially ostracizing bleeding disease for twelve years. All the doctors had failed her. She'd spent all of her money to seek answers, a cure, but their treatments had only made her worse. When she heard that Jesus was passing through her village, she pushed her way through the crowd, convinced that if she only touched his garment, she would be well. She was prepared to risk everything on that one touch.

I wasn't sure I could match her faith, but I understood her. She'd tried everything. Only Jesus had the power to save her.

The moment she touched the hem of Jesus's garment, the fountain of blood dried up. She might have turned home then, healing in hand, had Jesus not stopped. "Who touched me?" he asked as the mob pressed in around him.

His disciples teased him, but Jesus searched the crowd for the person who had taken some of his power. The woman came forward, trembling. She, a woman made unclean by disease, had touched a rabbi, but she fell down at his feet in the sight of all and told him the truth. Jesus, the representative of Father God, answered, "Daughter…"

The story reminded me of a Timothy Keller quote: "When you go to Jesus for help, you get from him far more than you had in mind. But when you go to Jesus for help, you also end up giving to him far more than you expected to give."

What did I really want? Physical healing, sure, but what else? And was I willing to give up my old life, my identity, to get it?

* * *

Mom took out the IV when I was well enough to drink and eat regular meals. After a few days of eating only warmed raw eggs, I muscle tested the first squash from our garden. To my surprise, they tested as "safe" despite the pesticide sprayed a month ago. I ate them boiled and pureed into a thick liquid.

My appetite grew. Concerned I might become sensitive to eggs from eating them so often, I tried ground beef, browned in the skillet and pureed with some boiled zucchini. Food had never tasted so good. Next, I added broccoli to the rotation—also boiled and pureed—and then added solid foods one at a time, beginning with carrot fries, mashed avocado, and what was supposed to be zucchini fritters but turned out to be zucchini mush.

My parents hadn't sold their house in West Monroe, so Dad drove out to the property most days to tend to Micah and Sara in the mornings while I performed my daily coffee enema and soaked in a detox bath. The process lasted two hours or more. I didn't enjoy the enemas, but they made me feel better. Without them, my bowels didn't want to move at all. Gone were the days of no movement for a week or more. To pass the time more pleasantly, I watched *Doctor Who* on Netflix.

When I finished my morning routine, Dad headed outside with an enthusiastic Micah trailing at his heels. Together, they tended the garden. Micah helped Dad pick squash and spot potato bugs and tomato worms. Since my reaction to the pesticide in May, Dad hadn't used any more chemicals. He deterred some critters by planting zinnias and mums at the ends of rows. Others he killed by hand. Micah thought it made a great game to point out a bug and watch Pops kill it, and his grin stretched from one ear to the other when he brought in the day's haul.

The garden grew the most colorful, tempting vegetables I'd ever seen. Squashes, peppers, tomatoes, tomatillos, eggplant, melons, beets. The abundance was enough to feed my parents, my family, Hannah's family, and friends, and there was still enough left over to sell. Several experienced gardeners in our circle commented that their gardens weren't doing half so well.

I'd never liked tomatoes. I never thought I would. And then one day in mid-June, Micah and Sara toddled inside, eyes bright with exciting secrets and tiny fists clutched tight around them. Each deposited a bright-red cherry tomato into my outstretched palm. There was nothing to do but pop them both into my mouth.

A bright, sweet flavor exploded over my tongue. I chewed, amazed. The kids grinned broadly. A gentle tingle spread through my body, as it did each time I ate produce from the garden. The first time I'd felt it, I had feared a reaction was coming on. Tingling had always been a sign of trouble, but this sensation was good and wholesome. Warm. Soothing. Life at work inside my body.

Each time I ate the fruit grown from the earth of Jubilee Farm, I felt good, a foreign experience. A little burst of energy accompanied each meal. My stomach hurt less often and with less intensity, and I sometimes went to the bathroom in addition to my daily enemas.

The prime ingredients and increased energy inspired creativity. Only two weeks after the prayer meeting, I made an eggplant lasagna out of eggplant slices fried golden in a pan of coconut oil and a meat sauce using ripe tomatoes, sweet peppers, and herbs from the garden. I ate my portion with a spoonful of goat cheese and a glass of fresh beet, carrot, and apple juice. For breakfast the following morning, I stuffed a few of our glossy jalapeno peppers with goat cheese, wrapped them in hormone- and antibiotic-free bacon—which I'd been sensitive to since January—and served them roasted and drizzled with honey. For the first time in my life, I made fried green tomatoes, battered in rice flour and fried in coconut oil. They became a fast favorite of both Brandon and me. I attempted Julia Child's ratatouille recipe, which took four hours to make but was worth every mite of effort.

All of the success I had at mealtime emboldened me. When the watermelon was ripe, I ate some. Mom watched wide eyed, waiting to see how I would do. No reaction. I hadn't been able to eat watermelon without Benadryl in five years or more.

My quick turnaround dumbfounded us all. Sure, we'd expected God to save my life, but we hadn't expected all this. I hadn't had a severe reaction in three weeks. I felt better and was gaining weight. It was exceedingly, abundantly more than we had asked or imagined. The garden had produced far more than healthful, beautiful food. It had brought forth the gift of hope.

23

Invasion

"Babe, I need you to wake up and listen to me." Brandon's tone was urgent.

I slid on my glasses and tried to focus.

"Fire ants are coming in through the kitchen wall," he said. "They must be under the trailer. I've killed several, but they just keep coming. Do what you can, and I'll try to figure out what to do."

I blinked at him. "We can't use poison."

"I know." He hurriedly kissed my mouth. "I'll think of something. I love you. Be careful."

He strode out of the room. The kitchen door opened and shut.

Fire ants. Lovely. Flipping marvelous.

Two years prior, Micah had suffered an anaphylactic reaction of his own to a few fire ant stings. No one in the house could afford to be stung. Slowly, so I wouldn't black out and fall to the floor, I rose from the bed. I paused, waiting for the spots in my vision to clear, and stepped into the bathroom. The ants would have to wait a minute.

I was unprepared for the sight in the kitchen. The ants poured in from the corner behind the counter and dispersed into trails that led in several directions like an army of tiny invaders. "Lord Jesus," I breathed. There were so many.

I prepped a bottle of vinegar and began to spray. The vinegar did little more than anger the ants. Dish soap, which killed wasps on contact, affected them even less.

A soft crash and musical babble to the tune of "Jesus Loves Me" told me the kids were awake. On the way to lift Sara out of her crib, I stopped at Micah's door. "Hey, baby."

"Hey, Mama," he said in his sweet husky voice.

"Mama needs you to stay out of the kitchen this morning. Fire ants are all over the place. Okay?"

"Okay," he answered cheerfully.

Sara wouldn't be so compliant, but there was little I could do.

Breakfast preparations made for a delicate dance. Everywhere I turned, there were ants. The kids were thrilled to eat their toast in the living room in front of the television, but I worried the crumbs would entice the ants to explore other parts of the trailer.

Out of ideas, I called Brandon. "Use your homemade shampoo," he said.

"I've already tried vinegar and dish soap. They did nothing."

"Trust me."

Armed with a spray bottle of mixed castile soap and apple cider vinegar, I made war. Brandon was right. The ants fell upon contact, but the concoction didn't stop them from coming in. Eventually, I tired and retreated to the recliner with Sara and a book.

Two pages in, I felt a familiar pain on my right side above my hip. Twisting, I spotted the ant and killed it before it was able to sting me again. Sara fussed, squirming in my lap. Assuming she wanted me to get on with reading, I picked up where I'd left off before being so rudely interrupted.

Sara wasn't pacified. I checked her for ants. Nothing. Memories of previous reactions flooded my mind. In the background of each one, my baby girl cried. I pulled up my shirt.

The skin around the ant sting had raised and turned scarlet, forming several large welts. Fear curled in my belly. Brandon was at work. Dad was in West Monroe. This reaction might be a bad one, and I was alone with the kids. My thoughts started going fuzzy as I dialed Dad's number.

"I'll be there as quick as I can," he said. The stress in his voice made me sad.

Each breath was accompanied by coughing and wheezing. My sinuses swelled shut. Sara was now hysterical. I slid her down onto the floor. It was uncanny how she knew I was reacting before I did. Stumbling into the kitchen in a stupor, I located the Acute Rescue, took several drops, and returned to the recliner to wait, an EpiPen in hand.

Dad walked through the door sooner than I had expected. God only knew how fast he'd driven. He didn't know the new acupressure sequence we used to treat my reactions, and I was too sick to explain. He helped me rise up in the chair and performed two rounds of BioSet, using swabs of my saliva and the fiery skin around the bite.

The procedure relieved my airways. Dad busied himself, firing my homemade shampoo at the ants, cursing them. "That's right, die. Die, you sorry sapsuckers!"

The urge to laugh surprised me, but though amusement pulled at my mouth, I couldn't muster the energy or heart to give myself over. This damnable illness affected everyone around me. It destroyed everything. And now, the confusion and dizziness returned. I coughed again.

Heat flooded my face, and my skin tightened. "Dad?" I mumbled through a swollen throat and mouth. "Is my face swelling?"

Dad looked up from battle and squinted at me. "Yeah."

He could see it. From across the room. So many times, my symptoms could only be felt. Alarm swept through me. Dad had done everything he could. For me, epinephrine was a last resort, but I was only getting worse. I didn't like the idea of using it, but if there was ever a time, it was now. Taking a deep breath, I reached for the auto-injector and stabbed my thigh.

Dad called Brandon, who left work when he heard what I'd done. We had to decide whether to follow protocol and drive to the emergency room or risk staying home. My heartbeat quickened and limbs quaked, but I felt better and breathed easier by the time Brandon had arrived. He didn't have to say anything. His very expression was a reproach. "What did you do?"

"I'm sorry," I said. Not for using the Epi but for ruining his day, his month, his year. Maybe his life.

He sighed. "If we take you in, you'll react to whatever is in the air, and they'll want to give you steroids. Neither Mom nor I are sure you're strong enough for all that."

My mom. She had good instincts. "I'm not."

"Okay then," he said, pressing his phone to his ear. "Hey, Dr. Yakaboski. This is Brandon. We have a situation over here again, and I was wondering if you're available to help."

When he hung up, I asked, "Is this real life?" It felt more like a strange alternate reality that I desperately needed to escape.

"If it is, I don't like it," he said.

When would we wake up from this nightmare?

* * *

Dr. Yakaboski had made a home visit twice before—once to teach Brandon how to perform the acupressure treatment and again to treat a reaction I had to the IV tubing—and here she was again. Brandon helped me to bed, where it was easier for her to perform her special combination of BioSet, TBM, and BEST. Brandon observed from the foot of the bed.

I felt better before she finished the first round. "We need to come up with a name for your treatment," I said as she massaged a pressure point in my hand. "You need to teach it to people. It's amazing."

"Get better, and you can help me do just that." With a sad smile, she finished her work and patted my hand.

I knew that look. It was the same look she'd given me when I'd entered her office after the pesticide exposure. She didn't say it out loud because she understood the power of spoken words, but she didn't believe I would survive this illness. She was preparing herself, as I sometimes felt Brandon doing. As I did with Jenny.

What I believed about my survival changed from day to day. Just yesterday, I was certain God was healing me. And then today happened.

"Thank you," I said. "I appreciate everything you do for me."

"You're very welcome."

After she left, Brandon pulled the bed away from the wall. "I don't want ants in the bed with us tonight."

The war continued the next morning. We couldn't poison them while I was present, so Brandon decided I needed to be removed from the house. Mom and Dad offered their spare rooms. Brandon drove me and the kids to West Monroe, where we would be safe, on Saturday morning. He returned to the property, where he met our friend Eddie Davis, who helped him pack what we needed and spray the ants outside.

Visiting my parents in their home was different from living there again. I had difficulty relaxing and was allergic to the dogs. Mom and Dad had two Australian shepherds and Hannah's terrier, Precious. My nose ran and grew stuffy, sometimes at the same time. Mom put the dogs out, which helped, but I felt bad for them. July in Louisiana was brutal.

Brandon's workdays increased in length by an hour. He left earlier and arrived home later. Dad was usually within reach, but he continued to drive out to the property every day to pick vegetables and check on everything.

Rather than focus on the negatives, I capitalized on the gifts. Staying with my parents meant I could sleep in almost every morning. I rose, ate a late breakfast of rice cereal, and savored some prolonged time in God's word. On days that Mom was home, we shared long talks in the kitchen. There hadn't been many opportunities to do so since I'd become sick. There was always an emergency or a pressing need in the way.

The kids enjoyed Grandma's toys as well as their own, and we maintained our rhythm of cuddles in front of the television and reading twice a day. While they napped in the afternoon, I took my daily enema and detox bath and was sometimes able to catch a nap of my own. In the evening, I cooked dinner for everyone, using the vibrant vegetables pouring in from Jubilee Farm. Mom and Dad praised my cooking, which had improved since they'd last sampled it, and

I was thankful to serve them.

We attempted to return the night of July 4, but our stay was short-lived. We were there maybe twelve hours before Sara was stung multiple times. Rather than congregating in the kitchen, the ants were now spread out. Though fewer in number, they were every bit as dangerous. We'd learned from experience—it only took one. We moved back in with Mom and Dad.

The debate didn't last long. We decided to hire a professional to spray inside the house. The poison posed as significant a threat as the ants, so we didn't know how long it would be before we could return home.

I mentioned the conundrum to Dr. Yakaboski. "Set out jars of water," she advised. "Place a jar in each room where you spray, and muscle test the jars every few days. Make sure you fill them with enough water to account for evaporation, and use fresh water each time." When all the jars muscle tested as "safe and tolerable," I would know I could go home.

I didn't understand muscle testing or how it worked, but it did work. God was good to hand me such a simple, clever tool. I thanked him for provision and comfort amid our losses. My parents hadn't sold their house yet, so I had a safe place to stay. Their home was comfortable, beautiful, and spacious. We had good food to eat, and Brandon didn't have to worry so much while he was at work.

Still, the loss of my home, even temporarily, stung. Though I could look at it as a prison, it had become a sanctuary. My personal refuge. A safe place. And ants had invaded it in relentless ranks. I'd lost my home, food, health, money, comfort, friends, family, and fun in the warpath of this disease. What else would it take before it was through with me?

* * *

Micah and Sara played at Mom's feet while she packed for a ten-day mission trip to inner city Atlanta with her church. Mom and Dad had signed up in the spring. There was no valid reason for them to back out now. I sprawled out on their bed, where Brandon and I would sleep while she and Dad were gone. I tried not to think about how lonely I would feel without them or what would take place while they were gone.

I wouldn't be without help or support. We'd arranged "mom care" over the next few days. Kaylee Aulds, a young friend and former music student of mine, would come several afternoons to watch the kids so that I could get an enema, a bath, and a nap. Nona, Debbie, or Brandon would fill in the gaps. I would need to wake up earlier, but neither my schedule nor my responsibilities would change much beyond Brandon's need for special care following his upcoming procedure.

Brandon had made the decision I had no strength to. "I gotta get fixed."

The grief of it threatened to sink me, but the facts had left us with limited choices. I couldn't afford to become pregnant. To sustain a pregnancy in my state would be a rare miracle. The baby, and possibly I, could die in the process. Brandon and I weren't willing to forgo sexual intimacy, no matter how difficult it was. While the non-latex condoms hadn't yet triggered a serious reaction, I had noticed an increasing sensitivity over time. We suspected the lubricants on the condoms.

I'd hoped to one day be healthy enough to carry and deliver another child. Sometimes I dreamed of a houseful. I'd always wanted at least three. We weren't finished. I felt it in my marrow. But the alternatives were simple—risk my life and the life of any child I might carry, or stop having sex with my husband. According to my understanding of biblical marriage, children were an important, joyous gift, but sexual intimacy was vital. As a covenantal act, almost a sacrament.

Besides, we liked each other. Celibacy wouldn't work for us. We'd cave.

Brandon was agitated and curt when the day arrived. Eddie picked him up since I was too fragile to go with him myself. I thanked God for a friend like Eddie who would take a day off from work for something like this. There was no one else like him.

My prayers for peace chased the truck down the driveway. It turned the corner, and to my relief and surprise, I was okay. Grace was a mysterious thing.

When they returned, Brandon was loopy but not much worse for the wear. The doctor reported that it had been a textbook procedure. Brandon only needed to rest and be careful for a few days. It would take a few weeks for him to be declared sterile.

To fight off the encroaching heaviness in my chest, I cared for Brandon as well as I was able, pressed into gratitude, and added to the list of gifts in my journal.

A few good, nausea-free days for Jenny.

Kaylee Aulds—a perfect fit for our family.

New music on my iPod.

The happy songs Sara sang upon waking up.

Mom and Dad arrived home from their mission trip with cool stories and fresh excitement. I prayed that nothing would happen to ruin it. Fortunately, I'd suffered no major upsets since the ant sting, but smaller daily reactions continued to plague me, accompanied by fear and doubts that sounded like my own voice but felt like an assault.

I may never get well. Sure—my allergies are better, but will I ever be able to rejoin the world? Those NAD supplements didn't work out. I may need the IV treatment after all. But if I get it, it will probably kill me, and then Brandon would be left with a dead wife and a $10,000 bill.

Each day, I fought an internal battle between hopelessness and the choice to worship, trust, and do the next right thing. I repeated the words "I trust you" aloud as I cooked, changed diapers, and took enemas—until I believed them. When I lost connection with the Holy Spirit, I whispered the words. When I made a stupid mistake—like forgetting to muscle test the goat cheese before I ate it—and suffered a systemic reaction, I said them again.

As I read the book of Genesis, God reminded me that he keeps every promise but that the fulfillment sometimes takes decades. *My faithfulness is best measured over time.*

One thing about all the voices in my head—God's voice was becoming more recognizable. It usually came from a truth found in the Bible. Each word accompanied a peace that calmed the tempest within. It offered me a hand up out of the pit.

Over the next few weeks, my prayers began to change. God had already promised healing, so I didn't have to beg for it. He'd also said that the healing would take time, so I decided to pursue contentment in my circumstances—as they were—without accepting them or being defined by them. I stopped praying for patience because contentment was patience with a genuine smile. I stopped believing in setbacks and set my hope on the journey, my Fellow Traveler, and the promised destination, not of healing alone but of complete wholeness in him.

* * *

I wasn't surprised, only dismayed, when I spotted the fire ant from the other side of my parents' bathtub. He stood guard over my water glass like a tiny soldier. This whole ant thing wasn't normal. I smashed him with my towel.

Stepping out of the tub, I saw three more crawling on the bathroom floor near my shoes. Glaring, I preached at them. "Though an army may encamp against me, my heart shall not fear; though war may rise against me, I will be confident."

More ants appeared in my parents' home over the next few days. Dad was ready to spray, but he couldn't as long as I was there. To save Dad unnecessary worry, Brandon brought me the water jars he had placed throughout the trailer a couple of days early. They tested as safe! After nearly a month of living with my parents, we packed up our belongings and drove home to Jubilee.

I was unprepared for the rush of emotion when my little mobile home came into view. The next hour was all work, tears, and happy singing. After putting Sara down for her nap, I climbed into bed and attempted a nap of my own. Relishing the soft cotton sheets, I dozed.

An old enemy crept into the room, slithered into my bed, and pounced. The very part of me which had been pounding with hot joy only moments before froze, bound in place by black winding tentacles. Fear made no sense at all. God had crowned the day with goodness. My tired, aching body rested in a warm pool of afternoon sun. I breathed familiar, safe scents I had missed for weeks. But there he was, haunting me.

Alone, he whispered. *You may be home, but now you are alone.*

It was an absurd lie. Brandon was sitting in the living room even as he hissed. *Your mother will begin teaching soon. Hunting season is on the horizon. Your well of helpers is about to dry up, and you will have to navigate life alone.*

Distraction. That was what I needed. I turned on the television. Fear continued to whisper, but now he had to compete with my favorite programs.

Inevitably, time to prepare dinner arrived. I sighed, turning off the TV. Fear still had my heart in its icy grip. *Alone, alone…*

It would be nice if *he* would leave me alone. I was going to have to fight. I pulled out a favorite weapon and silently reviewed Psalm 27:1. "The Lord is my light and my salvation. Whom shall I fear? The Lord is the strength of my life. Of whom shall I be afraid?"

You know you aren't ready to parent your children and manage your home. You can't even manage yourself.

"Fear not, for I am with you," I countered again in my mind. "'Be not dismayed, for I am your God. I will strengthen you. Yes, I will help you, I will uphold you with my righteous right hand.' God will send strength or help. So there." I almost stuck out my tongue.

Fear was quiet for a while, but he would not release me, and I couldn't wriggle out of his grasp. I prepared and ate dinner his prisoner, alternately praying and reminding myself of things that were true and real. By the time I began working on the dishes, I was tired of the struggle.

I doubled my efforts. "Why are you cast down, O my soul? And why are you disquieted within me? Hope in God, for I shall yet praise Him, for the help of His presence," I preached to myself aloud. "Grace, grace. Sufficient grace. Your grace is sufficient for me."

Brandon, who browsed a catalog at the table, raised his eyebrows and continued reading. The man was becoming difficult to weird out. He'd seen and heard too much.

I remembered the promise of James 5:16—"Confess your trespasses to one another, and pray for one another, that you may be healed"—and offered him context. "Hey, babe? I'm struggling."

As I told him about Fear and how he had attacked without a scrap of reverence for my joy, I realized something. This always happened. For every happiness, there was an equivalent assault. A price.

Today, Fear had paid me a visit. Of course, it was my choice whether I made a pet of him. Whether I fed him, sheltered him, and excused his mess. It was my job to turn him away. A moment of fear was only a weakness. Granting it entry was sin.

After my confession, I felt Fear's tentacles slip a bit. I preached on from the pulpit of my kitchen sink and could breathe again. I recounted truths about God's abiding presence. My soul remembered it was never alone. I shuffled my "Worship Mix" playlist and sang the lyrics like a battle cry. It wasn't pretty, but it was effective.

An inexplicable, unseen weight lifted off of me. Fear fled.

My mind was quiet and peaceful when I crawled into bed that night. Recounting the battle, I noted that confession and worship had been the most powerful weapons in my arsenal. Fear would likely come looking for me again, and I would need to remember how to fight.

24

Epinephrine

How I could feel so tired and not be able to nap was beyond me. I'd been a champion napper since my early teens. Nighttime insomnia wasn't a complete stranger, but lately it had become a regular visitor. I should be sleepy. Instead, I was only exhausted and heavy.

I drew the blankets up to my chin and shivered. Even in my sweatpants, I was cold. In August. Despite the weight I'd gained over the past few weeks. Something new was amiss. I tried not to feel anxious about it, but lately anxiety seemed to rule my body even when I suppressed it in my mind.

I mentioned the new symptoms to Dr. Yakaboski, who now insisted I call her Carolyne. "Let's check you out," she said, leading me to her testing equipment.

The computer hummed a dreary report as she poked and prodded. "Hmm...," she said. "Your thyroid isn't doing too well, which isn't a surprise. Your adrenals aren't functioning properly at all. When did the new symptoms start?"

It hadn't happened all at once. "The insomnia started while I was at Mom and Dad's. After the ant sting."

"After the epinephrine," Carolyne said quietly.

As she spoke the words, I knew she was right.

"Your constant reactions probably keep your adrenals

stressed out."

My recent reactions flashed through my memories—the balloon the kids had brought home from a birthday party and a menstrual pad, something I hadn't needed until recently after gaining weight.

"Do you have any sources of iodine in your diet?"

"I became allergic to the kelp."

Her cool fingers massaged my throat. "You may be developing a goiter."

Lovely. "Could that be why I'm getting hoarse when I read to the kids?" I asked.

She shrugged. "It could be inflammation in general. It's hard to know with you." She muscle tested my tolerance to a couple of supplements she had on hand, but neither worked. "Let's start you on some trace minerals for now. You can add them to your water. I'll look into a few alternatives to support your thyroid and adrenals."

A couple of days later, she stopped by the house with liquid iodine and several homeopathics that she'd made in her office. Homeopathics were no problem as long as I boiled out the preservative alcohol, and the iodine I could paint on my throat before bed each night, bypassing my temperamental gut.

On her way out the door, she said, "You should consider seeing Dr. Frieden. I don't know if your insurance will cover it, but I think she would be a real help to you."

Two phone calls later, I discovered that appointments with Dr. Frieden would cost less without insurance. Brandon drooped over the table, massaging his face when I reported the actual figure.

"Don't worry about it," I said, unwilling to stress him out further.

Brandon lifted his eyes to mine. "No. You don't worry about it. Do what you need to do. We'll make it work."

I made an appointment the next day. Darlene, the receptionist, told me that Dr. Yakaboski had already called and told them they might hear from me. She informed me that there was a space open on the day of my treatments with Carolyne and that they would be sure not to burn any candles or spray air fresheners before I came or while I was there.

Everyone needed a friend like Carolyne.

Dr. Frieden was as delightfully quirky as I remembered her. She performed acupressure sequences that targeted the thyroid, adrenals, and liver, all of which tested poorly, and gave me a chiropractic adjustment that immediately relieved some of my pain. I left her office to see Carolyne, who performed BEST and hooked me up to the infrared machine that helped to drain my chronically swollen lymph nodes.

That afternoon, I felt like a new woman. My pain was hardly noticeable, and I had energy. Taking advantage, I cleaned, whipped up a new batch of deodorant, and took the kids on a walk.

When I woke the next morning, I was sure I'd contracted the flu. Fatigue and aches racked my body. Nausea rolled my stomach before breakfast and after. A coffee enema and detox bath improved my condition, but only a little.

I called Carolyne to ask her opinion. "Detox," she said without hesitation. "It's a sign that the treatments worked, but we need to be careful. Maybe we won't put you on the lymphatic machine for so long next week."

The reduced time didn't help. After I prayed about whether to continue the treatments, I didn't feel I should stop. The overall benefits outweighed the unpleasant side effects. For one day, I felt good. Without the treatments, I never felt good. And there was something to be said for treatments I could tolerate at all. Who knew? Maybe they would improve my health over time.

Everything these days seemed to require faith—the substance of things hoped for, things yet unseen. I was so ready to see something. Anything.

Look at me.

Everything led back to worship. God didn't suggest it as a solution only for the moment. It was the reasonable answer to every circumstance.

* * *

Every time I gained ground, I declined again. Reactions often followed detox days, granting me no time to recover from one misery before the next. Discouragement stalked me like a hungry wolf. On my worst days, I scrolled my Facebook feed for long stretches of time to avoid myself. But scrolling didn't numb the ache; it made me restless, which led to sin.

Envy ate at my insides as I admired the fabulous food my friends were eating, the incredible trips they were taking, and the beautiful babies they were having. They looked so attractive and healthy and happy. I was even jealous of my sick friends who could take medicine, feel better, and get back to life as usual.

After being absent from the outside world for nearly two years, I'd become separate. Alone. Forgotten. Left behind. Invisible. My friends smiled in photos with other friends. Did they ever think of me? Even Brandon, my best friend, was so busy taking care of everything that I rarely saw him. A starving cavern opened inside me.

I stopped scrolling. I'd survived this long; envy wasn't going to take me out. I would learn the secret art of contentment if it was literally the last thing I did on this earth. My affections needed a reset.

So I fixed my eyes on the cross of Christ—proof of God's love for me, provision for jealousy, anger, fear, and depression. I worshiped, gazing at the beauty of Jesus, fixating on his goodness, reciting his word. I asked him to be for me what Brandon couldn't at the moment—my abiding companion, soul mate, and lover—knowing that he alone could satisfy my overwhelming need. That burden was too heavy even for Superman.

My list of gifts grew, though I ran out of wall space to post them.

A dusty walk on a warm summer morning.

The song of the locusts, the soundtrack of the South.

Small shoe prints in the red clay dirt.

Dirty little hands.

Flushed cheeks.

Sweaty ringlets at the nape of a sweet neck.

A pile of books and toys in my lap.

An unexpected visit with Jenny at the lake house.

I reminded myself of what I could do instead of what I couldn't. I could cook, wash dishes, and do laundry. I could smile at my babies and kiss them as often as I liked. I could listen to and answer the unending questions of a four-year-old and arrange happy faces on his toast with bananas and raisins. I could sing hymns, read books, hide naughty haiku in Brandon's lunch box. I could write.

As a special gift, the Lord planted a picture in my mind while I was reading Sarah Young's devotional, *Jesus Calling*, one afternoon. The vision inspired a fairy tale, which expanded into an idea for a fantasy novel. On days I had to lie in bed, ill from a reaction, I took out my speckled notebook and sketched out maps, characters, and plot ideas.

Months ago, I had laid my desire to be a novelist on the altar and thought it had burned up. In a way, it had. The desire to be known as a novelist was gone. Now, I was just a girl having fun writing a story she wanted to read. God had given me a fruitful way to use my imagination.

Of course, it was easy to lose touch with the good after hours of battling pain, fatigue, and depression. One night, I stared into a pot of boiling squash, kicking myself for my irritability with Brandon and the kids and for writing so little that day. The Lord spoke into it all—the novel, my health, our marriage, and life in general.

Trust me in the process.

I blinked, and the squash came into focus. Our Jubilee squashes were long withered and gone. For me to be boiling that squash, someone somewhere had planted a squash seed. They had watered it and protected it from predatory bugs. Someone had harvested it, packaged it, and shipped it so that I could bring it home. I had peeled and cut it and tossed it into boiling water. It must have hurt.

In a moment, I would drain out the water, mash the squash, and mix it with eggs and coconut flour. I'd roll it out and place it in the oven to bake until golden brown. When it was done, I would have something delicious. Something like bread. I would eat, and the squash would break down in my digestive system and become nourishment for my body.

Peeled, cut, boiled, baked, and digested. Process.

The Lord had said it before with the sauerkraut. He reminded me of it now.

I wasn't sure I liked process. Process felt a lot like death. But without death, there was no resurrection. Without loss, there was no jubilee.

25

Wedding Bells

After my third appointment with Dr. Frieden, my days were marked by more energy and less pain. The essential oils I'd bought in January no longer triggered anaphylaxis, allowing me to use them from time to time. My peripheral nerves calmed and ceased firing stinging sensations down my legs and into my feet. My next menstrual cycle presented without the familiar sciatic and pelvic floor pain that made standing for an hour or more over the stove so challenging. I also began to sleep a bit better.

When Jenny called and asked me to stand in her wedding, I felt confident I could actually do it. Months ago, she'd told me that she and Drew had never had a wedding. They'd been married in a court of law, and she felt she'd missed something by not stating her vows before friends and family.

"Let me talk to Brandon," I told her. "He has to be on board. I can't drive myself, and he'll be the one to take care of me if something happens." *When* something happened. I couldn't help but remember the previous year's drive home from Houston.

"Of course," she said, "but we're going to pray for a perfect day."

Amen. After all she'd been through, I wanted her to feel well, look gorgeous, and get everything she wanted.

To my surprise, Brandon agreed to take me to the wedding, which would be held during the second weekend of hunting season. Brandon never traveled anywhere during October. His yes came so easily that it could only mean one thing.

Sure, he loved me. He always loved me, but in the past, he'd denied me smaller and less risky pleasures due to inconvenience. It wasn't love alone. He was also afraid. He didn't want to withhold anything in his power to give, not when I could die at any time, not while watching Jenny waste with cancer. With her, every visit might be my last.

He was such a good man, especially good to me. He'd given so much, and still, he stayed when so many others would have run like hell in the opposite direction. He took me in his arms when other men would have gone looking for someone healthier, prettier, and more able to fulfill their desires. So often, it was in the warmth and safety of Brandon's arms that I glimpsed Christ's heart for me.

Our marriage had improved over the past few weeks. The timing felt relevant to my decision to look to Jesus to fulfill my needs and relieve Brandon from the pressure of being my everything. Still, the fear behind Brandon's yes saddened me. I couldn't refute it because it was based in legitimate possibility. I had no platitudes to offer him. Who didn't fear loss?

Three days after I spoke with Jenny, Hannah called. "I'm getting married! Rich finally popped the question!"

She too asked me to stand in her wedding. "I'd love to," I told her, trying not to think of all the festivities I would likely miss.

With two weddings looming, I needed better protection from fragrances than my cotton mask if I didn't want to end up as the brides' "something blue." I researched and found a mask with a filter. In lace. "Well," I said to the computer screen, "I'll be fancy."

In his goodness, the Lord sent us some encouragement before we left for Jenny and Drew's wedding. A friend from college sent me a message about a dream she'd had. In the dream, I was standing in a crowd of people, smelling a wildflower, perfectly healthy.

The next day, the organist from the church I'd attended as a child reported that she'd dreamed of me as well. She'd seen me in my home among a crowd of people. Lots of children were running around and having fun. What amazed me is that neither woman knew the other, and their dreams occurred on two consecutive nights.

To me, the dreams meant that healing was coming. I wouldn't die in Houston at Jenny's wedding. I even worked up enough pluck to attempt church the following Sunday. A surprising wave of emotion smacked me on the drive, and it took a few moments to sort out what I was feeling.

Life, as it was, had become my new normal. I'd accepted it and forgotten that I should be miserable all the time. Sure—there was loss, pain, disappointment, and crippling loneliness, but Christ was always present. Despite everything, I liked my life.

Today, God was returning something that had been stolen from me. I had no idea how much I'd missed it. Hot tears and sloppy sobs escaped from a deep hidden vault in my soul. I grieved what had been lost and thanked God for the gift. Even if my attempt at faith turned out to be a bust, I had this moment. I had today. Jenny had taught me that.

Brandon had intentionally left the house late so that we would be able to find a seat where there weren't many people. More people meant more triggers. Not everyone was in service when we arrived, so stares followed me as I made my way through the foyer. Their looks were full of questions they didn't have the courage, time, or interest to ask. I smiled back at them until I realized they couldn't see anything through my mask, glasses, and dark thick curls. Sometimes I wished for an invisibility cloak like Harry Potter had.

Once we were seated, I looked around the sanctuary. Many faces were new. After the service, most kept their distance, which was good. Already, my head swam and throat swelled. A few people who recognized me came close, but Brandon intercepted them with a hug before they could embrace me. Hugs were dangerous, as they left behind fragrant residue.

On the walk to the car, a conglomerate of odors attacked my senses, even through my masks. Every breath of fresh air smelled like an attack. I ripped off my mask only to walk through a cloud of cologne and caught the scent of car exhaust. Each smell screamed up my nose, clawed through my sinuses, and mauled my brain.

Brandon buckled the kids into their car seats, and then opened my car door to perform the acupressure treatment that had become a part of daily life. I hadn't asked him to. He just knew I needed it.

He extracted a cotton swab from the sandwich bag in my purse and extended it. Leaning forward, I opened my mouth and soaked the tip in my saliva. An occasional cough barked out of my chest while he tapped and prodded pressure points, but I smiled. I might be sick, but the reaction wasn't life threatening.

Brandon finished his work and planted a kiss on my brow. "Thank you for being so brave and trying something so scary."

I tried to focus on his face. "You're welcome."

Fatigue, pain, and aches pounced on the ride home, and I spent the remainder of the day in bed. All in all, I counted the adventure as a win. If I could survive church, I would survive Jenny's wedding.

* * *

I crossed my legs, gritting my teeth. Even if there was a public restroom available on this rural Texas highway, I wouldn't be able to use it. For so many reasons, public restrooms were out of the question. There was nowhere to pull over—no place safe from snakes, fire ants, chiggers, and poison ivy, no tree line or patch of brush that would offer a shadow of privacy. Brandon said I was too picky, but I was eying an empty mason jar, considering something I'd never before attempted.

"I'm doing it." I unbuckled. Even if I splattered, it would be better than being caught with my pants down on the roadside, getting sick because I'd entered a public restroom, or waiting so long I leaked all over the seat.

Peeing in a mason jar while traveling eighty miles per hour down a Texas highway proved trickier than I had anticipated. I'd waited so long that I filled the quart-size jar almost to the brim. Before I could close it properly, I sloshed urine onto my seat.

"Well, shit," I said.

"Nope. Piss," Brandon answered.

I daggered him with a look. He just laughed.

"The car is going to smell like it too," I said, disgusted.

Sighing, Brandon reached into the back seat for one of the towels we had packed.

"We need that for showers."

"You and I can share. Raise up." I lifted my bottom, and he stretched the towel over the seat. "Now then. I'll clean it up after we arrive at the condo."

I felt my own frown as I buckled. I was twenty-nine—too young to have my husband clean up my pee for me.

"Laugh," he said. "It's how we're going to beat this thing."

Some days, I hated how perfect he was.

We had no further hiccups until we arrived at the condo, which smelled of air freshener and fabric softener. My face began to swell, and my signature seal-bark cough geared up. "I asked them not to use air freshener," he muttered. "Let me treat you real quick, and then I'll replace the sheets so you can lie down."

I plopped onto the couch. "I don't think the chemicals are fresh. If they were, the smell would hurt more, and my symptoms would be worse."

Brandon handed me my purse, where I kept the bottle of Acute Rescue and a stash of cotton swabs for the acupressure treatment. I dug out what we needed while Brandon opened the windows.

"Lean into me," Brandon said, ready to begin.

"Always." I grinned and leaned forward as commanded. "Do you know why God had you bring me and not Mom or Dad?" I asked as he tugged, rubbed, and tapped.

"Why don't you tell me since you already know?"

"Redemption. This trip is about more than a wedding. It's going to be the opposite of the trip last year. Just you wait."

He didn't say anything. If he didn't agree, God would show him.

The next morning, Brandon and I woke early on our own and passed the time in each other's arms. Sexual intimacy didn't happen as often as either of us would have liked. As it turned out, I actually was allergic to sex. Even after the vasectomy, I suffered both local and systemic reactions that caused swelling, itching, and insomnia. The insomnia was sometimes severe, robbing me of sleep entirely. Because it was morning, I didn't have to worry about insomnia, but I took some Acute Rescue and allowed Brandon to treat me afterward to alleviate the other symptoms.

"Romance is hard," I said.

Brandon shot me a naughty look as he helped me to my feet. "Sometimes…usually."

I had plenty of time to shower, dress, make myself look as nice as I could without makeup or proper hair care, and still arrive early. God smiled on the day just as Jenny had hoped. The air was cool and crisp. Sunrays glowed golden, slipping through morning shadows to dry the dew and warm our shoulders. Slipping on my lacy mask, I took Brandon's arm and let him lead me inside.

Jenny took my breath away. She radiated strength and beauty and looked gorgeous in her white gown. Light shone from her blue eyes, transfixing me. I noticed the toll cancer and chemo had taken on her body since our visit two months prior. She'd lost more weight, and her skin had developed more brown splotches, but none of that mattered. She was as beautiful a bride as any I'd seen.

My groomsman escort and all the bridesmaids had collectively decided not to wear any fragrances on my behalf. Jenny whispered, "I didn't even ask them. They just did it."

Their thoughtfulness stunned me. Only a handful of people made that accommodation for me. The hospitality of strangers brought me to tears. I thanked each one personally.

God's seal of approval was apparent in every detail. His Spirit hung quietly about us all, manifesting in joy, calm, intentional moments, and physical strength for Jenny. I generally didn't cry at weddings, but today I couldn't help myself. It was lovely in its simplicity and impossibly sweet. Every expression, word, musical choice, and ceremonial symbol bore significance. The congregation was called to sing "Ode to Joy"—a fitting song for the event. When the chorus began, angelic voices rang from the loft above. The church had granted Drew and Jenny an unexpected gift of a women's choir to bless them. They blessed us all.

After the ceremony, we lingered for photos. I felt out of place being photographed with half my face covered, but I survived knowing that I was the only one bothered by it. On the walk to the reception, one of the bridesmaids that had kept me engaged in friendly conversation throughout the day asked, "So what is your illness exactly?"

I inwardly cringed. There wasn't an ounce of ill intent or incredulity behind the question, but that didn't make it any easier to answer. People had no context for the craziness I had going on. I couldn't just say "allergies" with an ironic smile. She'd asked in earnest. Discussion about immunity caused people's eyes to glaze over. No one knew what methylation was. My disease was a mystery to me. I didn't even have a name for it. There was no way to help her understand.

"We don't know," I said, "but we suspect it's some immunological or genetic disease that's made me allergic to everything."

Her eyes softened with empathy. "Wow. So how do you treat it?"

When there was no name for the disease, there was no established protocol. All I knew to do had been discovered through trial and error. "For the most part, I try to eat nutritious food, rest, and avoid triggers."

"Have you gotten better over time?"

I pondered the question. "In some ways. But when it comes down to it, I need a miracle."

The young woman paused before entering the fellowship hall where the reception was held. "I'll be praying you get one."

"Thank you."

"Thanks for answering my questions," she said. "I didn't know if you would."

"Thanks for asking. Not many people do." I hoped she could tell I was smiling.

Brandon caught up to me as she walked into the room full of milling, fragrant people. "Think you should go in there?" he asked.

"Probably not," I said, "but I want to say goodbye to Jenny."

He clenched his jaw and breathed hard out of his nose. "Okay."

On the way to see my friend, I passed a lady who wore an intense floral perfume. Three masks wouldn't have been enough to protect me from the stench. Determined, I found my friend, said goodbye, and told her how beautiful she was, how perfect the service had been, and how much I loved her.

Brandon and I said goodbye to Drew and his mother and made a quick exit.

"Oh my gosh," Brandon said when we had left the crowd. "Did you smell that?"

"I think all of Texas smells it." I coughed.

"How bad are you?" he asked, taking my hand.

"Not terrible. I might be okay after a treatment."

Brandon helped me into the passenger seat of the car. His gaze held mine as he performed the treatment. "You're welcome," he said.

"Thank you. You're the best."

He kissed me. "I know."

26

Intervention

Mom sat across the kitchen table from me, her gaze intense. "I think it's time to look into a major research clinic like Johns Hopkins or Mayo."

Ignoring the burning and nausea, I chugged another half glass of water, determined not to become dehydrated this time. For unknown reasons, my body had gone into another hyperimmune state, and I was unable to eat. Again.

"Nona agrees," she continued. "I didn't mention anything about Mayo when I saw her yesterday. She came to the conclusion on her own."

I didn't like what I was hearing. "No more doctors," I'd said. Now it felt like my most faithful prayer warriors had aligned themselves against me.

"You have to do something," she said. "You can't go on like this."

The words resonated, but I was afraid.

Silence settled over the kitchen. Mom waited. I swallowed the last of the water in my glass. "I don't know, Mom. Going to a place like Mayo would be a big dangerous deal."

"Living like this is dangerous."

Touché. "I'll pray about it and talk to B," I promised.

As I expected, Brandon agreed with me.

Mom called again the next day. "Have you decided?"

"Um, no," I said. "Brandon and I are against it, but I asked God to change our minds if we're wrong."

"Maybe this will help," Mom said.

Moms. When they got something in their craw, they didn't let go.

"I've been doing some research," she said. "I think you have some kind of mast cell disease. Maybe mastocytosis. It's unlikely because it's rare, so rare the textbooks here don't say much about it. The symptoms do match up though. It would explain why you react so fast. Mast cells are everywhere."

"Mastocytosis," I repeated. "How did you…"

"A former coworker mentioned that your symptoms sounded like mast cell stuff, so I researched it. Look it up on Mayo's site, and tell me what you think."

I began researching immediately. The list of symptoms read like a summary of my life—flushing, itching, hives, diarrhea, constipation, bloating, nausea, reflux, hypotension, shortness of breath, bone pain, brain fog, fatigue, enlarged lymph nodes, headaches, body aches, neuropathic pain, decreased attention span, difficulty in concentration, forgetfulness, anxiety, insomnia, depression, arthritis, muscle pain, uterine cramps, cough, asthma, throat itching, throat swelling, sinusitis, interstitial cystitis, angioedema, anaphylaxis.

Based on the articles I read, mast cell diseases were managed by a long list of medications and avoidance of triggers. I couldn't tolerate medication. I already avoided triggers as well as I knew how. Furthermore, there was no cure. What could Mayo do for me?

Brandon and I talked things over and decided there would be no harm in running a few preliminary tests locally. Elevated tryptase levels would point to systemic mastocytosis. As clear as a whisper, I heard God say, *Dr. Humble.*

"Oh, Jesus. Are you sure?" Of all the doctors I had seen, he was my least favorite.

I scheduled the appointment. When I told Mom who I would see, she advised, "Pretend to be unintelligent, and maybe he'll help you."

Unfortunately, I ruined the appointment before it began. Unaware that I was speaking to a nurse, I said some snarky things about my previous experience at the office. Not that anything I said was untrue. From the moment the nurse attached my face to my name and voice, she was cold. As was Dr. Humble. Even though I set aside my inner Hermione Granger and pretended to be clueless, I'd blown any chance I'd had at a pleasant appointment.

Before I finished reciting my long list of symptoms, which he was hearing for the second time, he called my bluff. "So what would you like me to do? Why are you here?"

I'd told the nurse which tests I wanted him to run when I scheduled the appointment. He already knew the answer to the question and wanted to jump straight to the point. The entire exercise was uncomfortable, and it was all my fault.

"Can you check my tryptase?"

He shrugged. "I tried to run that test a year ago. You wouldn't let me."

"Oh," I said. I didn't remember that.

"I have it right here in your records. But we can run them now." His pen danced across the paper attached to his clipboard. "Is that all you want?"

"Yes. Thank you. I appreciate your help," I said. And I did. Whether he liked me or not, whether or not he thought I was a hypochondriac, I needed him, and he'd agreed to help me.

On the ride home from the clinic, I realized there was an underlying reason for the way I'd acted. I'd been hurt, and I blamed the doctors. That wasn't fair. Doctors may not always know how to help, but they didn't go around intentionally hurting their patients. They hadn't caused my suffering. They were just…human.

In truth, God could've turned on a light bulb for any one of them. The only logical conclusion was that it wasn't time. He had me on a journey, and the destination wasn't all about physical healing. He had some purpose in mind, and his purposes were good whether or not they included a diagnosis, treatment, or healing. It was time to let go of the anger, defensiveness, and blame I felt toward the medical community.

Doctors aren't your enemy. Neither am I.

"I know," I said aloud. "I know."

That afternoon, I called Mayo Clinic in Rochester, Minnesota, to inquire about the process of scheduling an appointment.

* * *

Dr. Humble's nurse called two days later. "All your levels, including tryptase, came back normal."

I thanked her and hung up. The only thing a normal tryptase level indicated was that I didn't have systemic mastocytosis and would receive no further help from Dr. Humble—unless I wanted allergy shots or a psychiatric referral. Mom had offered to travel with me to Mayo in late May of 2014 after the spring semester ended at the university. Unable to schedule anything this far in advance, I set aside the decision of whether to go until after Hannah's wedding in mid-December. All of my energy and focus went into being healthy enough to attend.

I drank plenty of water and kept my fast short. Small meals eaten often seemed to help my digestive system accept food with less discomfort. My appointments with Dr. Frieden and Carolyne were the only risks I took. When the day of the wedding arrived, I felt strong enough to try it.

Brandon helped me into the strapless turquoise bridesmaid gown and pulled up the zipper. The gown dropped off my breasts and down my thinning torso. The dress had fit before my last little health crisis. I frowned at my reflection in the mirror.

"Hot," Brandon said.

"More like inappropriate. I'll have to figure out something else."

Brandon's arms wrapped around my waist from behind. "Who am I?"

Smirking, I rolled my eyes. "Superman."

"I'm also a redneck. I can rig this dress."

After a bit of tugging and pinning, the dress stayed in place well enough. "You may want to keep your arms tucked in, but I think you should be fine," Brandon said. "Let me know if it starts feeling loose." He wiggled his eyebrows.

We arrived at the venue a few moments before I was needed for photos. Musk and floral scents penetrated my masks, but they didn't overpower me. Again, the bridesmaids had forgone perfume for my sake, as had the groomsman who would escort me. "Think you can try a few photos without the mask?" Mom asked.

I pulled down one and then the other, tentatively sniffing the air. Removing the masks would improve the photos despite my puffy face and swollen eyes. "Maybe just a few."

Micah looked adorable in his turquoise shirt and brown bow-tie. Sara traipsed around like a little princess in her brown satin gown. My twin nieces looked like a pair of miniature angels in their white dresses. Hannah was radiant. Brandon looked as handsome as he ever had.

"How does it feel to be sexier than your wife?" I whispered to him as we posed for a family photo.

"I'll never know," he said with a wink.

As we posed for the last of the photographs, guests began to arrive and fill up the empty seats. I expected the smells to compound and trigger a reaction, but a bubble of supernatural protection enclosed me.

The ceremony was brief, but I collected each beautiful moment for the list of gifts in my journal at home—

Hannah's exuberance.

The quiet joy shining in Rich's eyes.

Covenant.

The girls' excitement.

A father who would love, protect, and raise my nieces to know the Lord.

Grace.

As soon as the ceremony ended, the chairs were cleared to make room for a dance floor. Music began to play, and the celebration began. Micah danced with me and then joined the growing conga line of tiny dancers. Sara darted here and there, eyes bright and fists full of snacks. Brandon pulled me into his arms and swayed to the beat of a love song. I even joined a few line dances with family members and friends I hadn't seen in a long while.

During a rest, Brandon handed me a cup of water. "Don't overdo it," he said.

Analyzing the cost and benefits, I said, "It'll be worth it if I do."

Tomorrow would come soon enough with all its hardship and big decisions, if it came at all. This moment was all I had. "Now" was all I ever had. Joy and food-free revelry was the proper response to God for his goodness—to Hannah, to Rich, to my family, to me. My laughter was a rebellion against the cold night that awaited me just outside after the last song ended.

* * *

A series of reactions pockmarked the days leading up to Christmas, creating unwelcome drama and an exacerbation of all my chronic symptoms, which planted me in bed. I'd already missed Thanksgiving celebrations and wouldn't be able to participate in the big family Christmas festivities, so Brandon and I had decided to host a come-and-go gift exchange on Christmas Eve for our immediate families. As simple as our plans were, they might have fallen apart if Carolyne hadn't invited me to her house for a much-needed treatment the day before the party.

The next morning, I felt well enough to perform the most basic tasks of hospitality—attend, wear decent clothing, and offer something to eat. Debbie arrived not long after the kids had finished their breakfast. She greeted us with a bright smile and asked, "Want me to clean house and play with the kids while you get your enema and do what you have to do for tonight?"

"Oh my gosh, yes," I said. "Thank you!"

She scooped Sara into her arms. "Brandon said you had a rough week. I'm just happy to help."

Encouraged by my improved state and Debbie's cheerful presence, I baked cookie bars, cooked dinner, and prepared homemade gifts of roasted almonds and body butter that afternoon. By the time family arrived, our little trailer was neat and sparkling clean, and the subtle scents of cocoa butter, cinnamon, and nuts warmed the air. Micah and Sara scurried round and round the open space, providing a soundtrack of belly laughter.

We gathered in the living room to open gifts. Brandon offered me the recliner and perched on one of the barstools we rarely used, leaving the sofas to our parents, Hannah, and Rich. The children congregated in the floor, eagerly awaiting their gifts.

Giggles, exclamations, and the ripping and crinkling of wrapping paper filled my ears and heart as would a lovely piece of music. Sara squealed in delight over her Mrs. Potato Head. Micah gasped, opening a large tin of Lincoln Logs. He huffed and grunted, wrestling with the lid so he could play with them right away.

"No, buddy. Not in here," Brandon said. "They smell. Let's take them to your room."

Micah said nothing but locked eyes with me from across the room, which fell silent at the intrusion. His brown pools were wide with disappointment and concern too weighty for a four-year-old to bear. I almost died where I sat. Without a word, he followed his daddy down the hall.

If Mayo could erase the emotional devastation of this disease, I would have left at the first opportunity. It couldn't, of course. The best I could hope for was a diagnosis and maybe some miraculous treatment that my body would accept.

No one understood the complicated nature of medical risk versus payoff as well as Jenny. I waited until after the New Year to call so that I wouldn't accidentally infringe on precious family time. When she didn't answer her cell, I tried her home phone as she'd instructed me to do.

"Hello?"

"Jenny?" The voice sounded like hers and didn't.

"Melissa!" I heard the smile in her voice, but she sounded tired. "How was your Christmas?"

We swapped holiday stories. She'd managed to visit every family gathering but hadn't lingered long at any. "Did you eat anything good?" I asked. We shared a mutual passion for holiday menus.

"A little, but I'm mostly back to baby food now."

"Oh."

"The chemo isn't really working anymore," she said. "It's just buying me some time. I'm in the grips of the disease now."

My throat grew hot and thick as if I were having an allergic reaction to her news. I swallowed. "How...how are you and Drew doing with that?"

"Drew's quiet, but I know he's sad. I hate to leave him and Matthew and Julia, but I've made my peace with everything. I'm just working on my book for the kids. Yesterday, I finished my entries about discovering music and the perfect shade of red lipstick." She laughed.

"That's amazing. They'll love that."

Silence.

I took a deep breath and said the words I'd planned to say if and when she reached this point. "Listen. No matter what, I will keep praying for Drew and your family. I'll even stay in contact if I can."

"That is so kind. I love you and am so thankful for our friendship," she said.

"I love you, too. So much." I'd thought I'd prepared myself for this news months ago.

"We found an older house nearby," Jenny said. "Drew's going to do some renovations, and we'll move in the spring. I've been thinking up different color schemes and decorative styles."

"Fun!" My voice sounded too bright to my own ears. "What colors are you thinking?"

Voices chattered in the background. Jenny paused to answer them. "Melissa? I'm sorry, but I need to go."

"Sure thing," I said. "Thanks for catching up with me."

"Thanks for calling. It's always good to hear your sweet voice."

The line clicked. Stricken, I set down my phone and stared at the wall. I couldn't breathe for the lead in my chest.

Hours passed before I realized I'd forgotten to ask Jenny what she thought about me going to Mayo. Funny—it didn't seem to matter anymore.

* * *

By mid-January, I'd become an uninspired, joyless shell of a woman. Maybe it was the cold holding me captive indoors, or that I couldn't remember my last "good day." Maybe it was that I knew Jenny would be leaving soon, and I couldn't imagine life without her. And Dixie, my mentor, had just buried a grandson after we'd all prayed long and hard for a miracle that hadn't come.

Poor January. It was such a buzzkill. Every. Single. Year. I kept looking for something or Someone to shake me out of my stupor, but no such luck.

My insomnia worsened. Some nights I couldn't sleep until four in the morning. To pass the hours, I prayed. I prayed for others who were sick and those like Dixie and her family who had suffered loss. I prayed for opportunities to be used by God. As a shut-in and allergic to the world, I couldn't do much, but I now had a specific skill set to offer.

A couple of days passed, and I heard that a friend from church had a little girl who suffered from mysterious reactions to different foods. I reached out to offer what help I could, and my friend accepted. I taught them to muscle test and perform the acupressure treatment Dr. Yakaboski had developed. I gave them some Acute Rescue, a few gut-healing herbs, and my copy of *Gut and Psychology Syndrome*. Before I left, I prayed for the little girl and my new friends, asking the Lord to reveal the hope and grace available to them as they suffered.

That night, the kids' cold symptoms took a turn for the worse, and I had the privilege of serving them in their sickness. I made chicken soup from bone broth, gave them homemade elderberry syrup and homeopathics, applied essential oils, performed acupressure treatments, massaged their lymph nodes, and gave them lavender baths, after which I wrapped them in warm towels I'd heated in the dryer. The hard work satisfied me in a way I hadn't anticipated, and they loved all the attention and affection I poured on them.

The work wore me down, but I experienced the truth of Deuteronomy 33:25: "As your days, so shall your strength be." There was always grace for the moment, and it never failed.

The question of traveling to Mayo lingered unresolved as I ventured into the book of Judges, which tells the story of Gideon. At a time when the Midianites were oppressing Israel, God encountered Gideon, who was threshing grain in secret out of fear of his enemies. After a greeting that didn't seem to fit the man—"The Lord is with you, mighty man of valor!"—God told Gideon he would save Israel from the Midianites, but Gideon was slow to believe. He was least in his father's house, of the weakest clan in his tribe, and very like me—lily-livered. He sensed the enormity of God's call, and it terrified him. He couldn't take the first step until he was beyond certain the Lord was with him. So he asked for a sign. And another. And another—until he was forced to believe the word of God.

Encouraged by God's patience with Gideon, I asked him to give me a personal sign—a good word about Mayo Clinic from a source outside of our circle who had no personal agenda. I asked that the word be reported directly to Brandon or me and told the Lord I would not schedule my visit until I received it. I had to be sure the trip was God's idea and not some desperate attempt to take matters into my own hands.

Later that week, during an impromptu Skype session with my longtime friend, Madonna, she mentioned that she was considering going to Mayo but wasn't sure what they could do for her there. Before I could voice my agreement, she said, "But my roommate's parents have both been. They love it. Think it's the best thing ever. They encourage everyone to go."

I couldn't breathe. God had just delivered my request—a positive unbiased word. I hadn't known how badly I didn't want to go until that moment.

A corner of my mind fretted. Surely that wasn't my sign. This was hearsay, not Madonna's personal experience. Besides, I may have brought up the topic of Mayo, which meant the mention didn't count.

Then I remembered Gideon and his fleece. As little as I wanted it to, it counted.

I took a deep breath as our conversation wound down. Before I hung up, I told her, "You were the mouthpiece of God for me today, and I hate you just a little bit for it."

She laughed. "What do you mean?"

I explained and said, "I'd hoped the answer would be no."

"If you think they can help, you should go," she said.

"I don't know what I think. All I know is that I need to obey," I said.

Tossing in bed that night, I battled an acute panic attack. How was I going to get to Minnesota safely and strong enough to withstand all the testing they would want to do? I couldn't fly. Too many triggers. The drive would require an overnight stay and would lengthen the trip. Once I arrived, how would the staff treat me? Like a committable lunatic, that's what.

The next morning, I read further into the book of Judges. In chapter 13, the Angel of the Lord visited Manoah and his wife to tell them they would bear a son who would begin to deliver the Israelites from the Philistines. Manoah didn't know who had spoken to him and offered to cook the prophet a meal. The Lord told him to provide a burnt offering instead. When the Lord ascended to heaven on the flame of the offering, Manoah realized he had spoken to God himself and feared that he and his wife would die because they had seen the glory of the Lord. Verse 23 stopped me cold. "But his wife said to him, 'If the Lord had desired to kill us, he would not have accepted a burnt offering and a grain offering from our hands, nor would he have shown us all these things, nor would he have told us such things as these at this time.'"

Peace, my child. Remember, it is my will that you live.

I expected Fear to leave with the assurance God didn't plan to kill me, but I feared something more than death, something I couldn't quite put a name to.

Trust me.

After all I'd been through, trust seemed so hard. If I leaped into the dark, I had no idea how far I'd fall or what the terrain was like at the bottom of the abyss.

Underneath are my everlasting arms.

"Do you know what you ask of me, God?"

Yes. Everything.

27

Homegoing

Communications with Jenny became briefer and more irregular as January lapsed into February. I sent a text on Julia's birthday to ask how she was doing and how they had celebrated. Her response saddened me. "I don't feel too good. I spend a lot of time in bed now. Caught a respiratory virus from the kids."

I prayed, sometimes with words.

We celebrated Micah's fifth birthday with a special pancake breakfast on the nineteenth. Jenny hovered in my thoughts throughout the morning. I called that afternoon and left a voice mail, letting her know that I was thinking about her and praying for her and her family. A few moments later, my phone rang.

For the first time in six weeks, Jenny's number flashed on the screen. My heart skittered in excitement. I snatched up the phone and answered.

"Melissa." The voice was a frail shadow of Jenny's usual sparkle and shine.

"What a treat," I said, determined not to lose the gift of the moment. "I had no idea I would get to talk to you."

"The treat is mine," Jenny said. She asked how I was feeling and how my family was doing.

"We're good. We finally decided I should go to Mayo to find out what's going on."

"Oh, good," she said. "Mayo is wonderful. How would you like me to pray?"

"I don't know." I sighed. "For my family, of course, and for my safety."

"And while you're there? What do you want to happen?"

"You know, I don't know what to hope for, so I'm just putting all my hope in God. You can pray that I'll keep my focus on him no matter what."

"I'll do that," she said. "I have lots of time to pray now."

"Enough about me," I said. "How are you? I wish I could be there to help you."

"I'm okay. Someone is always here for the kids. I don't do much more than rest. Hospice will probably start coming soon."

I fought to keep the sound of tears out of my throat. "I'm still praying for a miracle."

"I know," she said. "Thank you for that. Thank you for believing with me for so long. But listen—you don't have to keep your promise to pray for my family. I don't want you to live with that burden."

"Praying for your family isn't a burden. It never will be."

She hesitated. "Just the same. I won't hold you to that promise. Jesus will take care of Drew and the kids."

I couldn't breathe to sigh. "I love you."

"I love you too. I need to let you go now. It's hard to hold up the phone."

Only two minutes had passed since my phone had rung. "Sure thing. I might call you again in a minute and leave a song on your voice mail."

"Sounds good. Bye, Melissa."

"Goodbye."

I called back. Her cheery healthy voice answered. "This is Jenny..."

That Jenny was slipping away like air through my fingers. The recording ended, followed by a beep. I swallowed the coal in my throat and began to sing. "Precious Lord, take my hand; lead me on, help me stand. I am tired, I am weak, I am worn..."

* * *

"I love you so much." Jenny's text read like a farewell.

Everything this world had to offer a cancer patient had failed her. Nothing could help her now except for prayer. She needed the God of all comfort, the Resurrection and the Life.

Micah had a hard day, which I chalked up to too much sugar and birthday fun. He complained and whined incessantly, determined to be unhappy, which seemed to add to my own unhappiness. "But Saaawa..."

I'd had enough. I set my grief aside. "What is the issue, son?"

"Sawa won't come with me to my room," he whined.

"Okay. So go alone."

"I'm too scared!"

"Be strong and of good courage. The Lord your God is with you."

"But I can't *see* him!"

I softened. "That's the essence of faith, Bubs. Believing who you can't see."

Micah resumed fussing at Sara. Something was off. Micah was usually a cheerful, compliant child.

I stood. "Micah, Mama's not talking to you, okay?"

He paused mid-tantrum and cocked his head.

"I rebuke you, complaining spirit, and I command you to leave my son in Jesus's name. Jesus, please bring your joy and peace into our midst."

Micah crossed the room toward me. Halfway to the couch where I sat, he stepped on a plastic toy cup. "Ouch!"

"Ouch!" I echoed, extending my arms toward him.

He ran into my embrace and buried his face in my shoulder. "It's gone, Mama! It went away when I stepped on that cup!"

He leaned back, and his face beamed into mine. God had answered my prayer, and my little boy had felt it. God would do the same for Jenny. All that was required of me was a little faith.

I planted a kiss on Micah's soft cheek. "Yes, Bubs. Pain often precedes joy."

* * *

Jenny's friends and family scheduled a candlelight prayer vigil. Those who loved her gathered in her front yard to pray as she said goodbye to her family and closest friends inside. Her best friend in Houston had invited me, but I couldn't attend. No one was available to drive me.

The pain had become too great for Jenny, and soon hospice would grant her relief. Our time as friends on earth had ended unless Jesus showed up and pulled off another grave-robbing miracle. I still believed he could but had accepted that he probably wouldn't.

Jenny's mother-in-law, Lindy, kept me updated on her condition. Hospice arrived on the first of March and put her on a medication schedule that allowed her to rest uninterrupted and pain-free.

I wrestled with how to say goodbye—attend the funeral or try to make it to Houston before she died? When I posed the question to Lindy, she told me Jenny would be buried in Louisiana less than an hour from our home. I would be invited to the outdoor memorial service. The unexpected provision staggered me. How odd and precious were the kindnesses of God.

During these slow days of waiting, I scheduled my appointment at Mayo Clinic with Dr. Miguel Park, an immunologist recommended by a friend I'd met in one of the mast cell activation disease groups on Facebook. When it was done, hot grief squeezed my throat. I couldn't tell Jenny. She couldn't share her colorful thoughts.

On the morning of March ninth, I received a message from Lindy. "Sweet Jenny isn't suffering anymore. She passed on late in the night."

The expected tears didn't come. After two years of intense suffering, my Jenny was with our Jesus, her true home. I couldn't begrudge her the joy of her reward.

A gentle peace settled over me like a warm blanket as I lifted her family to the Lord in prayer.

* * *

Spring had come upon us suddenly and all at once, bedecked in all her youthful splendor. Life burst from the ground in fresh, vibrant blooms. New calves chewed bright-green grass near their mothers' knees in pastures nestled between rolling hills. Warm sunlight poured from the heavens—a smile of victory from my yellow-souled friend. Wind rushed through the trees, making music in honor of her free spirit. I had prayed for perfect weather. God had delivered.

Brandon led me by the arm to the outskirts of the group huddled around that horrid coffin perched above the black hole in the ground. Part of me was glad I couldn't see her. She wouldn't have looked anything like my friend anyway.

The fifteen-minute ceremony felt anticlimactic after a transformative friendship like ours. I appreciated the comforting words and personal touches, but none of it felt like Jenny to me. Her absence was a presence.

Someone handed me a palm-size stone and a marker with which to write a message. "You'll always be my Jonathan. Love, David," I wrote and placed the stone on the ground.

After embracing her family one by one, I exited through the gates of the small country graveyard feeling like an outsider. I was, really. Jenny's little daughter was older than our friendship. Some of them had known and loved her for thirty-eight years. What was my loss compared to theirs?

Tears finally came on the ride home—and with it a reaction to a perfume left on the coat I was wearing. Brandon stopped the car on the side of the highway, stashed my coat in the trunk, and performed an acupressure treatment.

My breathing regulated. I gazed out of the window at the budding pear trees and was reminded of the resurrection to come. When I saw her again, Jenny wouldn't be some sad ethereal wisp. She would be a perfected version of herself in physical form. She would laugh, dance, sing, and feast. Her face would be as recognizable as her spirit, and she would recognize me.

Jubilee was coming. It just wasn't here yet. Not for her family, and not for me.

28

Grief and Sardines

Grief rolled over me in unpredictable waves. Most of the time, my head stayed above water. I could see the world around me. The scent of Sara's soft curls anchored me. The breeze caressed my face. Micah sang an original composition at full voice. The sunlight warmed my skin, imploring me to remain present. My children were here, now, and I was with them. A moment of happiness would light upon my shoulder, and then, without warning, another wave hit, washing it out to sea, tossing me in the undertow until my lungs burned and ached.

My duties helped to distract me, but quiet moments in which my hands were busy and mind was still created the perfect conditions for an ambush. The hours I spent hand-washing dishes were the worst.

And so raged the battle for joy. If I looked intentionally, I could find it in freckled noses and blooming cherry trees. On days my joy-eyes didn't work so well, I worked through my list of gifts, thanking God for each one.

A living list surrounded me in human form. Micah and Sara, two of God's greatest blessings, gave me a sense of purpose just by breathing and needing me. Brandon provided faithfully, doing his best to make sure we wanted for nothing.

Mom and Dad joined us out on the farm and made themselves available whenever possible, with Debbie, Nona, and Honey filling the spaces between. Regular treatments with Carolyne and Dr. Frieden relieved my physical symptoms, which kept the emotional ones from crushing me. And then Jennifer Nervo, a friend whose natural healing blog I followed, made an incredible offer I couldn't refuse.

Some time ago, she had enrolled in a nutritional therapy program. I'd followed her journey through Facebook, inspired by not only her determination to acquire healing tools but also her passion to help others along the way. At the completion of the program, she reached out, offering me an exclusive spot as a pro bono client. Astounded, I accepted her generous offer.

She requested a list of the foods I was eating along with the findings of Dr. Jess Armine. I sent her everything I had. From the hodgepodge of test results and notes, she constructed a low-histamine, nutrient-dense, autoimmune-friendly menu, complete with five small daily meals set on a four-day rotation. Days one and three provided me with lots of calories. Days two and four gave my body an opportunity to cleanse. It was all there in front of me. All I had to do was follow it.

Real tears of gratitude ran down my face when I read it. No one else had been able to accomplish anything like this. Not even me. Truly, I wasn't sure how she'd done it, so I chalked it up to God looking out for me again.

The meal plan included lots of tasty options and the opportunity to try new foods. Parsnips, plantains, and cassava were all unfamiliar carbohydrate sources. Lamb and radishes were new to me. Kale, massaged with olive oil and served with pomegranate seeds, quickly became my favorite breakfast, while frozen blueberries were an instant favorite sweet treat. Juices made from romaine lettuce, celery, and cucumber provided me with refreshing bursts of energy with a side effect of gentle detox. Eggs were no longer a part of my diet, but I wasn't worried. The food was nourishing and filling.

Only the sardines were suspect. There was little calcium in my diet, and milk and multivitamins were out. Chock-full of calcium, sardines made an excellent supplement. I just didn't know if I could stomach them.

Leery, I opened a can and tried not to inhale, afraid a fishy smell might turn me off. Sardines were meant to be eaten straight out of the can, but I couldn't do it. Not on my first try. Brandon smirked from his seat at the kitchen table as I warmed them in a skillet with a little rice.

In silence, I sat, sensing his intense gaze but refusing to meet it. I closed my eyes and took a bite.

"Well?" he asked.

"Not bad." I kept chewing, trying to decide what I thought. I opened my eyes to see his expression. He didn't believe me. "Pretty good, actually."

Brandon shivered and grimaced. "If you say so."

"You should try some." Snickering, I held out the tiny silver fish on my fork.

"Babe, there's no way I would take your food. You need all you can get."

"You don't mind eating my homemade beef sausage patties or the sweet potatoes or the roast," I said. "Come on."

"Believe it or not, I'm not hungry." He rose and kissed my forehead.

"If you say so." I took another bite. They really weren't bad at all. Given some time, I might even learn to like them.

Brandon left, and I polished off the rest of my dish.

The next time I searched for sardines online, I couldn't find the brand that I'd tried previously. Hoping the taste didn't vary much from brand to brand, I clicked "add to cart" and hoped for the best.

The sardines in the new can were larger, but I managed to eat them without heating them up. I liked how salty they were. These days, I craved salt. I never seemed to get enough, even by drinking saltwater throughout the day.

The swelling began before I finished eating. Heaving a sigh, I stood and raked the remaining sardines into the trash. My vision blurred, and a wave of intense sleepiness swept over me. A familiar drunken feeling made my work in the kitchen more difficult. My gastrointestinal tract began to burn. Scores of tiny red bumps popped up on my skin and with them that deep itch that always grew worse the more I scratched.

My throat continued to swell, but I didn't have trouble breathing outside of a persistent cough. Acute Rescue drops and a capsule of DAO enzyme kept me stable until Brandon arrived home from work.

He drew back when he saw me.

"I need a treatment," I said.

"You think?" He set down his lunch box and the mail and followed me to the bedroom. "What happened?"

"Sardines."

"Those things you tried to get me to eat?" He helped me onto the bed. "You have a bunch of red bumps on the back of your neck," he said as he worked.

"Yeah, they itch. A lot."

"No more sardines for you." Brandon finished the treatment and left me in bed, where I must have fallen asleep.

A figure overshadowed me when I woke the next morning. I swallowed and wished I hadn't. Not even strep throat felt like this. Groaning, I tried to focus my swollen eyes. A pair of rough hands gently slid my glasses over my ears.

Brandon grinned down at me. "Hey there, sexy. You look like you've got the mumps."

I fought a laugh. Laughing would be too painful. "I feel sexy."

My voice didn't sound like my own. Liquid leaked from my left tear duct, which itched as badly as the rest of my body. I wiped and scratched.

Brandon helped me to my feet. "Your dad's here to watch the kids. I need to head out. You might feel a bit better if you stand and move around a bit. Your lymph nodes have to be the size of tennis balls right now."

"I believe you." I swallowed again and cringed.

I messaged Jennifer while I boiled the enema coffee. After a detox bath, she had me drink a glass of activated charcoal, mix poultices of clay and marshmallow root for the rash on the back of my neck, roll out herbal lozenges to calm my stomach, and perform a lengthy lymph-drainage massage. Everything provided some degree of relief.

When a smoothie made of frozen blueberries and canned coconut milk triggered a fresh reaction, Jennifer advised me to avoid all processed foods for a few days. The reactions took such a toll that I slept nearly twelve hours per night, waking at nine in the morning only to feel tired again by noon. The simplest tasks exhausted me, but the time spent in bed gave me an opportunity to try something that had been on my mind for several weeks.

Until recently, Netflix had made unpleasant tasks like

coffee enemas and sitting still while I poached in my own filth more bearable. Entertainment numbed the pain of Jenny's absence in otherwise quiet moments. I'd come to depend on it. But lately, I'd felt an invitation to something far better.

Rather than rush through reading my Bible in the middle of the day, I taught myself to study during the hour I took my enema. Instead of watching a forty-five-minute show while I soaked in the tub, I talked to the Lord about the burdens of my heart. It wasn't long before he called me to carry the burdens of others.

I prayed daily for Jenny's family and for the young pastor at my church who had recently been diagnosed with leukemia. Friends I hadn't seen in some time reached out to ask for prayer. One had begun to react to small amounts of gluten for the first time. Another began having regular, unexplained seizures. A friend's daughter was suffering from a neurological reaction after ingesting fertilizer. My young friend Caroline told me she was the sickest she'd ever been and now had difficulty getting out of bed for any length of time. The more I prayed, the more people contacted me to ask for prayer.

After several days of extra rest and eating small amounts of cooked rice blended into porridge, my system calmed down, and the lymph nodes in my face reduced to their usual size. Less than a week later, I tried my hand at making cassava fries, praying while I worked.

As I cut away the tough waxy skin, my vision turned watery. My thoughts and sentences muddled until I could no longer speak. Brandon helped me to bed, treated me, and left me to rest. When my mind had cleared, I thought about the odd reaction.

For the life of me, I couldn't figure it out. What had caused it? Maybe the reaction had been a spiritual attack. Because I'd been praying. Satan didn't like it, I was sure, which encouraged me to pray all the more. Right then, in the thick of the reaction. Even if my thoughts weren't clear to me, my heart was seen by God. He'd take my little offering and make something of it.

Before I resumed praying for others, I prayed for myself. Things were better than they had been a year ago. I wasn't having life-threatening reactions several times a week anymore. Nutritional therapy might prove to be another dead end, but how could I know until I gave God time to work? He'd provided the service unexpectedly free of charge with a friend who I respected and valued.

I couldn't allow Jennifer to be more committed to my healing than I was. She'd worked hard on that meal plan. Not many people would have undertaken a patient like me. The least I could do was persevere through these early trial-and-error reactions.

Failure only meant I was learning, and the fruits of failure gave me more opportunities to intercede in the quiet of my bedroom. Grace was with me. I could do this. I had survived reactions, hunger, pain, difficulty, loneliness, loss, grief, rejection, scorn, and daily coffee enemas for this long. I could survive nutritional therapy and all its learning curves for a few weeks. By my God, I could even survive the upcoming trip to Mayo.

29

Mayo

Mom and I booked a hotel room in Rochester, Minnesota, that had a kitchenette and was on the shuttle route for Mayo Clinic. We hadn't yet decided whether to risk the shuttle, but it was an option we wanted. A trickier question lay before us—how to get there?

A commercial flight was out of the question. Private flights were out of our price range. Driving wouldn't be easy, but we could do it with some careful planning.

When I posted a few questions to Facebook, Hope, a friend from college, commented that I should contact Wings of Hope, a charity that offered medical transport to people who lacked the income or health to fly commercially. As a recent winner of the Miss Louisiana pageant, she knew several of the pilots and organizers. She called ahead to let them know I would be in contact. Within a few days, I had emailed my application, praying that I would be accepted despite Brandon's annual income.

A representative called to let me know that I'd been accepted and a pilot had volunteered to fly me on the dates I needed to travel. I immediately sent Hope a thank-you message. So many times during my illness, friends, acquaintances, and even strangers had extended compassion and services I would never be able to repay. Hope didn't know me well, but she'd offered me a set of much-needed wings. I thanked God for her, for Wings of Hope, their generous donors who made the mission possible, and for the pilot I hadn't yet met who would fly me.

The next debate centered around the economical and safety points of taxis versus rental cars. Mom and I came to different conclusions. She thought a taxi was the way to go. I wanted to book a rental.

I'd been studying the books of 1 Kings and Acts in the Bible. In both books, believers cast lots to determine God's will on trivial matters that didn't fall under a specific law. As Proverbs 16:33 said, "The lot is cast into the lap, but its every decision is from the Lord." At my request, Brandon flipped a coin.

Tails. I sent Mom a text. "We'll take a taxi."

The small planes that would carry us to Minnesota and back couldn't sustain much heavy luggage, so I devised a way to pack light and still have room for a couple of pots and pans. Even if the hotel had cookware, it would likely be cheap nonstick, and that kind had triggered reactions in the past. The pantry items I needed would be shipped directly to the hotel where we'd be staying. Either Mom or I would cook our meals and pack lunches for the long days at the clinic.

For my family, I created a childcare schedule and a daily menu. The kids and I prepared and froze snacks and meals the week before I left. Trying very hard not to stress over the mess they made in the kitchen, I drank up every sweet moment. They were my littlest friends, nearest neighbors, greatest earthly sources of joy, and my reason to get up in the morning. I would miss them terribly, likely more than they would miss me.

The day of departure arrived sooner than I had anticipated. Brandon packed my single piece of luggage into the trunk as I buckled Sara into her car seat. "As long as I've known you, you've never packed this light," he said.

"I've never been concerned about keeping a plane in the air before either." I walked around to the passenger side of my silver Malibu and gazed at the piece of land I'd come to love. When I got back, Jubilee Farm would be producing the first fruits of our second crop of summer vegetables.

"Got your Acute Rescue?" he asked before pulling out of the driveway.

I opened my purse. "Check."

"Swabs?"

"Check."

"EpiPens?"

"Yep.

"Inhaler?"

"Ten-four."

"Extra masks?"

I pulled them out to show him. "And my enema bucket, magnesium salt, and bentonite clay." Anything else I forgot would be easy to buy.

He rolled out of the gravel onto the red dirt road. Dad pulled out behind us.

Our plane was scheduled to depart from the Monroe airport at noon. We would fly to St. Louis, Missouri, where we'd refuel and then continue on to Rochester. Ten days later, someone would pick us up from the Rochester airport to fly us back home.

Hannah met us at the airport with the girls so they could watch our plane take off. The kids were all excited to see one another and eat snacks while they waited for our pilot to arrive. Brandon stayed nearby and held me close. "I'm going to miss you," he whispered into my hair.

"Not more than I'll miss you," I said.

He grunted.

A pair of strawberry-blond pilots in tan polos walked through the doors leading out to the hangar. The Wings of Hope insignia was embroidered on the lapels of the polos. "Melissa Keaster?" one said.

"That's me," I said, my voice muffled by my mask.

The men grinned, each holding out a hand for me to shake. "We're going to stretch our legs for just a minute, and then we'll be ready to head out."

The noise level rose as the kids anticipated the takeoff they would witness from the roof of the building. Brandon held me in earnest. "I can't believe you're leaving me with these kids."

I laughed. "They'll be fine."

"But will I?"

The pilots rejoined us. One took my bag. The other took Mom's, and Mom extracted her pink ice chest from Sara's grasp. "My ice chest," Sara said.

Mom laughed. "Actually, this is mine, but you're welcome to borrow it when we come back."

I picked up Sara and kissed her squishy cheeks. "I love you."

"I luh you," she said.

I set her down and wrapped Micah in my arms. "I love you, too, bud. I'll miss you bunches."

"I love you, Mama," he said.

Before I followed the pilots out the door, Brandon said, "Take a deep breath."

I obeyed. He unhooked a loop of my mask to steal a kiss and set it back in place. "Come back to me," he said.

"Yes, sir," I answered with a salute and followed the pilots out to the plane. The propeller was already running.

Mom and I settled into the tiny cabin. She said something to me, but the noise of the engine drowned out her voice. A moment later, I spotted Dad and Brandon on the bright-red roof of the building. Little hands waved above the railing.

The door slammed shut. The pilot shouted back, "Ready to go?"

We answered with a thumbs-up. We were off.

* * *

We landed in Rochester without incident. We thanked our kind and capable angel pilots and went in search of a bathroom. The scent of floral air freshener ambushed me. I held my breath as long as I could, but my efforts weren't enough to save me from a reaction. Mom offered to treat me. "I'll just take some Acute Rescue for now. I bet we'll come across a few more triggers before we make it to the hotel. You can treat me there."

Mom nodded and called for a cab. We didn't wait long.

The driver wore cologne but left the windows rolled down. The fresh air kept my reaction from progressing further. Mom treated me when we made it to our hotel room. After a short rest, I felt well enough to prepare a simple dinner from the groceries we'd brought in the ice chest. The sun hadn't set when we crawled into bed after nine o'clock and had already risen when we woke before seven the next morning.

The plan for the day was to grocery shop, as we were now out of groceries, and rest before appointments began on Thursday. Mom called for another cab to take us to a grocery store several people had recommended. There, I was sure to find fresh organic produce and a selection of high-quality meats.

Today's driver was a middle-aged man with a kind face. Smiling, he held the door open for me. On the ride to the grocery store, he asked, "Are you here for Mayo?"

I hoped he could feel my smile. "Did my mask give it away?"

He grinned into the rearview mirror. "That, and your accent. People from out of town are almost always here for Mayo. It's a great clinic."

The grocery store was better than anything I'd imagined. Strolling the aisles full of specialty items and all-natural body care products, I might have felt like I was on vacation had I not been in gastrointestinal distress. For whatever reason, my stomach had decided to be unhappy. Bloating accompanied stabbing pains. The pain spread and grew in intensity until my breath sped into shallow pants.

It was a relief to return to the taxi. Mom chatted with the driver as I drew into myself. Through my discomfort, I felt a familiar sensation in my spirit, as if the Holy Spirit had poked me. *Pay attention. Things are about to get interesting.*

When we'd almost reached the hotel, the driver began to share some of his experiences with us. "Not everyone likes this job, but I love it," he said. "I've laughed. I've cried. I've prayed with sick people."

"Cool!" Mom said. "Do you believe in Jesus?"

"Oh, yes. I used to be the pastor of an Assembly of God church. Now, I have church in my car. I once prayed for this one guy with cancer. He went to the doctor, and the cancer had disappeared. They were totally confused. Another time, I had this girl ride up front with me. She was going somewhere an hour away. I led her to Jesus that day. If you want, I can pray for you."

My spirit stirred again. "I would love that," I said.

He parked the cab underneath the overhang at the hotel, grabbed my hand and Mom's, and began to pray. His words felt secondary to the shift in atmosphere in the vehicle. The Holy Spirit fell like a soft blanket, bringing peace and comfort. Warmth spread through my chest and torso. I no longer hunched, clutching my rib cage in a makeshift fetal position. All my pain had vanished. In an instant.

Never had I experienced anything like this. Stunned, I asked him for his name.

"Arthur."

"Thank you, Arthur. You just prayed all my pain away."

"Wow," he said. "That's so encouraging. I've been having a hard time for a while now. It's always great to see God move." He offered no further details.

"Can we pray for you?" I asked.

"Of course!"

Mom and I grabbed his hands again, praying blessings and grace upon him. Tears dripped down his cheeks. I handed him a handkerchief. "Please keep it," I said.

He helped me out of the car, and I threw my arms around him. I couldn't help myself. I loved him. He was my brother. Forever. "Thank you so much."

Cleaning chemicals and air freshener assailed me as we walked back to our room, but I suffered no reaction and enjoyed pain relief throughout the evening. The last traces of my fear fled. I was right where God wanted me to be.

* * *

On Thursday morning after a late breakfast, we packed a lunch and headed downstairs to catch the shuttle to Mayo Clinic. The campus stretched out for blocks. All of it was kept clean and attractive with pristine landscaping. The shuttle dropped us off at the lobby of what we thought was the main building, even though it was difficult to be sure. Each one was named after different people. We rode an elevator to reach the floor where I would see Dr. Park. I checked in at the reception desk of the large waiting room and sat with Mom.

From everything I observed, Mayo worked like cogs in a clock. A patient was called. A few moments later, he returned to his seat to wait a short while longer. A nurse called my name. I followed her to a room where she checked my weight, temperature, blood pressure, and the medical documentation they already had stored in the computer. I, too, returned to my seat, but I didn't wait long.

Another nurse led me to a private room where she asked about my symptoms and how I was feeling at the moment. She jotted some notes. "Dr. Park will be with you shortly."

A commanding voice spoke in sharp tones outside my door. I heard the name of the doctor several mast cell patients had warned me about. He was very good, they'd said, but his bedside manner left something to be desired. I was too worn down and sick of doctors to deal with the likes of him, so I'd requested Dr. Park instead. The doctor's voice and footsteps faded, and we waited.

A few minutes later, the door opened, and a short man with dark hair stepped into the room. He smiled warmly and offered his hand to my mom and me. A sense of peace gently wafted through the space. He listened with quiet interest as I shared my symptoms, occasionally asking questions. Without comment, he asked me to lie down on the exam table and inspected my skin and abdomen.

When he was finished, he sat down. "Well, your symptoms are consistent with a disease called systemic mastocytosis, but the chances of you having that disease are very low." He went on to explain that the disease was extremely rare and that other diseases could mimic some of my symptoms.

After recommending I see a dermatologist and a gastroenterologist, he ordered tests that would begin an elimination process and gave me instructions to pick up a urine receptacle before I left the clinic. Further testing and appointments would resume early in the morning.

He stood and said, "Melissa, I know this has been very hard. I understand that you came a long way. But some diseases can be tricky to diagnose."

In other words, I might have come all this way, might have spent a lot of my husband's hard-earned money, and could still leave this fancy clinic without a diagnosis. But I knew that already. I was here because God had ordained it. No other reason. If I left without a diagnosis, a diagnosis wasn't the reason he'd sent me, and the facts weren't more complicated than that.

"I understand," I said.

He shook my hand again. "We will try our best to figure this out. God bless you, Melissa."

"God bless you, Dr. Park."

30

Naked

On Friday morning, we left the hotel at 6:00 a.m. with my urine receptacle in tow. I would begin the day with blood work followed by a photo op. Had I been well enough to enjoy a cup of coffee, I might not have minded the early morning. Still, I couldn't help but appreciate the way Mayo managed their laboratory. It was a masterpiece of efficiency.

After the photo, we took the elevator to the dermatology department. There were no openings until June 23, but Dr. Park's nurse had been confident we could be worked in on a Friday before a holiday. Mom and I had brought books to pass the time, and I was able to finish Timothy Keller's small volume *The Freedom of Self-Forgetfulness* before my name was called.

The dermatologist's gaze swept over me from head to foot as he walked in the little exam room where I waited. He was a short man with sharp blue eyes, very handsome and so well dressed that I felt self-conscious in my casual attire and poor appearance. He didn't smile but seemed very attentive as he listened to my symptoms and concern over some of the spots on my skin.

When I finished, he said, "Thank you. I'm going to read my notes back to you. Please correct any mistakes." He began, "This delightful twenty-nine-year-old Caucasian female presented for general skin examination."

He read everything I'd said back to me almost verbatim. After I authenticated the accuracy of his notes, he said, "Excellent. I'll give you a moment to undress. When I come back, I'll give you a thorough check."

The paper cape the nurse handed me felt like the punch line to a joke of which I was the subject. Why anyone had gone to the trouble of manufacturing it was beyond me. Nonetheless, I did what was expected of me, ashamed of my hairy legs and threadbare panties with holes at the elastic seam. Some time had passed since I'd thought to buy new underwear, and I rarely spent my precious energy shaving.

I rubbed my bumpy skin gently so as not to create too much friction and leave a rash but enough to provide some heat so that I wouldn't shiver. It was cold enough to hang meat if they wanted. The doctor returned. "I'll need you to take off your underwear."

Mortified, I obeyed. Sure, I had a husband. I'd gone to the gynecologist for years. Small audiences had watched me push out a baby on two separate occasions, but there was something exquisitely humiliating about standing before this strange man baring it all underneath the scrutiny of his assessing gaze and ultraviolet flashlight. Just when I was certain it couldn't get any worse, he said, "Please bend over and spread your buttocks."

Oh. My. Jesus, come back! Now, Jesus! Now would be good!

He didn't, though I couldn't have imagined a timelier moment.

The doctor told me I could dress, and he hadn't left when I began scrambling for my underwear. I'd been fully clothed at least five minutes before he returned.

He looked me in the eyes, which was big of him. I wasn't sure I could look anyone in the eye after inspecting their butt crack. Good thing I hadn't pursued a career in medicine. I fought a shudder.

"I see no evidence of cutaneous mastocytosis. The new brown spots you spoke of appear to be benign nevi. However, I'm happy to do a skin biopsy and stain the mast cells for tryptase," he said.

My brain struggled to follow. It was still reeling from the recent trauma. No mastocytosis—good. Benign—good. Skin biopsy—hmm. My system may not love that, but then again, I'd come all this way and taken off all my clothes. Why not? "Yes. Thank you," I said.

"We'll take care of that in just a moment. Would you like to see psychology for your anxiety?" he asked, his blue eyes penetrating the skin he'd just inspected.

My friend Caroline had warned me that someone would recommend I see psychology. She had refused, a decision she'd later regretted. But I understood her. A psychology referral poked at the wound everyone with an invisible illness had. In our own voice, the wound said, "You're crazy, and no one believes you."

After Caroline's refusal, her internist had not been as helpful and seemed to suggest she was a hypochondriac. "Seemed"—because accusations like that were usually communicated through body language and medical recommendations rather than literal words.

I didn't want Caroline's experience. Though I didn't believe a psychologist could do much for the anxiety my illness caused from time to time, I preferred to take the path of least resistance and the most help. I would be at the clinic until that afternoon's appointment with the gastroenterologist anyway, and it might be nice to talk to an outsider about the insanity of my life. "Yes. Thank you," I said again.

"Wonderful." He turned to his computer. His fingers clicked against the keys. A nurse entered the room and administered a local anesthesia to prep me for the biopsy. I worried it might trigger a reaction but then realized if that happened, there were far worse places to be. They had my medical history and the means to save my life.

Something pricked my hip. A moment later, heat flushed under my skin, and my mind began to swim. An overwhelming sense of sleepiness settled over me until I felt I could fall asleep on the table. Something cold pressed against the spot where I'd been pricked. A click followed.

"All done," said the nurse. "I'll suture you up, show you how to care for the biopsy site, and let you go."

Mom looked up from her book when I reached the lobby. "Well?"

"There was never a better exercise in humiliation," I said. "I'll tell you about it over lunch."

* * *

We made our way to the quiet courtyard we'd discovered the day before. In the ground floor lobby, we encountered a small crowd enjoying a musical performance. A mezzo-soprano belted show tunes above the skilled accompaniment of the pianist, who sat at the shiny black grand. We paused to listen before moving on.

The cool air mixed with Minnesota sunshine made for a perfect day. The trees and flowers that surrounded our little courtyard caught the breeze and performed a gentle song of their own. Church bells chimed, joining the chorus on the hour. Although the space didn't seem to be the most popular spot on campus, there was ample seating, and someone had erected an interesting piece of metal art. From the adept management to the aesthetic appeal, the clinic had been designed to make patients' experience as pleasant as possible.

Mom and I ate, enjoying the lovely day, until it was time to drop off my urine receptacle, which I referred to as "the Container of Shame." I wasn't sad to be rid of it.

Though I'd been added to the schedule just that morning, my wait in the psychology department was a small fraction of what it had been in dermatology. A pleasant-faced woman, who didn't smell too strongly of fragrance, greeted me and led me to her office. She gestured to the sofa against the wall and took a seat behind her large mahogany desk. Feeling more and more like a cliché, I plopped down onto the psychologist's sofa and studied the books lining the shelves. I recognized a few of the titles.

The doctor pulled out a yellow legal pad and pen and began asking questions intentionally phrased to set me at ease. To my surprise, I didn't need that touch. The couch was comfortable. The view through the window was peaceful. The books made me feel at home, and I wasn't reacting to anything.

As I answered her questions, I found myself telling my story, which I'd done often but in blog post–sized fragments. It was interesting to hear it all come from my mouth as a whole. The woman never appeared distracted or bored. She peered at me keenly from behind her glasses. "This illness has left you disabled, hasn't it?"

I hadn't thought of it that way. "I suppose it has."

"Do you feel sad, depressed, or hopeless?"

"Sometimes. More so in the past," I said, making several connections at once. It was true. I had felt hopeless at times, but not for several months now. Not even when Jenny had died. I would almost say that I felt...happy. I gave credit where credit was due. "I probably still would if it weren't for Jesus. He's changed me through all of this. I take joy in my life as small as it is, and I believe it's valuable."

Her expression froze. After a moment, she looked down to write, a gentle smile spreading across her face.

At the end of the appointment, the psychologist fetched a psychiatrist from a neighboring office. They weren't concerned about my anxiety or depression. "We believe that you should make an appointment with our behavior modification specialist for your migraine headaches. He could really help you," the psychologist said.

Migraines. I blinked, baffled. Yes, I had migraines. I'd had them for almost ten years. But migraines didn't even make the top ten of my most-pressing complaints.

I allowed them to make the appointment, though I hadn't decided whether to attend. To do so, I would have to extend my stay in Minnesota, something I wasn't sure I was willing to do. As they led me back to the lobby, the psychiatrist said, "You should visit Silver Lake Park while you're here. It's lovely."

The tip was much appreciated. It would be nice to get out.

A thousand pounds of fatigue weighed me down as Mom and I walked out of the psychology department, but we couldn't go back to the hotel yet. I had an appointment with gastroenterology in an hour.

On the ground floor, we found the quiet room a nurse had told us about the day before. We walked into blissful darkness that hid hospital-grade recliners and blankets. The room was empty. We each found a recliner and settled in. I took several deep diaphragmatic breaths to calm my wired system and drifted off to sleep. Half an hour later, I startled awake. Nothing had happened, but there was a foreboding in my spirit about the next appointment.

I prayed, reminding myself of how God had been with me every step. He hadn't abandoned me yet. He wouldn't abandon me now. I closed my eyes and made myself rest for the remainder of the hour.

We arrived on time, but we waited a while to be seen. Mom walked back with me, for which I was grateful. The doctor fidgeted and didn't often look me in the eye. He seemed bored by my list of symptoms. He mentioned an endoscopy and a colonoscopy, which I suspected would be disasters. When he recommended a gastric emptying test, I wondered whether he had read my chart. That test required me to eat bread, milk, and eggs and drink radioactive water. I could die on the table.

"Will you stain for mast cells?" I asked.

He gave me a blank look. "I'll biopsy anything that looks abnormal. I'd also like to run a simple blood test to check for celiac sprue."

Did he know what Dr. Park was looking for? Did he care? He didn't seem to, but I knew better than to voice the question. "When do you leave town?" he asked.

"We leave next Friday on the thirtieth."

I left his office with test schedules and instructions. He'd scheduled the scopes for the Friday we would leave, which I'd told him wouldn't work. Even if I could delay the flight, I wouldn't be well enough to travel after the procedure.

Maybe I'd caught him on a bad day, but I wasn't too impressed with the man. I left his office crushed, too tired to fight the feeling.

I trudged back to the laboratory with Mom at my side. I had one more round of blood work to do before this ridiculous day was over. As I sat waiting to hear my name called for the last time that day, I knew there was only one way to fight the thing trying to take me under. Not really caring whether anyone overheard, I softly sang lines from a favorite hymn:

> Jesus, Jesus, how I trust him,
> How I've proved him o'er and o'er;
> Jesus, Jesus, precious Jesus,
> O, for grace to trust him more.

Half-aware, I followed the phlebotomist to the lab, dropped into the seat, and made it outside to catch the shuttle. On the ride back to the hotel, Mom put her clever mind to work. "No gastric emptying test," she said. "Too dangerous, and not the most pressing problem."

I nodded, too exhausted to talk.

"We'll wait to see what Dr. Park says about the scopes. If he thinks we need them, we can schedule those at home."

A weight lifted off my chest. If I'd had the energy, I would have high-fived Mom for still being able to think. I made a mental note to thank her later.

Mom helped me to the elevator. I was too tired for stairs. When I finally collapsed onto the bed, I realized it had been an eleven-hour day. I had no idea how I'd managed it. Thankfully, I had a long weekend to reflect, recover, and process through all that had happened.

* * *

Test results trickled in over the next three days. I trembled inwardly each time I opened the online portal, feeling a mixture of relief and frustration at each normal lab result. Why I reacted that way, I couldn't yet guess.

We rested all day on Saturday, reading and watching *Call the Midwife* on Netflix. On Sunday, we followed the advice of the psychiatrist and visited Silver Lake Park. We walked along a paved path that bordered the shore of the small lake, watching mother geese teaching their tiny young to swim, eat, and follow. Our cab driver had agreed to return at a set time, so we found a bench nestled in the shade of a large tree by the water. I wasn't very knowledgeable about trees and had no idea what kind it was. Mom guessed it was a willow.

"If I was a tree, I would want to be this one," I told her.

The roots sank thick and sturdy into soft lakeside soil. It stood fat and strong at the bottom until one trunk became two. Two branched off into three, and three became four. Supple boughs hung from limbs that stretched outward, forming a thorough canopy. They came to life as the wind rushed off the water and proposed a dance. We were mesmerized by the waltz. Sway, two, three. Sway, two, three.

How many long seasons of nakedness, of bone-crushing winters had she endured by the water, waiting, waiting to achieve such poise and grace? Why must she be naked when it was so cold out? Whatever the reason, the Lord required the same vulnerability of me. The winter had already been long, and here we were waiting, waiting on test results. On answers.

My dermatology appointment came to mind. I wasn't like the tree in front of me. I was more like the trees in

Louisiana, shedding my clothes in stages, hanging on to my last layers as long as I could, afraid to expose too much, afraid of being hurt.

"Blessed is the man who trusts in the Lord, and whose hope is the Lord. For he shall be like a tree planted by the waters," I whispered.

If I truly trusted God, would I feel so afraid?

That night, I shed my clothing and stepped into a hot magnesium salt bath. I reached for my iPod and opened the portal to see if any new results had come in. Again, my heart raced and breath sped as I waited for the page to load. And suddenly, I knew.

I'd been lying to myself.

"The heart is deceitful above all things," I said to no one in particular.

I'd been telling everyone that I was going to Mayo "out of obedience to God," that a diagnosis didn't matter, but if that was the whole truth, my heart wouldn't pound so hard every time I accessed my records. I'd repeated the insipid platitude countless times—"I don't know what I hope for, so I will hope in God." But what did that mean, really?

The truth was that I hadn't allowed myself to want anything too much. Experience had taught me well. With a disease like mine, hope was the most dangerous thing of all. Every time I mustered up a little, it was snatched out of my reach like a carrot on a string. Leaving with a diagnosis was unlikely, and the odds of finding a medication I could tolerate were dismal.

I couldn't afford hope. It was too costly. Hope led to disappointment. Disappointment after disappointment wore on a soul. It wounded. It might even kill.

Friends had lauded my stoicism, mistaking it for faith. Stoicism might look like faith, but it was counterfeit. Faith required risk. Stuffing desire was not risk. It was self-preservation, the very opposite of faith.

Sudden raw desire sprang from my chest like a sob. There, in my nakedness, I could finally be honest. I wanted answers, and I wanted them desperately.

Words tumbled from my lips, dissolving into groans of the spirit. For the first time in two years, I begged God for an answer.

"Vindicate me! Let me not be ashamed!" I cried, echoing the words of David. Because I would be ashamed if I had come all the way to Minnesota for nothing, risking my small measure of health and abandoning my family for ten days on a fool's errand. I had prayed for God to be glorified. "How can you be glorified unless you act for me?" I asked.

Honesty felt good. Nakedness had felt wrong in the dermatologist's office, where I was examined by indifferent clinical eyes. In a hotel bathtub, God looked on me with the greatest love in the universe. He saw me to the core and loved me still. Love like that made one bold. Bold enough to let go and hope.

The bathwater cooled. I stepped out of the tub, dressed, and confessed to Mom everything God had revealed. She smiled. "Perfect love casts out all fear," she reminded me.

Together, we knelt on the floor and asked God for the answer for which we'd come. When I stood to cook dinner, I believed God would grant my request.

"Lord, help my trust to stay put," I said.

For she shall be like a tree planted by the waters...

The God who gave the gift of faith could surely keep it.

* * *

The hours of Monday stretched long as they always did. I suppose Monday didn't know it was on holiday and had permission to speed up. After what seemed like a week, Tuesday dawned, audaciously supposing it had arrived on time.

Today would be easy—I had one short appointment with Dr. Park. It would also be life changing—I would either receive a diagnosis or the grace to go home empty handed.

I measured the wait to see the doctor in long deep breaths, losing the count but never the rhythm. One of these breaths would be the lucky one. On one of these breaths, someone would call my name.

"Melissa Keaster."

Mom and I were escorted to the same room we'd visited days before. Dr. Park joined us a moment later, his expression sober with compassion. "Hi, Melissa. Most of the results from your tests have come in. They all appear to be within the normal range. The biopsy may take another day or two, but Dr. Davis doesn't expect the lab to find anything abnormal."

I knew all of this, of course, from my obsessive portal checks throughout the weekend. I was thrilled not to have a progressive malignant disease, but the way he shared the findings cast a splash of doubt that I would receive what I expected.

A sweet invisible presence surrounded me. My heart quieted. I was held by everlasting arms.

Because moms will be moms, Mom asked, "So what is the diagnosis?"

He inhaled a shallow breath. "After eliminating other possibilities, I think you have mast cell activation disease."

Something alive leaped in my chest.

Shock. Relief. Gratitude. Praise. Joy. All came bursting from my stretch-marked heart.

Never had I prayed a do-or-die prayer quite like the one I had prayed on Sunday. Never had I been so confident I would be answered. Never had I felt so brave.

God had delivered. After years of bewildering symptoms, I finally had a name.

A name said, "You're not crazy. You are not alone," which were comforting truths when the disease was isolating and the symptoms left you questioning your own sanity.

Dr. Park continued, his voice soft. "Unfortunately, mast cell activation disease has no cure, but it can be managed through medication, diet, and lifestyle modifications. Your quality of life can improve."

He delivered the verdict like it was bad news. If he thought the idea of no cure would devastate me, he underestimated the value of an answer.

He recommended I begin a light medication regimen that included an antihistamine and montelukast. "I remember you saying that you sometimes have difficulty with medication fillers. Maybe you can try a liquid version or contact a compounding pharmacy."

Thank God I was married to a pharmacist who could help me sort that out.

"If these medications don't offer you enough support, we can try an antidepressant that has been proven to relieve symptoms in mast cell patients."

"What about cromolyn sodium? To ingest?" I asked. Several sensitive patients in the mast cell community had taken it safely, and it had helped.

"I'm happy to prescribe it," he said, "but let's see what the antihistamines can do for you first. I think we need to approach things slowly with you."

Thank God for a doctor who got it.

Mom asked about the importance of an endoscopy. "You can do that locally if you like, when you're ready," he said, closing the folder containing my records. "Would you like me to pray for you?"

I smiled beneath my mask. I'd thought he might be a Christian. "Yes, please."

He thanked God for sending me to the clinic and to his office. He asked that I would begin to experience healing, not just for my body, but also for my spirit and emotions. The prayer was sweet, poignant, and perfect.

Mom thanked him with tears in her eyes and asked to take a photo of us both.

"Sure," he said and moved by my side.

I slipped off my mask. With a press of the screen, Mom captured the moment for which I'd waited nearly a decade.

31

Breathe

We tried to reschedule our flight home for a day or two earlier than planned, but it didn't work out. For two full days, there was nothing to do but rest. Mom and I spent the time reading, praying, writing, talking, eating good food, and watching *Call the Midwife*.

The return flight took longer than expected due to a large storm system that stretched from Missouri all the way home. Brandon, Dad, and the kids met us at the airport that evening. Sara rushed out through the automatic doors, ahead of the pack. I opened my arms, expecting a Hallmark-worthy moment.

She flew past me toward Grandma, but she didn't leap into Mom's arms either. No. That tiny heifer snatched the pink ice chest from Mom's grip. "My ice chest!" she exclaimed.

We all laughed, and I learned that I placed after an ice chest in importance.

Burying my face in Brandon's shoulder, I breathed in his clean earthy scent. It was the smell of home and safety, a signal that I could relax a little. Mom and I thanked the pilots no less than three times before we left with our people.

Lively chatter replaced the quiet of the last few days. Brandon's hand held mine. Taking in the familiar sights on the ride home, I considered God's faithfulness. He'd brought me home, a diagnosis and prescriptions in tow. I could get better.

We pulled onto our red dirt road, and Micah said, "We have a surprise, Mama."

I glanced from him to Brandon, whose mouth curved into a droll grin. The trailer came into view, and I gasped. While I was gone, Brandon had covered both porches and painted them dark brown. A bright-hued garden featuring sunflowers and roses colored the end facing the drive. A raised herb garden had been built at the bottom of the porch steps.

Brandon stopped the car and walked around to open my door. "Happy birthday," he said, as he helped me out.

I threw my arms around his neck and planted a sloppy kiss on his mouth. "Thank you! I love it!"

Everything looked so beautiful that I decided to host a tea party for my thirtieth birthday. "You get to do that when you're too sick to go out and are a little eccentric anyway," I told Brandon.

Brandon cocked a brow. "You have to be old or rich to be eccentric."

"Not when you're a thirty-year-old shut-in hippy who makes her own deodorant and owns a Squatty Potty," I retorted.

The menu for the tea included three herbal blends, which I created from loose herbs—rhubarb and hibiscus, raspberry leaf and peppermint, nettle and rosehip. I made gluten-free zucchini cake, almond flour thumbprint cookies filled with dark chocolate and homemade raspberry jam, and my friend Caroline's recipe for grain-free lemon bars.

Of everyone invited, only Honey was unable to attend. I set a table of fine china for Mom, Debbie, Nona, Hannah, my cousin Lisa, Aunt Suzonne, and my cousin Morgan. For our children, I brought out a couple of small tables and let them enjoy their tea from miniature china cups.

God sweetened the gathering with his presence. All three teas were the perfect strength. My favorite was the raspberry leaf and peppermint. Unsweetened, it paired perfectly with the treats. Everyone enjoyed one another, and I was thankful to finally serve and honor my caretakers.

As the conversation wound down, my head swam and stomach bloated painfully. I was suddenly very aware of my colon, which ached with heat. Coughing, I excused myself. A powerful wave of listlessness washed over me as I made my way to the sofa inside, and I was good for nothing for the duration of the night. Mom, Nona, and Debbie saw to the clean-up, hushing me every time I told them to leave the mess for tomorrow.

Over the next few days, Brandon and I studied ingredients and muscle tested several versions of the drugs Dr. Park had prescribed. Neither the pills nor the liquid forms worked. Several people in the mast cell disease community on Facebook shared my conundrum. Though I wasn't a total anomaly, I couldn't help but laugh that I was allergic to antihistamines.

Brandon checked with the compounding pharmacies in the area. Obtaining pure forms of the drugs would be cost prohibitive. In the end, I asked Dr. Yakaboski to use her handy-dandy energy machine and create a homeopathic form of loratadine, which I tolerated very well. I didn't, however, notice much change in my condition.

Having attempted Dr. Park's first recommendations, I emailed him requesting a prescription for ingestible cromolyn sodium. Brandon brought it home from work the next evening. Though the medication muscle tested as safe, I was still concerned that it could trigger a reaction. Some mast cell patients couldn't tolerate it. Some found it a miracle drug.

When I didn't react at all after three days, I celebrated, but a minimum of two weeks would pass before we could determine whether the medication helped.

* * *

Nicole, the laboratory scientist who had encouraged me in the emergency room last year, messaged me, asking if she could buy some fresh tomatoes from the garden. "No," I replied, "but you can have some." We planned to meet on Brandon's next day off.

Nicole greeted us with a bright grin. "I'm so glad Mayo was able to figure things out. Are any of the medicines working?"

"Not yet," I said, handing her a bag of fresh tomatoes. "The one I'm trying now takes time to work."

"Well, good luck. And thanks for these!"

"Thank you for encouraging us last year. You have no idea what it meant to us."

When I returned to the car, Brandon whispered, "Eskamoe's is right over there. Want to get the kids a treat?"

"They'd love that," I whispered back.

There was no line, so we pulled right up to the window. Brandon gave his order and handed the cashier his card. Something shifted in my body. I frowned. Was my face swelling?

You're not sick, I told myself. *You're fine*. I continued this silent self-talk all the way home and had almost convinced myself when I nearly fainted trying to get out of the car.

Brandon was at my side in a second. "What's wrong?"

"I'm sick, but I'll be all right," I said, still hoping I could talk myself out of anaphylaxis.

Brandon helped me inside and then went back out to talk to my parents, who were picking tomatoes and peppers in the garden. The voices of the children traveled through the thin exterior wall. I focused on the sweet sound.

The reaction progressed. Soon, things would get bad. I took a dropper full of Acute Rescue and sent an emergency text to Brandon.

Shock sang its siren song. By the time Brandon had determined the culprit was peanuts through muscle testing, I was exiting reality—that cold place where it was painful to breathe, think, move, obey.

The burning in my chest eased. Brandon's face blurred and shimmered. Muffled sounds reached my ears. Enclosed in a womb of peace, I drifted toward the ceiling. I also lay on the bed below, Brandon at my side.

"Breathe!" he commanded. His fist pounded my chest. He was afraid.

Two paths opened before me. I couldn't stay in this strange in-between place. I was on the move. The paths stretched in different directions, one below, the other someplace in the far distance to my right. I couldn't quite see where it led, but it went somewhere good and full of light. That, I knew.

I could rest and let my family rest, or I could continue to fight. If I stayed, the battles might never end. I was so tired— a tired that went beyond flesh and bone. We all were. Letting go would be easy, especially with Jesus so near.

His fragrance permeated everything. I could almost taste him.

Fear didn't exist here. Only a choice. Brandon would be okay. The kids, too. They'd be loved and cared for. The war could end.

But Brandon would be broken. He loved me. I loved him, and I had promised him for as long as I lived.

As much as it was up to me.

I gasped. Everything hurt. A warm hand pulled at mine. Another karate chopped my spine. Breath came more easily.

Brandon's body sagged over my abdomen. His face pressed into the coverlet. "You weren't breathing. I thought I'd lost you there for a minute."

I rubbed his spiky hair as he gave himself permission to be human. The last few years had turned it into more salt and less pepper. He'd probably earned a few new gray hairs just now. "I think you did," I said when I could talk. "You brought me back."

"Let's not do this again, okay?" he said.

"Okay," I said.

"Okay."

32

Mixed Bag

For days after the shock episode, my vision turned black and legs lost feeling every time I stood. Once, when I thought the moment had passed, I walked into the kitchen and woke up on the floor with a throbbing arm and hip. No one was home to witness what had happened, but I could only assume I'd fainted.

When I had recovered some strength, I noticed a little relief from gastrointestinal pain. Slowly, eating became almost pleasant again. Most of the time.

With relief came inspiration. After a year of note-taking, character development, and creating backstory, I began actually writing my fantasy novel, which I'd titled *Eleora*. Every day during the kids' nap time, I pulled out my speckled notebook and favorite gel ink pen and scribed the story one cursive sentence at a time. Some days I wrote for an hour. Other days I wrote for two. After a couple of weeks of feeling discouraged about my slow progress, the Lord prompted me to observe Sabbath in my writing work. Funny—I became more productive after that.

Grief continued to rock my boat. In many ways, I felt Jenny's loss more profoundly than I had at the beginning. There was so much I wanted to tell her. I longed to hear her unique perspective phrased in artful sentences, to see the light in her eyes, to grin at her laugh.

It helped that Mom now lived on the property and was home for the summer. She paid me almost-daily visits. Similar in personality and interests, we'd always been close and had never struggled for topics to discuss. These days, we almost always spoke of what God was doing or teaching us.

"How is your study of Acts coming?" she asked one morning. Amber, a longtime friend of mine, had recently called asking what I knew about the baptism of the Holy Spirit. Having grown up in the same church she had, I admitted, "Not much."

Amber had shared several passages of scripture she was studying with a small group at her nondenominational church. The passages all came from the book of Acts, so I read the entire thing in a couple of days, determined to take it in with an unbiased mind. Several passages proved extremely difficult to explain if there wasn't a baptism of the Spirit that followed or accompanied the believer's baptism of water.

Having decided long ago that the simplest explanation of any given scripture was probably the truest, I'd prayed a simple prayer in the bathtub one morning. "God, I grew up Baptist, but your word indicates that the disciples prayed for new believers to receive the Spirit after they already believed in Christ. So if there is more of your Spirit to be experienced, I want it. Baptize me in your Holy Spirit."

There were no gusts of wind or flashes of lightning. As far as I knew, no flame danced above my head. But something had changed.

I grinned at Mom's question. "I think God has me in a practicum of sorts. He's showing me things when I pray. Pictures and little movies. Sometimes he tells me things.

Actually, I think he shared something with me about you."

"Oh?" she asked.

I pulled a book from the shelf and handed it to her. "After we talked yesterday about the trauma you've gone through these past few years, I opened this book and read about this oil blend. It was like God highlighted it or something. I can't explain what I mean. Anyway, it's an oil that supposedly targets trauma, and I think God wants to use it to heal your pain."

She read the information about the oil and shrugged. "I'll try it," she said, so I ordered the oil.

The day it arrived in the mail, I messaged Mom. Before I let her leave with it, I laid a hand on her head and prayed over the oil. She opened the bottle and breathed in the scent. The words of Psalm 103 burst from her lips. "Bless the Lord, O my soul...forget not all his benefits, who forgives all your iniquity, who heals all your diseases."

A few days later, Mom told me she was healed. "Every time I would smell it, I would pray Psalm 103. The pain I thought I would always carry is gone."

Mom's experience was the first of many like it. Somehow, though I was a shut-in, God brought people to me. Some called. Some messaged me on social media. Others went to extensive lengths to see me in person. I prayed. God would act. If God shared a scripture with me while I was praying for someone, I passed it on to that person. I had no idea what I was doing. Everything was new.

God's presence became everything to me. I didn't even miss television. Every spare moment was spent on him. In that place, I became happy—happy with my life, happy with everything. The feeling was something like falling in love but more. It didn't make sense. In light of my circumstances, joy seemed ridiculous. But there it was with me, all day every day.

In terms of physical health, Brandon and I decided that in some ways I was better, and in others, I was worse. Anaphylaxis didn't occur as often, but when it did, the effects seemed more severe. New symptoms popped up here and there, and my food sensitivities compounded.

The previous summer had been nothing short of miraculous. I'd gone from lounging on death's stoop to eating foods I hadn't tolerated in years without the slightest issue. Healthful tingles had followed each meal. The garden itself had been a miracle. Dad and Brandon had been untried gardeners, and yet the crops had thrived. Rains had come at the right times. Bugs had been only a minor nuisance. This year was different.

Squash bugs destroyed our crop. Tomato worms had a heyday. After the broccoli and cauliflower were gone, I didn't tolerate anything well. I didn't understand, but neither did I despair. I was too happy.

One afternoon, Micah and I sat on the back porch and watched an afternoon thunderstorm roll in while Sara napped late. The wind cooled the summer heat. Heavy drops pounded the tin roof.

"God brings the rain and makes it stop and makes the garden grow," Micah observed sagely.

"That's right," I said. "He brings rain and sunshine and gives growth to the seeds we plant. He makes all gardens grow, even the ones hidden inside of us." I touched the center of his chest.

"What kind of garden is inside of me?" he asked, eyes wide. "Will I grow vegetables?"

I laughed. Laughter came easily these days, even in a land of sparse gardens, daily reactions, and no proof of improvement. "No. You will grow fruit. Mommy plants the seed of the Gospel in your heart. Then God sends rain and sunshine and gives increase, just like he does for our garden out there." I pointed. "After some time, you will bear lots of good fruit—love, joy, peace, goodness, and faithfulness, to name a few."

I didn't understand everything that was happening, and I didn't have to. In a fallen world, life was a mixed bag of happiness and disappointments, successes and failures, new discoveries and long waits, pain and healing, death and life. Through it all, God was growing something good. Today, we could only see in part. One day, we would see the whole.

August found me doing very well, all things considered. Despite my inability to eat from the garden, I'd gained weight, my energy was up, my pain was more manageable, and I was sleeping better. Dr. Yakaboski and Dr. Frieden reported improvement in my adrenals and thyroid. I no longer tested positive for an overgrowth of *Candida albicans*. Detox reactions weren't the problem they once were. Drinking more saltwater relieved the drops in blood pressure that blacked out my vision and sometimes sent me to the floor.

Micah started kindergarten. I'd always wanted to homeschool him when the time came, but I didn't have enough good days to be sure he would receive what he needed. We found a great little classical Christian school about a half-hour drive from the house. It was the kind of school that softened the loss of not being able to homeschool, offering small classes, half days, reasonable homework loads, and godly staff. Mom dropped him off on her way to the university, and I picked him up in the afternoon. The transition made my days fuller, but God granted me the grace to keep up.

Caroline Lunger called one afternoon. A pastor from Wisconsin had driven four hours to pray for her. "I'm not reacting to smells anymore!" she exclaimed.

Joyful tears burst from my eyes. I'd been praying for this news since I'd met her. "Praise God! I'm so happy for you!"

And I was. Later though, there was a tiny voice inside that whispered, "What about me?"

The question sounded harsher in Brandon's wounded voice. "That's great, but what about you? What about us?"

I didn't have answers. Though I felt better overall, little reactions plagued me daily, requiring at least one acupressure treatment each. Nothing had threatened my life since the recent peanut exposure, but small reactions were enough to make me miserable with fatigue, brain fog, insomnia, and pain of all kinds.

There was little I could do to relieve Brandon's load. I did everything I could at home, but errands like grocery shopping were out of the question. Even if it had lost some of its shock value, mast cell activation disease continued to ruin his life.

A second fire ant invasion didn't help matters. He woke one August morning to find them streaming in from the wall behind the washing machine. Leaving me a note to be careful, he left for work, promising to take care of the problem when he returned home.

"Nothing is going right," he said that night, his glazed eyes staring past me. "You may feel fine today, but I could lose you tomorrow because someone makes a stupid mistake. Things are tense at work. We're thousands of dollars in debt. We're still in this trailer with no real plans to build, and these damned ants won't quit. It's like they're sent by the devil to take you from me."

As if to prove his point, a fire ant crawled up my arm. He flicked it with his finger. "Sometimes I swear God is playing with me."

The pain behind his words broke my heart. "These ants aren't from God," I reminded him.

He huffed an unintelligible response. Unwilling to preach at him, I prayed for him instead. Brandon was on his own road, and I couldn't walk it for him.

Jenny's birthday approached, and over the next few days, my mind went back and forth, deciding whether to visit her grave. It felt silly—bringing flowers to someone who was too happy to care. But Jenny's resting place was important because her body was important enough to Jesus to raise up and restore to everlasting perfection one day. Either way, I needed to honor her memory.

We left late in the afternoon and rode into the sun all the way there. Brandon drove the winding roads a little too quickly. The bouquet of spray roses sat in a vase of cold water anchored between my feet, beating themselves senseless at each turn in the road. Everything looked different after six months' time. Green grass and vines grew thick and close on either side of the highway. Cows, lethargic in the September heat, flicked their tails and shook their heads to shoo pestering flies.

We arrived at St. Rest Cemetery, relying on Brandon's memory of a single trip, and parked beneath the shade of an oak. We passed through the gate and walked up the hill to a spot where the red dirt was packed tight. No grass. No headstone either. Someone had lovingly marked the spot with one of those gaudy funeral wreaths made of silk flowers in various shades of pink, a potted plant now dead, and a sun-faded, plastic bouquet of something that had probably been nice once but now looked like weeds.

Death was sad, and every attempt we made to preserve our memories was sad. Like flowers, they faded. This scared me most of all. I wanted to remember the one who had shown me what it was to be brave, what it was to forget myself in suffering. I didn't want to forget her face or her voice, her best qualities or darkest secrets. I didn't want to forget what she'd meant to me.

Fire ants were busy in the dirt. Brandon brushed several off my shoes, admonishing me to be careful, and walked back to the car while I tried to figure out what one was supposed to do at the graveside of a beloved.

Standing right above her decaying body, feeling a connection so strong it was almost physical—even in death—I didn't cry. Or talk. There was no point. No one could hear my words but God, and he knew my every thought. So I thought at him.

I thought about Jesus weeping at Lazarus's tomb. He wept knowing what he was about to do—at his friend's graveside and on the hill outside of Jerusalem not long after.

Why did he weep?

Because death was an enemy. Death tore souls apart, souls once knitted together, and the tearing always left at least one soul mortally wounded, so much so she was afraid to stay the bleeding because it didn't feel right to heal. Because everything going back into place just as it was felt like a lie—a heinous, blasphemous lie.

Jesus wept at death because he had created everything for life unto life. Because decay wasn't the intention. *Forever* was. A broken world, a broken order deserved our grief.

Even if it all would be made right one day.

The eastern sky offered a welcome respite for my aching eyes. Wiping sweat from my neck, I noticed the foot of her grave pointed east. When the Savior returned, Jenny would be facing the right direction. Were all Christian boneyards designed this way? Would we rise as bones, ashes, and dust and be restored in the air, or would we rise perfect and beautiful? Would the soil cling or fall away?

A stinging pain on my shin pulled me out of my reverie. I brushed the ant away and placed my bouquet of roses and goldenrod where I imagined Jenny's hands were clasped over her chest. The flowers, so alive today, would be as dead as she was by tomorrow. Life was so god-awfully short.

Sweating and swelling, my body interrupted my prayers for Jenny's family. Funny how I'd almost convinced myself not to come, and now I didn't want to leave. Brandon perched lazily on top of the car in the shade of the oak. The tightness in my chest sent me to him.

"I got stung," I said, and he came to life. Scolding me for standing still too long, he took my shoes and began the treatment with that look his face always made when something like this happened, the one full of irritation and blame I'd learned to ignore. The look wasn't for me. It was like Jesus's tears. Every little thing would be all right, but disease and death were still enemies worthy of tears and anger.

"It wouldn't be a trip to see Jenny without something interesting happening," I said.

He didn't reply. An hour-long drive through the middle of nowhere with me reacting was on his mind, and he was not ready to joke. The comedian had been beaten out of him in the last few months. Now I was the one more likely to laugh at the ridiculousness of this disease. Of course, no one would ever see me laugh at cancer.

The Lord spared us both a shock reaction.

My iPod shuffled to the song "I Love It," by Stephanie Treo. I turned up the volume, remembering Jenny's defiance of disease and missing her sassy side. Brandon and I crossed Lake D'Arbonne at that royal moment when the sun sinks behind the trees, casting rays of pink and gold above its head like a crown. The reflection on the smooth water undulated like a moving royal train. Jenny felt closer in this moment than she had at her gravesite.

God was so good.

Because of Jesus, the evils of disease and death were nothing more than a fire ant sting. Restoration was coming. I believed it like I believed the sun would rise the next morning. In the meantime, his presence was enough. It would always be enough.

33

Communion

The posts about my trip to Mayo Clinic and subsequent diagnosis of mast cell activation disease drew new readers to my blog. Not long before, comments had been rare. Now, one or two were common. I tried to reply to each one. Some days, online connection was the best connection I experienced. Brandon had retreated into his shell under the pressures of work and homelife, and while I enjoyed my children, they couldn't meet my needs.

One comment, in particular, caught my attention— "Dear Melissa, my name is Melissa. A lady at my dentist's office told me of your blog, since I am also in the midst of a healing journey." She went on to describe the uncanny similarities between us. Not only did we share the same name, but we both had brown curly hair, a son and a daughter of similar ages, and birthdays on June 3. The most important commonality was that we were both followers of Christ. After reading my blog, she had made an appointment with Dr. Yakaboski. She thanked me for the recommendation and the encouragement my posts had offered.

Instead of simply replying to her comment, I emailed her at the address she left. We made plans to meet at Dr. Yakaboski's office the following week.

When I arrived, Melissa and her husband were waiting for me in one of the center's office spaces, painted a pale sea green. They sat shoulder to shoulder at a table. An empty chair waited for me on the other side.

Melissa's doe eyes followed me. Her glowing countenance drew me at once. For someone so ill, she was surprisingly joyful and winsome. I immediately loved her sweet husband, Michael, whose strong and gentle presence reminded me so much of Brandon. We enjoyed a half-hour "getting to know you" conversation between our appointments and swapped cell phone numbers before we parted ways.

Our friendship developed too fast for my comfort, reminding me of the early days of my friendship with Jenny. One day, she said, "I think our souls are knitted together like Jonathan and David."

My throat squeezed, and for a moment, I couldn't talk. "I can't do this again, God," I said upon hanging up. "I'm not ready."

Love her.

I wanted to love her as fiercely as I was capable, but my heart hadn't recovered from the blow of losing Jenny. It might never. Of course, it was impossible to withhold love completely. She was always so chipper and easy to talk to. She loved my Jesus and loved to talk about him, and we shared an undeniable amount of common ground beyond that.

"Do you think God speaks to us?" she asked one day over the phone.

Smiling, I rinsed suds off another pan and set it aside. "Absolutely."

"How do you know you're hearing from God, and that you're not just hearing your own thoughts?"

"Well, his voice always agrees with his written word. I can't say that for mine. He usually says something that surprises me or convicts me. Not in a way that beats me down but in a way that empowers me to change." I offered her a few examples. "Sometimes he shows me how to pray for people or gives me a scripture to share with them. I've even wondered if I have the gift of prophecy."

"Wow," she said. "I'm so glad I asked." She explained how God was constantly giving her little directives concerning health and life management, even where to put certain cups in her cabinets. "He's also revealing a ton of sin in my life."

I didn't want to shoot her down. Satan wasn't known for revealing sin, but something didn't feel right. "That's cool. But remember, God is rest. He doesn't keep us busy all the time."

"Oh, I love that," she said. "Let me tell you what else. God's been healing me!"

My stomach dropped. "Awesome!" I said as cheerfully as I could, trying to quench the longing within. Would another chronically ill friend receive healing while I still waited?

"I have been so anxious about having a bad reaction to food that I've been starving myself without knowing it. Last week, God took away all my anxiety, and I ate store-bought bread and a store-bought shake, and even ate out at a restaurant!"

I rebuked myself for feeling as I did and chose to enter into her joy. "Praise God! That's so wonderful, Melissa!"

"And guess what else."

"What?" What could be better than being well enough to drink a milkshake without dying or wanting to die?

"God gave me a word for you. After what you said, I think I might have the gift of prophecy too. God says that he loves you and that you are healed."

My visceral reaction was extreme caution, like I needed to shield myself from what she'd said. But that was hypocrisy.

"I know you still have symptoms, but God says you are healed," she repeated when I didn't respond.

Wiping my hands, I sat. "He always told me he would heal me. In many ways, he has."

Melissa shared several other things she thought God had said about me. As she spoke, I realized how others must feel when I shared similar words with them. It was awkward being on this side of the conversation. I took a deep breath. "Thank you so much for sharing all of that with me. I'll be fasting tomorrow about several issues, including these."

I prayed as I had promised, putting several of her suggestions into practice. If she had indeed heard from God, something would come of it. I tried juicing again and muscle tested less often, relying more on prayer. I pricked my finger for blood samples each day, which I used in my acupressure treatments. Mast cell disease was a disease of the blood. What could a finger stick hurt other than my finger and squeamish nature? Though I couldn't tell that I improved, I didn't get worse.

I invited Melissa and her family to our home for a meal to celebrate her healing. She and her family walked through the door, the scent of laundry detergent trailing behind them. Brandon lifted his eyebrows at me. His sensitivity to smell could now rival my own. To my surprise, I didn't feel a reaction coming on. I shook my head and mouthed, "I'm okay."

Throughout the evening, the children enjoyed one another's company almost to the point they couldn't stop whispering and giggling to eat. Michael and Brandon seemed to understand one another without saying much. Melissa and I more than made up for their lack of words. My mind flashed to the memory of dinner with Drew and Jenny. Rather than feeling sad, I felt Jenny's smile on the whole thing, as if she looked on from my little cloud of witnesses.

Melissa left me with a gift of sauerkraut and herbal tea. "To remind you that healing is coming," she said. I hugged her goodbye, thankful for her friendship.

When they had gone and the house had fallen still, I filled the sink with hot soapy water and worshiped. Time passed quickly in that sweet place. I was surprised and sad to find all the dishes done.

Have communion with me?

"Yes, Lord."

My hands trembled as they poured bright-red hibiscus tea into a glass. Elements in hand, I sat on the couch and set "Ten Thousand Reasons" to play again. Oh, the crunch of that rice cracker—my Savior's broken body, the Bread of Heaven, come down to fill up my empty places, to heal me of unbelief, doubt, sin, and disease.

I wept.

Oh, his blood! His life's blood spilled for me. "Let it bring healing to mine."

I drank and waited, half expecting healing to come in that moment. When it didn't, I believed it would come during the night. When I woke the next morning, already too tired to face the day ahead, I knew it hadn't, but God had refreshed my belief.

He loved me. He would heal me. From his viewpoint, he already had.

* * *

A time of prayer and fasting followed. My body was too weak to fast as healthy people did. I couldn't go without food much past noon before having a reaction because I hadn't eaten, but I did what I could. Though I was largely trapped in my home, a long list of needs developed. It seemed like everyone I knew was fighting a battle of some kind. But God didn't talk much about them. He wanted to talk about me.

He came after my sarcasm, which I used as a coping mechanism. He wanted me soft, pliable. I prayed for people I loved to be delivered from pride, and God revealed telltale signs of the same sin in me. After reading a social media post by another mast cell disease sufferer, my instinct was to tell her she was looking at her situation all wrong and that she should look at it my way instead.

You need to learn how to weep with people.

God had a lot of work to do in me.

Our church announced a Thursday-night prayer and communion service. The gathering would be less dangerous than that of a Sunday morning and more intimate. Prayer meetings didn't draw crowds. The Lord filled me with an urgency to ask for prayer at the service, which excited me. Was God about to free me of this disease? Would he do it at the church?

The day of the prayer service arrived and brought with it a thousand fears. Would I get sick and have to leave? Even if I didn't get sick, there was still an emotional cost for going. By now, I was used to my role as a social outcast, but I still struggled with people's discomfort with my mask. Some couldn't even look at me. Others kept conversation short, glancing here and there, their feet itching to escape. I'm sure they wanted to respond well, but they didn't know how. In an intimate prayer service, I might be a distraction. A burden. And when I asked for prayer, what would I say? I wasn't so good at explaining myself to a group of strangers. What if I cried and made everyone uncomfortable?

When I shared my fears with Brandon, he blinked twice and said, "You're crazy, and we're late. Get in the car."

We were a couple of blocks from the church when I realized I had left my bottle of Acute Rescue on the counter at home. I panicked. It was a sign: I shouldn't have come. As the command to turn around perched on my tongue, I found an unopened bottle of the homeopathic in my purse. I relaxed. God had me covered.

The service wasn't what I had imagined it to be, although I was correct—not many people had come. We worshiped much more than we prayed, and the prayer time mostly consisted of a pastor announcing prompts as we prayed silently in our seats. During the final worship set, the pastor invited people to receive prayer from elders stationed at the back of the room.

Well, I'd come for prayer, and this, it seemed, was the only way I was going to get it.

I turned my head. I knew all three elders, and all three knew a little of my situation. I wouldn't have to explain much. "Which one, Lord?"

No answer.

I stepped into the aisle. All three were busy praying with someone else. I almost returned to my seat, but Brandon was behind me. Standing off to the side a little farther back, a couple roughly between the ages of my parents caught my gaze. I didn't know them, but that didn't matter. Without further deliberation, I approached and began to explain.

The man peered down at me with sharp blue eyes and an interested furrow in his brow. The woman's expression filled with compassion as I shared about my disease, its effects, and the good God had done in the midst of it. Neither had difficulty looking me in the eye, and I didn't feel awkward talking to them. A profound sense of safety set me at ease.

When I finished explaining, the woman looked at her husband. He took a slow breath. "Three things came to me as you shared your situation. First, I believe there is a huge emotional component to your disease. I don't know what happened to you before you were sick, but I imagine you probably need some emotional healing."

Emotional healing? What did he mean? My emotions were fine. I was Mayo Clinic psychologist approved.

"Second, there is some serious spiritual warfare surrounding you. This is more than a fight for your life. It's a fight for your future."

The words hit me like a cold splash of water to the face. I had been fighting for joy so long that I'd forgotten I was fighting against something. Demons had chased me in my dreams. They'd visited me in the night. I heard voices that weren't mine or God's. Every time something good happened, something awful followed. And those ants—it was creepy how they kept hunting me down. I'd seen the warfare surrounding others but had missed the warfare surrounding me.

The music stopped. Voices rippled behind us. The service was over.

The man continued. "Finally, fear plays a major part in all of this. Fear is your greatest foe."

The word was hard to receive. If he only knew how far I'd come. If he only knew what it had taken to stand there before him. If he knew that it would cost me a minimum of two days in bed to recover, would he still think me a coward?

"I would love to pray for you," he said.

I nodded. It was why I'd come.

As he prayed, the sense of being wrapped in a soft blanket of acceptance and peace couldn't be missed. When he finished, I asked his name.

"Matt Massingale." He smiled and extended his hand. "And this is my wife, Kathy."

I introduced myself and Brandon.

"You know," she said, squeezing my hand, "I think God sent us here just for you. We weren't going to come. Our TV repairman stayed late. We were on our way to get something to eat and decided to swing in. Not more than a minute later, you walked up."

The mask hid my grin. "God's pretty cool like that."

"You may want to read the book *Victory over the Darkness,* by Neil Anderson," Matt said. "There's a lot in there that might help you."

Brandon wrote down the title and muttered in my ear, "Neil Anderson is the author of the book I'm reading right now with Randy."

We thanked the Massingales, exchanged numbers, and left with a lot to think about.

"So I wasn't healed tonight," I said to Brandon on the way home.

"No, but I'd still call it a win."

"Yeah."

I fasted the next day. I needed to seek the Lord.

He confirmed all that Matt had said, and I was humbled. Then he led me to the book of a minor Old Testament prophet and offered it to me as a gift: "And the Lord answered me: 'Write the vision; make it plain on tablets, so he may run who reads it. For still the vision awaits its appointed time; it hastens to the end—it will not lie. If it seems slow, wait for it; it will surely come; it will not delay…the righteous shall live by his faith.'"

34

Encounters

Melissa's number flashed on the screen of my cell phone. She didn't usually call during the evening. It had been a long, hard day, and I was washing dishes. An emotional breakdown around noon had required me to repent and apologize to the kids. We'd recovered somewhat after exchanges of forgiveness and singing hymns of praise, but sinful anger always left me spent.

The kids ran wild circles in the living room, laughing in late-evening delirium. Brandon studied the screen of his phone as if it contained answers to all of his problems. It wasn't a good time.

I pushed the answer button and covered my free ear. "Hello?"

"Oh, Melissa. Good. I need you to pray for me."

A troubled feeling settled in my gut. "Okay."

"I must depend on the Lord alone. For food. For drink. For everything. I must depend on him. He will tell me what to do. He will tell me when to eat. To drink. I must depend on him alone. Pray for me." Her speech came in repetitive fragments.

I retreated to my bedroom. "How long has it been since you've eaten?"

"He will tell me when to eat. He will tell me what to eat. I must depend on him alone."

"Are you home alone?" I asked.

"Michael is at church with the kids," she said. "Pray for me. I must depend on him."

I sat down on my bed. "Why don't you go to the kitchen and get a snack while I pray?"

"Michael left food for me. Water too. I will eat and drink when he tells me to."

"So why don't you go ahead and take a bite?" I asked, fighting to remain calm. I prayed that God would release peace over my friend.

"Will you talk to Michael? He doesn't understand how much I need to depend on the Lord alone. Will you explain to him? Will you tell him I'm okay?" Her voice sounded urgent. "God will tell me what to do. Michael just needs to believe. God tells me when to sleep, when to go to the bathroom. He tells me what to do."

I swallowed. "Sure, Melissa. Can you give me Michael's number? I'll call and explain right now."

I jotted down the number she gave.

"Okay, I'm going to hang up now and call Michael. Why don't you eat the food he left for you while I'm on the phone?"

"I must depend on the Lord alone," she said.

"We all do. I'll call you back as soon as I've talked to Michael."

"Okay. Thank you, Melissa."

I dialed the number twice, but the call wouldn't go through. She'd either given me the wrong number, or something was wrong with the line. Taking my hair in my fists, I tried to think through the panic mounting inside my chest. I'd come to love Melissa, to value her as a friend. I might be the only person who knew how sick she was, and I couldn't help her.

I ran to Brandon, who always seemed to know what to do. "Hand me your laptop," he said.

A moment later, he pulled up Michael's number from his company's website. As I'd suspected, Melissa had mixed up a couple of the numbers. Brandon prayed silently for me as I dialed the new number. The call went through, but I had to leave a voice mail. I waited, perched on the edge of the bed, staring at my reflection in the mirror but not really seeing myself. Only minutes passed, but each one seemed to stretch beyond its normal limits.

Before the first tone of my phone's ring had played out, I answered. "Hi, Michael. This is Melissa Keaster. Have you spoken with Melissa today?"

"Yeah. I just got off the phone with her." He didn't sound adequately urgent to me. He sounded…cautious. "She said you would call."

I didn't waste time beating around the bush. "Listen, I spoke with her. I strongly urge you to call everyone you trust to pray for Melissa right now and get her to the emergency room as quickly as possible. Do not wait until tomorrow. Do it tonight."

A pause. "She told me you were calling to tell me everything was okay."

"Everything is not okay, and we both know it," I said. I repeated all I remembered of my conversation with Melissa and repeated my recommendation. "How long has it been since she's eaten?"

"I don't know." His voice sounded tired now. Hollow. "Three days?"

Not enough time to really hurt her unless she hadn't had a drink either. "Okay, I'm going to let you go now," I told him. "Call your prayer warriors. I'll be praying for you too."

He hung up, and I released a breath I didn't know I'd been holding. Brandon patted me on the back.

Dishes awaited me in the kitchen. My tears dripped into the cooling dishwater, drilling holes in what was left of the suds. The kids turned curious faces to me when a sob escaped my throat. But Mama had cried many times at the kitchen sink. It was nothing unusual.

* * *

Michael heeded my advice and took Melissa to the hospital. Overnight, the emergency room staff decided Melissa needed extended care. She was sent to a behavioral health facility upstate, where she stayed seven days. Michael visited Melissa as often as he could and posted updates on a social media group devoted to prayer for her. For a week, my own battle didn't matter to me. I only wanted my friend to get better.

The next time she called, Melissa sounded like herself. "I'm on my way home," she said, her voice strong and steady.

I, however, fell apart. Whatever current I'd ridden through the summer had blown out on the autumn wind. When Robert and Dixie made their first trip up to the farm, I could barely drag myself out of bed to say hello.

The visit was nothing like I'd envisioned. I fed them a tough dried-out ham over far more palatable conversation. Dixie shared her grief over the loss of her grandson last January, and I recounted what had happened with Melissa and my concern for her as she pursued healing.

"I remember taking my grandson, Sean, on a walk at the beach when he was little," she said, tears shining in her blue eyes. "I told him, 'God told the ocean it could only come this far.' God created everything with limits, including us. God loves us all, but he also loves us—you—in particular. You aren't the Savior. What your friends need is Jesus, so you need to get out of his way. Let him be who he is so they can see him. So you don't burn out, and so you don't suppose yourself to be more than you are—finite, divinely beloved dust."

I took her words to bed with me, where I stayed most of the weekend. Melissa was my friend, but I wasn't her savior. She needed Jesus more than she needed me. Playing the hero had only led to a serious crash and burn. It was time to let go and trust God to intervene. It was time to remember I was only dust.

* * *

Weeks passed before I stopped expecting a sudden miraculous healing. Something shifted in my body with the cooler weather, and my reactions increased in strength and number.

One Tuesday during school pick-up, I met Micah at the sidewalk, took his little hand in mine, and escorted him to his seat on the other side of the car. About a mile down the road, heat flashed through my body. My tongue swelled, and throat tightened.

Bewildered, I pulled over as quickly as I could and grabbed my phone. Both Mom and Debbie worked nearby. I'd stopped in a grocery store parking lot halfway between them. Debbie's number appeared first on my recent call list. I selected her name as my thoughts turned to soup.

Two rings. "Hello?" she said, her greeting taut with concern. My disease had trained everyone to answer with trepidation.

"I just picked up Micah from school. I'm reacting to something. I'm at Brookshire's on 165. Can you leave work?"

"Actually, I'm less than a block away. I'll be there in a minute."

As I reached for my Acute Rescue homeopathic, the mottled skin of my right palm caught my eye. The skin was raised and a shade of angry red. What had I touched?

Debbie tapped on my car window. "Grammy!" the kids exclaimed.

I was too muddled to coach her through the steps of the acupressure treatment, but she remembered most of them on her own, having practiced several times herself. When she finished, she said, "You don't look so good. How about I drive you home?"

"That would be amazing," I said. "Thank you."

"What do you think did it this time?" she asked as she pulled out of the parking lot.

"Something I touched." A picture of taking Micah's hand flashed through the haze in my brain. I needed to be cautious. Micah was very sensitive. "Bubs?"

"Mmm-hmm?" Micah answered from the back seat.

Peanuts were my first thought. "What did you eat today?"

He rattled off the list of snacks I'd packed.

"Any candy?"

"Not today," he said.

My mind clunked through the list of my most severe triggers. "Did you play with a balloon?"

"No." He paused. I could almost hear him think. "But I did play with rubber bands right before we lined up to come home."

Debbie and I swapped a glance. I made a mental note to buy latex-free rubber bands for his teacher to use in class.

My old friends arthritis, fibromyalgia, and fatigue mustered their resources and introduced a new friend. One evening during dinner prep, I fished a package of ground bison out of the sink where it had thawed and cut it open. As I worked the cold meat into patties, the skin of my palms began to itch and then burn.

"Here we go," I muttered. But nothing else happened. My tongue didn't swell. No cough developed. It was the weirdest thing.

Finishing my task, I washed my hands and studied them. The skin was raised into welts and mottled with shades of pink and bright red. I thought through the list of known triggers and assumed I'd reacted to the ink on the bison package label. Newspapers, magazines, construction paper, and crayons had all triggered my mast cells before. It seemed a reasonable conclusion.

Welts broke out on my palms and fingers every evening during meal prep for more than a week before I realized the new trigger wasn't ink or plastic packaging. It was the cold temperatures of the food I handled. Gloves helped a little, but burning, itching welts formed night after night without fail, adding a new measure of misery to cooking.

On Sara's birthday, I was hanging a banner when my breathing became labored. The resulting systemic reaction sent me to bed. Unable to form a more plausible explanation, we assumed the elastic bands on the banner must have been made of latex. Brandon, Debbie, and Nona set up everything without me. Once the party began, Brandon helped me to the porch steps, where I sat for the duration. I didn't usually cry over reactions, but this one crushed me. What had gone wrong with my hands?

The enemy then advanced on my children. Micah trembled in fear at the prospect of walking down the hall to his room alone. It wasn't a long hall. Our single-wide trailer was shorter than most. I prayed for him and taught him to preach truth to himself. "Be bold! Be strong! For the Lord is with you!" he would chant as he marched down the hall. Most of the time, it worked. Other times, he refused to go until either I or his baby sister accompanied him.

One night as I rocked Sara to sleep, she buried her face in my shoulder, grunting as if in pain. "What's wrong, baby?" I asked.

"I'm scared," she said.

"Scared of what?"

She pointed over my shoulder. "I'm scared of that thing looking at me."

Angry heat rushed from my neck into my face. I turned, knowing I wouldn't see anything. Good Lord, even the baby had to learn to fight. "Okay, love. Here's what we're going to do. Repeat after me: in Jesus's name…"

"In Jesus's name…"

"Go away."

"Go away!"

"Good. Is it gone?"

"No."

"Okay, let's sing some songs to Jesus."

We sang her favorite hymns, "Jesus Loves Me" and "There's Something About That Name."

"The songs are making it go away!" she said.

"Praise the Lord," I said, rubbing her back.

The next morning, I picked up the book Matt Massingale had recommended, *Victory over the Darkness.* I'd ordered it weeks ago. If this was the way things would be, I needed to brush up on my fighting skills and look deeper into the idea of emotional healing. I couldn't deny that I was wounded. Even if my disease wasn't rooted in emotional trauma, it had caused some.

The Christmas season offered me ample time to read. I'd finished my first draft of *Eleora* and was resting the manuscript before I began the rewrite. No one expected me to attend parties. Family gatherings were too risky. Each day while the kids napped, I made a cup of herbal tea and settled into the recliner with a blanket and the book.

While I read the chapter "You Must Be Real to Be Right," the Holy Spirit fell on me with such conviction that I set the book down and staggered to my bedside. My knees buckled underneath the weight of knowing I was both the prodigal and the son who'd stayed home—the foolish prostitute and the arrogant pharisee.

My list of offenses ran long—entitlement, envy, anger, fear, impatience, competition, unclean thoughts, unclean lips, pride, lack of love. A picture came to mind of a nervous chicken, scurrying around in a dither, eating up all the grain, afraid there wouldn't be enough. The chicken was me. I begrudged and envied the other chickens their grain, forgetting there was always enough, I'd never gone hungry, and the hand that fed me never ran out. No one wanted to be a fat, nervous, jealous chicken.

There was no excuse to offer, no explanation I could give. Two handkerchiefs weren't sufficient to catch the tears. I couldn't breathe through the weeping.

A soft gust of air entered my bedroom. With it, a Presence. The Presence carried peace and comfort on his breath. He knelt beside me in the posture I imagined he took all those years ago when he looked into the price for my soul and sweated blood. He grieved with me. He was so close that the bitter pain turned sweet. Unfurling my clenched fist, he wound invisible fingers around mine and whispered, "I love you. I accept you. We're going to fix this."

I leaned into the Presence, unable to speak. What was there to say to one so holy, so loving, so true? It wasn't time to speak. It was time to listen.

* * *

I tried to relive the holy experience the following day and failed. No one could manufacture moments like those. One could only make space for them. So I listened, I studied, I read.

God gave me a word for the new year—mercy.

A storm rolled in the night of January 1, 2015. I lay in bed, listening to the thunder that rolled and rolled like waves, and remembered a verse from the book of Job: "God thunders marvelously with his voice; he does great things which we cannot comprehend." God had a lot to say in the upcoming year, and he was clearing his throat. I might not understand his mind, but his heart was as kind as it was pure. It would all be mercy as it had been from the beginning.

35

Sheol

Winter stayed mild until school resumed in January, when icy winds swept down from the north into Louisiana. One Thursday afternoon, I dressed Sara and myself in layers to face the twenty-degree temperature outside, finishing off our outfits with knit caps. Welts broke out over the skin that grasped the frigid steering wheel, which was uncomfortable and annoying.

"Should've put on gloves," I muttered to myself. Otherwise, I was fine.

Micah huffed clouds of frosty breath as he hustled into the warm car. I closed his door and slid back into the driver's seat. Happy to see one another, Micah and Sara exchanged stories about their day. I enjoyed listening to their prattle until I reached the long isolated stretch of highway between town and the house.

My chest tightened.

Surely not.

It had to be the cold air.

I reached for the heater, but my arm was slow to respond. A telltale underwater feeling replaced clear thought. My feet. I wasn't in full control of my feet.

God in heaven. My kids.

I prayed, concentrated on taking slow breaths, and kept driving. There was no shoulder. My body wasn't obeying the commands I gave too well. If I pulled over, I could end up in the marshy ditch among the trees.

The church sign across the highway from our road signaled me to slow down. I would have to turn soon. I coasted down the road and into the driveway, afraid my useless foot might not lift off the gas at the right time. The car stopped. Micah helped Sara inside. Reality flashed through white noise in infrequent bursts until I dropped onto the bed like a rag doll.

An earthy, fresh-air scent wafted over me. A blurry figure leaned over the bed. A voice I knew. Brandon. Had I called him?

His questions garbled. The words came at me all out of order. I couldn't answer. I hadn't even understood what he'd said. He spoke louder. His urgency didn't help. I tried to pat his hand, console him. My hand wouldn't obey. His hands searched, pounded, chopped. Liquid, wet and sharp, ran over my tongue, down my throat.

A drawn brow was the first thing that came into focus. His brown eyes shone with a wild, harried light. I understood his questions. My wrist rotated when I asked it to, but every limb objected to movement.

"What happened?" he asked as if for the twelfth time.

"Not sure. Maybe the cold?" My tongue felt fat and lazy in my mouth, but I'd been coherent long enough to make some educated guesses. Cold and heat were known mast cell triggers. My hands had been reacting to cold for weeks now. The wind outside cut through cloth and skin and snaked around the bones. I shivered. What else could have done it?

Brandon sat, grazing my shin, which I could feel again. He massaged the back of his neck. "Well, at least we live in Louisiana."

"Maybe it was a fluke."

"Like the thing with your hands?"

One could always hope.

But it wasn't a fluke. The cold hung on, trapping me indoors. One cold day, I ventured near the front door to help Micah put on his shoes. On his way out, a gust of wind swept inside. The brisk air nipped at my face in a pleasant way. Our little mobile home wasn't insulated all that well, but Brandon kept the heat going as though my life depended on it. Warm and snug beneath layers of warm clothing, I had no idea the cold rush of air could be dangerous to me, but all the symptoms I experienced on my last drive home set in at once. I called Dad, who walked across the yard to treat me, and I made a mental note to stay away from the door when the temperatures dropped below freezing.

Previously, I'd joked about feeling like a prisoner in my own home. Now I was. Depression sucked me into the vortex of my Facebook newsfeed. Sometimes I didn't resurface for hours. Again my world had shrunk, but I wasn't even present for what God had given.

The kids would create something and say, "Look, Mom!" In response, they received little more than a perfunctory glance with an occasional side of grump. "Look, Mom!" was an invitation into their world. How many invitations had I missed? How many invitations from God did I miss every day because my eyes were glued to a screen that couldn't love me back?

It was time to set aside my online presence and detox. The decision, while simple, felt like a big deal. My online presence was the only presence I had in the world outside of the four walls of my home. I didn't work. I was separated from church. Facebook provided me with friendship, however shallow, and a space to be known. The desire to be known and understood by people was part of my problem. What I needed was to learn satisfaction in the intimate understanding of God.

With a farewell message, I signed off.

* * *

The next morning, Brandon was scheduled to interview for a position at work he'd been preparing for, for over a decade. As a young pharmacist, he'd taken on extra responsibilities that usually belonged to the pharmacy manager. He'd trained himself to make schedules, order inventory, evaluate employees, and provide excellent customer service so that he could become a pharmacy manager at the store he had served since he'd been in pharmacy school. He'd waited patiently and worked hard for this day.

"How do I look?" he asked, standing at the foot of the bed.

"Sharp and sexy," I said. "I'd hire you."

"Wish me luck." Not that he believed he needed luck. He was confident the position would be his.

I wasn't. Months ago, when the previous manager had announced his decision to retire, I'd felt impressed to pray for Brandon's heart, not that he would get the job. Still, I hoped. He deserved it and badly needed a win.

He kissed me and left. I prayed and waited for his call.

The phone rang that afternoon. I answered, breathless. "Well?"

"I didn't get it." His voice thinned and cracked.

The weight of his disappointment crashed onto me, and I couldn't speak at all. I knew what I had prayed, but it didn't make sense. Why couldn't he get this one break? He'd stayed late countless nights, taken patient calls at home, and driven back to work after hours to fill prescriptions. He'd served faithfully and had never received so much as a thank-you from the company. It wasn't fair.

The line was quiet. He waited for me to say something. "I'm so sorry, babe. Did they give a reason?"

"I'm not good with people, apparently."

"Well, that's the biggest load of bullshit I've ever heard," I said, heat rising to my face. Who had said that? On what grounds? I'd show them "not good with people."

He sighed. "I need to congratulate Jodi and get back to work."

There were individuals in that pharmacy who didn't like Brandon, who would rejoice in his devastation, and I couldn't do a thing to shield him from it. "Okay. I'm praying for you."

But when I hung up the phone, words wouldn't form. I could only weep.

* * *

Inhale. Exhale.

I lay in bed and stared at the ceiling as I'd done time and again. When I'd felt like I was dying. When I actually was. It was practically a ritual now.

The sheets released Brandon's earthy scent, reminding of the way he grounded me. He'd been so strong. Strong for us all. It was my turn to be strong for him, and I couldn't even be strong for myself.

Inhale.

A tear seeped out of the corner of my eye and rolled down my cheek. "What can I do for him, God? How do I help my husband with this?"

Exhale. Inhale.

Listen. Do not advise.

Exhale. I'd never had much success at keeping my mouth shut. Could I do it? Could I trust God to do all the talking that needed to be done?

Inhale. Exhale.

Cook him plenty of good food.

That I could do. The kids and I would make him a gluten-free zucchini cake before he arrived home from work. His favorite—fried deer steak, peas, and potatoes—for dinner.

Have sex with him often.

A sharp inhale.

"Okay, God, but you know sex comes at a pretty high price," I reminded him. Every time, I itched, flushed, swelled, and lost an entire night's sleep from the insomnia sex induced. "I'm not sure I can do it that often unless you relieve some of these symptoms."

It was too miserable, and no one wanted me to end up on TLC's *Sex Sent Me to the ER*.

Exhale.

I opened my Bible to Job 41. The words blurred behind the lens of tears that covered my eyes. I'd been studying the book for weeks, looking for the answers all God-loving sufferers wanted. If answers were there, I hadn't found them yet. "My heart isn't here. It's in the first three chapters," I prayed.

So go there.

Startled by the directive, I stopped crying. The thin pages clung to my damp fingers, rattling as I flipped back.

Inhale. Exhale.

Again, I introduced myself to Job of Uz and invited his hell to consume my own.

* * *

He wiped his feet on the mat as I fished golden brown deer steaks out of the sizzling coconut oil. The sag of his shoulders shattered me. The kids rushed to him before I could step away from the stove. "Daddy! Daddy! We made you a zucchini cake!"

"Because you had a bad day at work," Micah added.

He lifted Sara into his arms and drew Micah close. Moisture shone in his eyes, rimmed in red. "Thank you so much." The words came out half-choked and raspy.

I set aside the last of the deer steaks and went to him.

"Y'all go finish your movie," Brandon said, releasing the kids.

I wound my arms around him and held him as tightly as I was able. His lips were moist and salty with tears. They'd made him cry. They'd made my Superman cry. A flash of heat washed over my body, and it had nothing to do with mast cells.

Exhale.

Obeying, I released every murderous thought on a breath.

"What am I going to do now?"

I understood. He'd been working toward that position since before we were married, and they'd given it to someone else. Advice, unbidden, came to mind. God had known it would. I swallowed every religious platitude, every wild and vain imagination.

Locking eyes with him, I poured all the intensity I could muster into my next words. "Where you go, I will go. Where you live, I will live. Whatever you decide to do, I'm with you, and I support you."

He buried his face in the curve of my neck and pressed me into him.

At dinner, he wasn't as hungry as usual, but he ate. Afterward, Sara rushed a slice of cake to the table to replace his empty plate. He praised her baking prowess with each bite. The happy light beaming from her eyes made us both feel better.

After washing the dishes and tucking in the kids, I found him in bed, lost in Candy Crush. I lay next to him until he was ready to set it aside and then comforted him as only I could.

I drifted through the long tunnel toward sleep. No unpleasant symptoms troubled me. I hadn't offered one word of advice.

Inhale. Exhale.

I could do this.

One breath at a time.

By God's grace.

* * *

Violence seethed underneath my skin for days. Maybe that was why I'd started running a low-grade fever all the time. Weeks ago, it had hovered around 98.2. My new normal rose to 99.4, sometimes spiking to 100 degrees.

Everyone involved in Brandon's disappointment should feel the pain he felt. I hated them all, even though I knew I mustn't. Fantasies of revenge burned through my imagination. I blessed them all instead. I didn't feel it, but I said the words. Maybe that counted for something.

Blessing for them. Vindication for Brandon.

The rage evaporated, and I was left empty.

There was nothing left.

Rage had taken everything.

Except the fever.

* * *

My spirit lay in the ash heap with Job. I lacked the energy to hold my Bible, let alone read it. I didn't know what to pray. I couldn't coax myself to sing.

God hovered nearby. Above and beside. Somehow beneath me. Not saying a word. I acknowledged his presence and echoed the quiet.

Snow fell outside. Large flakes falling, falling from the Louisiana sky. A rare gift. The kids played in the drifts with my parents. Their laughter pierced the stillness.

Cold seeped through the window at my head. Not enough to make me sick. Not enough to make me care.

Why?

When Brandon had asked the age-old question, God had actually answered him. "To tear you down and remake you into something new," God had said.

What was left to tear down?

The only thing that mattered was God's presence—a rest sweeter than death.

Death, I might welcome if God offered another opportunity.

I meant to rise and make hot cocoa for the kids, but I fell asleep.

* * *

God didn't seem to mind my listlessness. He didn't speak, but he was there. He never left. Instead, he came closer.

Every morning, I woke aware of his presence. Every night, I fell asleep in his arms. Little by little, life seeped back into my dry bones.

From the sanctum of my bed, I sang a love song to my Savior. Cracks interrupted the light, airy flow. The sound blasphemed my classical training, but the Holy Spirit seemed to smile at the flaws.

* * *

The day of Micah's birthday party arrived, which meant I had to leave the bed and walk out into the cold. I'd scheduled the party at the local children's museum so that I wouldn't have much to do.

Cake and drinks were my only responsibilities. Good thing too. The evening grew cold. Despite several layers of clothes, topped with knitted hat, scarf, and blanket, my brain fuzzed out and limbs grew heavy. Breathing was labor.

Brandon stretched me out on the floor and performed the acupressure treatment as guests walked in without a proper greeting. We must have looked crazy. Looks weren't always deceiving.

* * *

In early March, Brandon made me leave my bed to travel to Branson with the family. I didn't want to go and resented him for making me, but the change of scenery, the presence of my parents, his parents, Nona, and Papaw—doing so well now though we'd almost lost him—the joy of my children, the good food, hymn singing, and fellowship were exactly what I needed.

On the ride home, I reached for Brandon's hand. "Thank you," I said without explaining myself.

He smiled as though I didn't have to.

The day after our return, I pulled out the three speckled notebooks containing the manuscript of *Eleora*. Nothing was usable. Garbage, all of it.

In bed, propped against two pillows, I grabbed my laptop, opened a new Word document, and began again.

36

Community

"I feel…lonely," I told Mom over a steaming cup of herbal tea. I'd finished typing the final words of the third draft to *Eleora* in mid-July, and it was now in the hands of beta readers. Two weeks later, with no new writing project, I'd awakened to a reality I'd previously been able to ignore.

Mom's dimple appeared. A certain glint in her eye warned me to brace myself. She was preparing to unload something that she'd been mulling over, waiting for an opportune moment to share. "Well," she said, "you've been in isolation—writing your book—for months. You haven't had time for people. Which is fine. It's the way things had to be. But now your book is finished, and you're left with the isolation."

It was as if she'd smacked me in the face with a pillow. It surprised me but didn't hurt too much. "So what do I do about it?" I asked.

Mom shrugged. "Tell people what you want. Invite them back in."

So, take initiative. "To start, I'd like to visit with you every day that you're available until you go back to work."

"I'd like the same," she said and sipped her tea.

Not long after our conversation, the theme of community began to appear everywhere. The message found me in scripture, blog posts about publishing and marketing, news articles, sermons, and conversations with Dixie and Robert the weekend Brandon drove us all down to Baton Rouge for a visit. Moms needed community. Writers needed community. Disciples of Jesus needed the body of Christ—the Church. Especially the sufferers. And the body of Christ needed them.

Seek community.

God's voice swept all the breadcrumbs into a neat discernible pile, but the message scared the ever-living day lights out of me.

"Umm, God? I know you know this, but I'm a shut-in," I said. "People literally make me sick. What do you expect me to do?"

No answer. I would have to try something and hope for the best.

Returning to Facebook would be a bad start. The last thing a lonely person needed was counterfeit community. Immediate family couldn't completely satisfy the depth of my need or sustain the weight of my burden. Besides, if I had all the community I needed within easy reach, God wouldn't have prompted me to seek it out.

I hadn't been to church in a while. My health remained somewhat stable at home, so I probably wouldn't die if the attempt didn't go well. Brandon liked for me to go, despite the fact he was the one who had to take care of me and two small children when something happened. I agreed to try, and Brandon came up with a plan.

After speaking with the church administrator, Brandon set out baby food jars of water in different locations throughout the sanctuary, each jar labeled according to the location where it was placed. After several days, he collected the jars, and I took them to Dr. Yakaboski. Jar by jar, we muscle tested the safety of the air in each section of the church. My muscles tested the strongest with the jar placed nearest stage left.

Each Sunday, we would rush to feed and dress the children and make the forty-five-minute drive to Ruston. Brandon would pull into the parking lot a few minutes late and send me to wait for him at a well-ventilated entrance. He would check the children into children's church and meet me in the empty corridor. Taking my hand, he'd lead me through the foyer to the sanctuary entrance farthest away from the thickest traffic flows. His sharp eyes would scan the foremost rows closest to stage left, and then he'd lead me to the least populated seats. We'd join the last song or two of worship time, listen to a sermon, and wait for the crowds to clear before exiting the building.

Something invariably happened each week. One Sunday, several heavily perfumed college girls arrived later than we had and took the seats in front of us. I began to wheeze within a few seconds and had to sit in the foyer alone for the remainder of the service. Another Sunday, we sat directly under the air-conditioning vents, and I reacted to the cold air. When I ventured too far from stage left, the change of air triggered a reaction. It was weird, but I was used to weird at this point.

I also had to be careful about the number of times I moved from sitting to standing and how quickly I did so. My blood pressure dropped and heart raced, numbing my legs and blacking out my vision. More than once, Brandon had to support me so that I wouldn't faint. Brandon would treat me once we were in the car, and I would spend the remainder of the day in bed.

There was an emotional toll in addition to the physical one. I'd grown used to strangers avoiding eye contact and not approaching me in public places—so used to it, in fact, that it startled me when someone looked me in the eye or smiled— yet it remained a mystery to me that people I'd known for years behaved like most strangers. Granted, Brandon played the role of my bodyguard with Oscar-winning intensity, but one wouldn't think that would stop a friend from smiling or saying hello.

As the service ended one Sunday in late August, I turned to see Hanna Peshoff several rows back. Catching my eye, she moved in my direction and draped an arm across my shoulders. "How are you?" she asked.

As I updated her, a young man approached us and waited for a pause in the conversation. Hanna turned her attention to him, answered his question, and introduced him to me.

"Hello," I said, offering my hand.

He wouldn't take it, nor did he return my greeting. Rather, he turned his shoulder away from me.

Hanna said, "You can shake her hand. You won't hurt her."

"I'm good. I'm good," he said and walked away.

This young stranger had little power to hurt me, but I still felt pain. His behavior had painted a potent caricature of the way people behaved toward me on a regular basis.

Hanna gasped and covered her mouth. "I am so sorry, Melissa. I don't know why he did that."

"Don't worry about it," I said, hoping to make her feel better. "I'm fine."

His behavior wasn't her fault. It was almost funny, really. I wouldn't tell her I was used to it. I didn't want pity.

Though I considered myself an intelligent woman, it took months for me to realize that church didn't necessarily equal community. The revelation landed on me during communion, which always took place at the end of the first service of the month. I'd brought my rice cracker and a small jar of hibiscus tea for Brandon and me to share. The teaching pastor asked everyone to move toward the center of the sanctuary for the sake of easy distribution of the elements.

Brandon and I exchanged a glance.

"I'm not sitting out here by myself," I told him.

"Then you can sit in the foyer or out in the car," he said.

"No. We're moving." I grabbed my bag and moved toward the center of the sanctuary with everyone else.

Brandon followed, his jaw clenched, frustration seething off his skin. He took the plate of crackers and passed them over me. "Please leave," he whispered. "These perfumes are going to kill you."

It was as if he knew I was trying to hold back the cough building in my chest. What he didn't understand was that I was already dying—of loneliness and isolation. For four years, I'd wasted, separated from the body from which life flowed. I couldn't leave. I couldn't sit away from everyone. I'd rather be sick.

Coughs erupted from my chest when the service ended and crowd dispersed. Brandon waited for the bodies to thin and then, grabbing my arm and bag, ushered me out of the building and into the car. In silence, he treated me and left to retrieve the children.

"You would think my opinion mattered," he said on the ride home. "I'm the one who has to take care of you when you're sick."

"You don't get it," I said, too ill and heartbroken to explain.

* * *

Church wasn't working out. Every Sunday, I suffered a reaction to at least one trigger, hurried home, and spent the day in bed. There was little opportunity for real community, and there wasn't much anyone could do about it. Still, God had given me a command. A strange command, which probably meant it was important. Surely there was a way to obey. October arrived before a possible solution came to mind.

Nearly a year ago, our church had released a video through the weekly newsletter about a group who met for prayer on Sunday mornings. I'd wanted to join at the time, but when Brandon checked into it for me, the room had been freshly waxed, rendering it unsafe for me. In the video, a middle-aged man with a pleasant face invited anyone interested to join them during the first worship service.

It seemed a good solution. The group couldn't be more than a few people. They met for prayer, after all. Fewer people meant fewer fragrances I had to contend with. In smaller groups, community formed organically. No one could conveniently ignore me, nor could I hide.

I contacted the church administrator who'd worked with Brandon and me to figure out how to attend on Sunday mornings safely. "I don't think they meet anymore, but I can give you the leader's information," he said.

"Perfect." I jotted down David Wheeler's name and number.

I dialed the number a couple of weeks later on a Thursday afternoon during business hours, thinking he wouldn't likely answer. By the fourth ring, I was thinking up a message I could leave on his voice mail without exceeding the time limit.

"Hello?"

"Oh! Um, hi. Is this David Wheeler?"

"Yes, it is."

"My name is Melissa Keaster. Jeremy Pendergrass gave me your number. I was calling to find out about the prayer group that meets on Sunday mornings."

"Yes. Well, we don't actually meet anymore," he said.

"Oh." The news pricked, deflating me like a balloon. The disappointment surprised me. Jeremy had told me they'd stopped meeting. I'd had this man's phone number for two weeks and hadn't called. The sense of loss wasn't logical.

David explained that he'd formed the group because several people in the church had felt burdened to pray for our pastor who had been diagnosed with leukemia. Now that he was in remission, they no longer met. The story made me smile. I'd felt that same burden to pray and had spent several days in deep intercession for our pastor's healing. Somehow, this man and I had been riding similar wavelengths in the Spirit, and we didn't even know one another. But now what?

"What's on your heart?" he asked.

Holy loaded question, Batman. Where did I start?

"I've been a shut-in for several years now, but this summer God began speaking to me about community. I've been trying, but the nature of my disease makes social interaction difficult." I explained my illness and symptoms, hoping I wasn't boring him or taking up too much of his time. He listened so quietly, I might have thought I'd lost him except for an occasional utterance of empathy.

"I'm just trying to be obedient and find out what it is that God has in mind," I said, unsure of the reason tears had formed in my eyes.

"Mmm. Several of us who met for prayer on Sunday morning continue to meet at the Siegmunds' house on Friday nights. We meet tomorrow night, actually. Do you know Bruce and Pamela?"

"No."

"Well, that doesn't matter. Anyone who wants to come is invited. This bunch loves to pray for people. We usually have a meal at six, followed by worship and prayer at seven."

"I need to speak with my husband," I said. "It isn't safe for me to drive a long distance alone. But could I come at seven just for the meeting?"

"Absolutely," he said.

I hesitated. Many triggers lurked in homes. If I didn't mention them, I could end up reacting during the meeting. My reactions could be frightening and disruptive. Preparation would be the lesser inconvenience. "I'm sorry to ask this, but could you let the Siegmunds know that I might be coming? I'm highly sensitive to candles, air fresheners, strong perfume, hand sanitizer, and peanut particles. I also can't do balloons. I will wear a mask, but if everyone knows, the chances of me getting sick will be a lot lower."

"Sure thing," he said. "Can you repeat that list? I'd like to write it down."

God, I'm such a burden.

I repeated the list. David thanked me, which made the tears spill down my cheeks. No one ever thanked me for telling them all the things they couldn't have or do in my presence. "I'll let you know whether or not I'm coming after I have a chance to talk to my husband."

"Sounds good," he said.

"Thank you."

"You're welcome. I hope to see you tomorrow night."

The call ended. What was it I was feeling?

David's final words described it best.

Hope. I hoped.

* * *

Brandon listened, but a wall of resistance rose in his eyes.

"I know it's risky, but so is church, and I really want to go," I said.

He finished chewing and swallowed slowly. In my impatience, I wondered if he really needed all that time to think or if he was just making me wait for kicks.

Warm pressure formed against the backs of my eyeballs. If he didn't answer soon, blood might shoot out.

"Tomorrow is the Big Serve," he said.

"I remember." Brandon had volunteered to help the students and staff at Micah's school build an exhibit at the local zoo as a service project.

"It'll be a long day. I have to get up early, and the labor will be fairly hard. How long will this meeting last?"

"David said it officially ends at nine, but that's when they usually start to pray for people. I'd like them to pray for me." A drop of warm moisture trickled down my cheek. "Ugh," I said, wiping it away. What was the deal with all these tears?

Brandon's wall melted from brick to mud. "You really want to go, don't you?"

"Yes. God has something for me there."

His long, slow sigh bespoke the weight of the sacrifice.

"Okay."

* * *

Brandon dragged in the next night later than either of us had anticipated, dusty and disheveled. One look at him almost convinced me to relent. Almost.

I handed him a dish of hot food. "Want to let me drive so you can eat?"

He took the dish and set it down. "I'll eat and drive. Just let me change my clothes."

We pulled into the driveway after seven. I braced myself to walk into a room full of strangers several minutes late wearing a mask. "Are you sure you won't come in?" I asked.

"I'm sure. It feels good out here. I'm going to lean back, read for a few, and take a nap," he said.

I didn't understand, but neither did I press the issue. He'd brought me here when he would have preferred to be at home in bed.

"Text me if you start to feel anything," he said.

"Okay."

He leaned toward me. "I'm serious."

I swallowed. "Okay."

His lips touched mine, and I stepped out into the cool October night, thankful the temperature hadn't dipped below sixty degrees. Had it been any colder, Brandon would have used the excuse to keep me at home.

A window revealed a man who wore thick-framed glasses and looked to be near my mom's age. He spoke to a group of about twenty people. With a trembling hand, I knocked at the front door. A beautiful woman with large dark eyes and a demure smile answered, radiating hospitality and peace. "Hello. Welcome. They are meeting in there," she said, pointing toward the hall. Her African accent and the rich timbre of her voice moved through my soul like music.

"Thank you." I stepped through the doorway and was met with a sensation unfamiliar yet clearly recognizable. The love of God was so thick inside the home that it fragranced the air. I tasted it. I waded through it as I made my way to the room.

The man who spoke paused midsentence and said, "Hi, Melissa. I'm Bruce. Make yourself comfortable."

I answered with a timid wave and spotted an empty seat. Several people made eye contact and offered warm smiles. A quick glance told me I knew none of them. Bruce resumed his speech, making jokes to which the group responded with soft laughter.

The attendees comprised children, middle-aged adults, and some with silver hair and wisdom carved into the lines of their faces. A Black couple who looked to be near my age sat in one corner. An Asian girl sat on the couch. A range of ages, different races, and multiple nationalities were represented in this small group.

I was trying to figure out which one might be David when Bruce said, "David is coming, but he'll be late. This afternoon on his way home from work, he witnessed a car accident. Someone was actually thrown from the vehicle. David stayed with him until paramedics arrived. I'd like to take some time to pray for that man and for a few others we know who need prayer."

My mask hid my delighted grin. What a bunch of weirdos we all were—misfits gathered to pray and worship on a Friday night.

And God responded. His presence felt corporeal. I'd never experienced him like this before. It was as though he was serving us all a tiny sliver of heaven in that place. How fantastic it was to be with people who recognized the gift and reveled in it with me.

After some time spent in intercessory prayer, we sang along to several older worship choruses. A local dentist led a Bible study about the kingdom that has come and the kingdom that is coming. His teaching was excellent, rooted deeply in the Word of God. No one cared that David came in late or that he spoke a soft greeting to me before he took a seat. No one minded that others left early.

At the close of the Bible study, Bruce moved a metal folding chair to the center of the room. "We're officially finished for the night, but we'll open up this extra-special holy chair for anyone who would like to receive prayer."

A chorus of snickers hung in the air in response to the joke. A couple of people rose from their seats. I expected them to sit in the chair, but they left the room. Seconds stretched into a minute. My insides fluttered as if they were keeping time. David had said these people loved to pray. I'd already seen that. God was here. And everyone was aware of the new girl wearing the mask in the back of the room. That empty chair was the reason I'd come.

I moved to the chair so quickly that my vision didn't black out from the drop in blood pressure until I'd plopped down. With no plan or filter, my story rushed out—my illness, the struggle, publishing decisions about my novel, Brandon's job disappointment. The last few sentences were a blubbered mess.

Some leaned forward in their seats. Others had gathered around me. Eyes shone with tears. I hadn't encountered such compassionate listeners in a long while. Each one took a turn praying. Others whispered behind me. It took me a moment to realize I couldn't comprehend what they were saying because they were praying in unknown tongues.

Years ago, I'd attended a service in which the pastor tried to force someone to pray in tongues to provide evidence of their salvation. I'd hated that. I'd left the service in a fury. He'd done this to a teenage girl my age. It was wrong. This, I liked. It sounded like peace, comfort, and love. It flowed like music. The presence of God thickened with the utterances. I released my theological prejudices and opened myself to whatever God wanted to give me. He would reveal anything that wasn't meant for me, and I would give it back to him.

The prayers were beautiful. God gave a man named Henry a picture for me. In the picture, Henry saw a dark room with a burning candle, dim at first, but slowly growing brighter until the whole room was filled with light. He said, "I believe that is what God has been doing in your life and what he will continue to do."

The picture immediately reminded me of something God had spoken to me early on in the illness. Healing would be a process. It would take a lot of hard work. But what if "hard work" hadn't meant what I'd thought?

A couple of people prayed I would leave without suffering from a reaction, and I immediately began to feel better. When they finished, I checked the time. The hour had grown late without me realizing it. I thanked them all for praying for me and walked outside to find Brandon asleep in the car. He stirred when I opened the door.

I poked him. "Want me to drive home?"

"That's okay." His words were thick with sleep as he adjusted his seat to an upright position. He yawned. "How was it?"

How did one describe the indescribable? "Amazing." Such a weak adjective. "I want to come back to the next meeting."

A deep noise rose from his throat. "And when is that?"

"Two weeks from tonight."

Regardless of how Brandon felt about it, I knew he would bring me back. He loved me more than he loved himself. He'd proved it time and again. And I had to come back. I'd discovered the thing for which God had sent me searching. He was just getting started showing me whatever good thing he had up his sleeve, and I had to see it through.

37

A New Family

Cars filled the driveway and spilled onto the street. Brandon whistled low. "Looks like more people this time. Sure you want to try this?"

"Yep!" I'd been looking forward to the meeting for two weeks. Crowded or not, I wasn't going to miss it.

"I'm going to run to Walmart for a few things. Text me if you need me," he said.

"Got it."

He puckered his lips.

"Thank you," I said and kissed him.

Bruce was introducing himself and the speaker for the night when I claimed the only empty seat in the room. He interrupted himself to say hello again and continued on. Glancing around, I noticed several new faces, some my own age. The man beside me was new. The scent of his cologne passed through my double-masked barrier into my sinuses, which began to swell.

God, please don't let this reaction get out of control. I want to stay.

Worship began, and the man stood and moved to the center of the room. He looked to be in his early fifties, like Bruce, and had a face like Woody Harrelson's with a pronounced chin. Fractals of light glinted off his glasses, at times obscuring his sharp blue eyes. Everyone else remained seated, so I felt free to do the same. Before the song began, the man prayed in a loud voice. "Holy Spirit, come more. You are welcome here."

Closing my eyes, I silently agreed with the prayer.

The man sang loudly off-key, spontaneously shouting, "Hallelujah!" and "Jesus!" here and there. Cool air rushed past my face. I opened my eyes to find him dancing. Once, he twirled.

Having grown up in a Baptist church, I'd never witnessed such demonstrative worship. Where I'd come from, some might've judged his behavior as showboating, an attempt to get attention. I didn't sense that at all, and I had an excellent nose for counterfeit. Only God could see our hearts, but his worship felt genuine to me. The passion behind it reminded me of David dancing before the ark of the covenant as it was carried into Jerusalem. I appreciated the freedom in the room to sit and receive, to sing from our seats, or to dance like fools before the Lord. The man obviously didn't care what anyone thought. I appreciated that too.

A young man from a church plant in Baton Rouge spoke about our authority in Christ, sharing testimonies of miraculous salvations, repentance, and healing. "We know it's God's will that everyone be restored and healed in heaven, so when we pray 'your kingdom come, your will be done on earth as it is in heaven,' we must realize that healing is a part of that," he said.

I'd never considered the topic of healing from that angle. Though I wasn't sure I agreed, I wanted to hear him out. He taught the importance of faith, with which I absolutely agreed. Why would anyone ask for something they didn't believe to be possible? This question led to another—did I believe? And another—was I somehow standing in the way of my own healing?

Theoretical belief came easily enough. Miracles had happened before; they could happen again. But what of applicable belief—belief that a miracle could happen to *me*? When I'd considered healing in the past, I believed God would lead me to the right doctor or diet or medication, and that I would improve over time. I had only recently considered the possibility of a sudden unexplainable healing.

The young man concluded his teaching and said, "I know it's getting late. How about we all pray with a neighbor?"

No one sat on my right. That left me with the neighbor to my left. The Woody Harrelson character who had twirled before the Lord. Of course. "I'm Melissa," I said, offering my hand.

He took it and gave it a single shake. "Tim. How can I pray for you?"

"Well, I've been sick with this crazy allergic disease for a long time. Hence, the mask." I tapped it and explained some of my symptoms. He listened quietly.

"I would love for God to heal me," I said. "After tonight, I can't help but wonder if my own lack of faith is getting in the way. But if God is most glorified in my sickness, I want to submit to that."

"May I put my hand on your shoulder?" he asked.

I hesitated. Throughout the night, my fibromyalgia had worsened. During flares like this, my skin was so sensitive that the lightest touch was painful. At home, I always let Brandon know when I felt like this so he wouldn't touch me. And yet I didn't want to miss a single thing God had for me, so I nodded.

He placed his hand on my left shoulder with no way to know that most of my pain concentrated there. "Lord, I ask you to release my sister from any burden of guilt or doubt that she isn't enough or that she doesn't have enough faith to be healed." Immediately, the feeling of not-enoughness dropped away.

He paused to pray in tongues. In that moment, a gentle heat spread from his hand into my shoulder and neck, erasing the pain as it went. He prayed for my digestive system. I didn't feel discomfort there, but my head cleared. I hadn't realized how fuzzy it was. The wheezy feeling in my chest dissipated. My sinuses opened.

If I hadn't been wearing my mask, he might have seen my jaw drop. I'd experienced something similar when Arthur, our taxi driver in Rochester, had prayed for me. I'd gotten some relief at the last meeting, but it had faded by the next morning. How long would it last this time? "How can I pray for you?" I asked.

"Just for more of God."

After I prayed for him, he said, "Earlier, you said you believed that God is glorified in your sickness. Answer me this—where in the Bible does sickness glorify God?"

"John 9. The blind man," I said.

A dimple formed in his cheek. "Was it the blindness that glorified God or the healing?"

My brow furrowed without my permission.

"Read it," he said and left before I could process what had happened.

As I sat in thought, David Wheeler joined me on the couch. I checked my phone but saw no messages from Brandon. Assuming he hadn't made it back, I shared with

David my exchange with Tim. "I have a friend who died of cancer last year," I told him. "If everything depended on faith, she would be healed, and I would be dead."

David nodded soberly. "That's part of the mystery. We don't know why God heals one person and not another, or why someone is born into disability while another child is born healthy."

David's phone dinged. He checked it and grinned. "Tim asks me to invite you to our Personal Prayer Ministry training class on Sunday night. It's based on a healing ministry out of Bethel Church in Redding, California. Would you like to come?"

The words "healing ministry" put together like that set off an alarm in my brain. "Maybe," I said.

"We meet this Sunday evening at my house. Five o'clock."

"Can I bring my mom?" Her BS detector was better than mine.

"Sure." He shrugged.

"Okay, then. I'll be there," I said, wondering what kind of whack-a-doo rabbit hole I'd just agreed to jump into.

* * *

Tim's parting question sent me to the Gospels. I read them all—Matthew, Mark, Luke, and John—pausing at each account of healing. In most cases, Jesus didn't approach the sick without some sort of invitation. The ones who were well enough congregated around him, waiting among the desperate masses to be touched. Blind men called out to him from the side of the road. Some were carried to him by friends and family. Others came to Jesus interceding on behalf of a beloved invalid.

There was no account in scripture of Jesus ever turning someone away empty handed. Not one. A very few, conditioned by decades of suffering to believe they would never be healed, he plucked out of the crowd. Because he was that good.

Another thing I noticed was that Jesus rarely stopped at restoring sick flesh. He forgave sin. He sent lepers and blind men to the priests, who had the power to restore them to worship with the congregation. When one father lacked faith, he addressed the father's lack with his abundance and healed his son. The woman with the bleeding issue, who had captured my attention for so long, would have been happy with a quick cure for her physical ailment, but for Jesus, physical healing wasn't enough.

I studied the passage in Luke 8 again the morning before the prayer ministry meeting at David's house. Jesus had been on his way to heal a sick child who would die without his touch, and he'd stopped for a woman who had suffered for twelve years with a chronic illness. Years of persistent pain. "Like me," I whispered.

Also like me, she'd believed in Jesus's power but doubted his kindness, and so—out of fear—had tried to remain hidden. Jesus called her out of the crowd, not because he hadn't known who had touched him, but because he wanted more for her than she'd wanted for herself. He knew her real freedom lay in stepping out of the shadows and into the light. It lay in deliverance from rejection and fear, in the comfort of being known and loved by God and the community in which he'd placed her.

The woman's illness, like mine, was hidden, but it kept her separated from everyone, ceremonially unclean. The moment of saving faith wasn't when she'd reached for the Savior's hem in secret; it was when she'd stepped out "in the presence of all the people," renouncing fear and isolation. The throng—the inconvenience, the roadblock, the thing crushing her and Jesus—was the very thing God employed to draw out a sidelined sick woman and the means by which she was restored, so that she could, as Jesus commanded, go in peace.

The story remained with me throughout the day. I shared my insights with Mom on the drive to David's house that afternoon.

"I could use some restoration," Mom said. "I'm absolutely empty. If I didn't love you so much and if I didn't feel like God wanted me to go, I would've stayed home tonight and rested."

Having noticed the bags under her eyes and the sag of her shoulders over the weekend, I had prayed for that very thing. I'd invited her because I wanted her help navigating any theologically unsound waters, but I hoped she would receive a personal touch from God as well. "Maybe you'll get some tonight," I said.

"That would be nice." Mom turned onto a long drive toward a beautiful old house set on a hill.

"Wow," I said.

"This is nice," Mom agreed.

David greeted us in the foyer painted in an inviting shade of yellow and led us into a room my brain wanted to label "parlor," which featured a grand piano and large windows that looked out into a well-kept yard. Everyone had already gathered and smiled in greeting. A young woman who looked to be in her twenties sat next to Tim. Her thick brown hair was pulled back into a ponytail that cascaded down her back.

She studied me with curious blue eyes. I smiled, knowing she might not be able to see it behind my mask but hoping she would feel it all the same. David took a seat at the piano and led us in worship.

A warm comforting presence enveloped me as we sang to the accompaniment of rhythmic chords. I'd sung with groups of great skill without this level of intimate fellowship with God. We would've sung the entire night had it been up to me, but after three songs, David played a recording of a teaching on forgiveness.

"The beginning of healing is forgiveness," the teacher said. I listened to the entire teaching with a discerning ear, following along in scripture, and found no fault with anything said. The teaching ended, and I made a silent request. *God, show me who I need to forgive, and grant me the grace and courage to do it.*

A throat cleared in the corner of the room. I looked up to see the young woman's hand raised. "David, I...um...I have a prayer word for Melissa."

David smiled. "Perfect. We're almost finished with training and ready to launch Personal Prayer Ministry. Tonight, we will split into small groups to practice some of the tools we've learned. Melanie and Melissa, if you're comfortable with it, Erica and Pamela can partner with you for practice."

I looked to Mom, who smiled and shrugged. "Sure," I said.

The young woman—Erica, I presumed—left the room for a moment. She returned, wiping her palms on her jeans, and looked as though she was trying to control her breath. "I'm Erica. Tim and Laura's daughter," she said.

"Nice to meet you. I'm Melissa," I said.

Pamela Siegmund, the beautiful Black woman I had met at the first meeting I'd attended, moved close and asked, "Is there anything you would like us to pray for?"

Mom remained silent and watchful. I mentioned Sara, who had recently shown several signs of rebellion, and asked for wisdom concerning how to meet her needs. They prayed, and then Erica cleared her throat again. I silently prayed for her courage and waited as she wiped her hands on her jeans one more time.

"I have trouble remembering things I read, even in the Bible," she said, "so I don't know all the stories or where they're found. But today, I was reading about the woman with the bleeding issue."

I glanced over my shoulder at Mom, who stared back at me with tears in her eyes.

"I believe you have that woman's faith," Erica continued. "I believe God will heal you. I don't know when, and I don't know how—whether it will happen over time or all at once—but healing is coming.

"God healed me all at once this past summer. I was like Humpty Dumpty. All the king's horses and all the king's men couldn't put Humpty Dumpty together again. But the King can. I believe God healed me on a molecular level, and I believe he will heal you on a molecular level."

Her words echoed my prayers. They addressed my fear of not having enough faith. They spoke of healing on the molecular level. Hadn't I prayed for God to heal my blood? Tears rolled down both of Mom's cheeks. I was so thankful to have her with me as a witness.

"You know, I don't know if I care whether God heals my food allergies," I said. "I'm used to them at this point, but I want to be free of this mask. I want to bear my own burdens and be free to minister to others. This mask gets in the way of that."

Erica moved from the end of the couch to kneel in front of me. Her eyes locked with mine. She took my hand and said, "This probably isn't what you want to hear, but I feel like God is saying that your mask isn't a hindrance to your ministry. It's part of your story, and you can minister just fine with it." Then she prayed the desire of my heart anyway, closing with, "And God, I ask that she will be able to have her cake and eat it too. May she be able to eat any kind of birthday cake she wants by her next birthday."

I smiled. That would be nice. Unlikely, but nice. I hadn't had a normal birthday cake since my wheat allergy emerged in 2005.

When Erica finished her prayer, I said, "You should know that I have identified with the woman with the bleeding issue since 2013. I wrote a poem about her and everything. Just this morning, I revisited that passage of scripture, and Mom and I were talking about it on the way here. That word you gave me—it was from God."

When we had returned to the car, Mom said, "Wow."

"Yeah. Wow." I chuckled in awe.

"We have to get those ministry materials and train with them. This is the missing link to what we're already doing. It's what the world needs," she said. "And oh my gosh! The worship!"

"I know, right?" I agreed.

"I've never had this happen before, but God restored me while we sang. I feel light and full of energy. Filled up instead of empty. Like, I can face the week now."

A soft laugh escaped my lips. "Praise God." It was about time she benefited from all the service she rendered to me.

"These people are the real deal," she said, pulling onto the highway.

"Believe me, I know."

God had sent me on a search for community, knowing all the while what I'd find—a family. A family who would see my tired faith, stand in the gap, and believe for me.

* * *

The prayer ministry team met again two weeks later. This time, Brandon let me attend alone. "If you react, I figure they'll pray for you, and you'll be fine," he said with a wink.

It was strange driving myself nearly an hour away from home. For fun. Of course, my idea of fun was rather peculiar in its own right. The only people I knew who got excited over prayer meetings were the weirdos I was on my way to meet.

The recorded teaching that night was on physical healing. Dr. Francis MacNutt of Christian Healing Ministries didn't spend much time making a theological case for healing. He was more concerned with the practical aspects of praying for healing, such as the roles of touch, words, and authority. His humility and blend of scripture and testimony made the instruction accessible despite my ignorance of the subject, and the simplicity with which he taught left me feeling like I could leave the meeting and pray for almost anyone.

When the recording ended, Tim asked David for permission to speak. David nodded.

"We have to get over this idea that God wants people to be sick and that it somehow brings him glory," Tim said. "God hates sickness. He used it in the Old Testament as judgment. In the New Testament, God's judgment fell on Jesus. Today, he disciplines us through circumstances—

consequences, financial hardship, and persecution—but he doesn't use sickness. We can pray for the sick with the assurance that it's always God's will to heal."

I recalled a question I'd been wrestling with. Trembling, I raised my hand. Tim nodded to me, and I took a steadying breath. "What about 2 Corinthians 12, where Paul asks God to remove the thorn in his flesh three times and God says no?"

Light reflected off the lenses of his glasses as he cocked his head. "What evidence do we have that the thorn was a physical ailment? The man had been beaten within an inch of his life multiple times. He'd been shipwrecked, stoned, and imprisoned. There were times he went hungry and didn't sleep. How would a sick man survive all that while traveling the world telling people about Jesus?"

The pitch of his voice rose with each phrase of his defense. I couldn't tell if he was angry or simply impassioned, and I couldn't answer his question.

Laura, his wife, placed a hand on his leg. He paused, blinked, and said softly, "If you will look at a few different commentaries, you'll find that many theologians believe the thorn was an agitating spirit. Does that answer your question?"

"For now," I said, amused at their exchange.

Tim continued his speech, and I flipped over to 2 Corinthians 12 in my John MacArthur study Bible. His notes on verse 7 read, "Paul's use of the word 'messenger'…from Satan suggests the 'thorn in the flesh'…was a demonized person, not a physical illness."

Well then.

"We're almost organized and ready to take applications for Personal Prayer Ministry," Tim said. "If any of you want a session, let Erica know. She'll send you a copy of the application and get a team together for you."

I raised my hand again.

"Yes?" Tim asked.

"I want an application and your first available time," I said.

Tim and Erica exchanged glances. "I'll be leading this one," Tim said to her.

"I'm on it too," Erica said, making a note.

"Me too," said Pamela.

"You can have the session at my office," David said. "I want to hang around to intercede anyway."

"All right then," Tim said. "Talk to Erica after the meeting, and we'll get you scheduled."

We moved through the conversation within seconds. It was as if they'd all expected this moment and had prepared for it in their own minds. In a snap, they'd assembled.

For me.

I fought to hold back the tears. Church hadn't trained me for this. To receive love. To witness people roll up their sleeves and make a plan to dig me out of my pit.

The whole prayer session thing was still a mystery to me. While I had only a vague idea of what to expect, God had sent me to these people so they could pray for me. Whatever I'd signed up for was the next step of the journey he had me on.

I felt it in my marrow—God was about to do something. Something big. Aslan was on the move.

38

Touched

The light of the computer screen mocked me. The application demanded information about all the things that hurt, like some kind of sadist that enjoyed my pain. How to bring all my darkness into the full view of my friends? What would they think of me after they read my rap sheet?

Excessive fear/anxiety. Check.

Depression. Check.

Grief/Loss. Check.

Pride. Ugh. Check.

Loneliness. Check.

Uncontrolled anger. Check.

Chronic illness. Duh.

Unforgiveness/Bitterness. Probably.

Sexual abuse. Cringe…check.

Compulsive sinful behaviors (e.g., sexual sin, anger, chemical indulgence). Guilty as charged.

Self-hatred. Well, now that you mention it—check.

Please list your most significant traumas.

Please describe some of your feelings.

Did I really want to go through with this? I didn't have long for internal debate. Erica had given me a time slot for Sunday night in lieu of training. "Jesus, help me," I said, beginning to type.

That morning, I'd read Jesus's words in Luke 11—
"Therefore take heed that the light which is in you is not
darkness"—which indicated that we had some responsibility
for our own blindness. I wanted to be full of light, like the
room in Henry's vision, but I harbored dark corners in my
soul. Fear, anger, shame, and lust had held on to me since
childhood. The cycle of "sin, repent, repeat" had grown old,
and I was sick of it.

Each question brought events and people to mind.
Betrayals, attacks, wound after wound. The police officer
who had pulled me over that night for no legitimate reason
and had terrorized me with threats of jail and gestures to his
gun. The teacher who had watched little boys molest me and
hadn't stopped them. The pastor who had accused me of
insanity and witchcraft to my grandmother.

My answers were a drawn map to the skeletons in my
closets, but God was about to deep clean the whole house,
which was something I wanted more than physical healing at
this point. Mast cell activation disease I could live with. The
darkness had become unbearable.

After emailing the completed application to Erica, I had
nothing to do but wait. One might think I'd be accustomed
to waiting after all this time, but a week had never lasted so
long or given me so much creative space to overthink the
moment my new friends would discover how awful I really
was. Finally, Saturday night arrived. One more sleep, and I
would be free.

I sat down with the kids to read a Bible story and pray
with them before bed, as I always did when I was well
enough. After the story, I closed the Bible and said,
"Tomorrow, some people are going to pray for me. They're

going to ask God to heal me. It will be an important and special day."

"Mama, I'm going to pray for you," Sara said. She cuddled up next to me, laid a hand on my shoulder, and prayed in a strong voice. "Dear Jesus, please help Mama be able to handle da cold so she can go to church wiff us and so she can play in da snow wiff me."

Micah wouldn't be outdone. "Please help Mama to feel better soon," he prayed simply.

Those sweet little prayers carried holy weight. I tucked them into my heart to ponder as I drifted off to sleep.

The next morning, the Holy Spirit led me to Joel 2:25—"So I will restore to you the years that the swarming locust has eaten"—and gave it to me as a promise. I stared at the words on the page, which compelled me to speak out my own. "Mast cell activation disease, it's been quite a ride, but today I say goodbye."

I briefly wondered whether I should fast to prepare for the session but then realized any fast today would be nothing more than an attempt to make a deal with God. I couldn't earn my freedom any more than I could've earned my salvation. Jubilee was a gift. The only proper response was celebration.

* * *

"It's going to get down to thirty-nine tonight," Brandon said, an edge in his voice.

"I'll be sure to layer up," I said. Nothing would keep me from going. "Besides, you'll be there to take care of my sick keister if anything goes wrong."

"Is this place you're going even safe?" he asked.

"They know I can't tolerate air fresheners or perfume. That should cover it."

He sighed.

I turned into him and wrapped my arms around his waist. "Please don't worry. Something amazing is going to happen tonight. God has me. You can hang your cape, Superman."

With a grunt, he went outside to clear the passenger seat in his truck.

I understood. For years, he'd watched me improve an inch and then lose a foot. Experience had conditioned him to be wary of any hint of good. Tonight, experience wasn't allowed to dictate my expectation.

"Lord, don't disappoint him. He needs this as much as I do," I prayed.

Brandon held my gloved hand for the entire drive. It was cold, but I hadn't reacted on the walk to the truck. Brandon had had it running and warm when I'd climbed in.

We parked in front of the office building several minutes before the session was scheduled to begin. Tim and Erica pulled in behind us. Tim stepped out of his truck, introduced himself to Brandon, and shook his hand. After they exchanged a few words, Brandon looked at me intently and said, "Text me when you're done."

I kissed him and followed Tim and Erica up the steps to the entrance.

David greeted us in the foyer. "Follow me. All the air fresheners are turned off, and the office is warm. You can let me know if we need to adjust the temperature. I'll be in the foyer praying," he said, leading us down a dimly lit hallway.

The office was cozy and comfortable, not messy or too neat, as I would expect of a psychologist. I detected a faint fragrance in the air and decided to wear my masks to prevent the interruption of a reaction. Pamela arrived as I shed my coat, hat, and gloves.

Tim pulled out a copy of my application and squinted down at it. "I will lead your session today. Pamela will act as a second, and Erica will write down all the good things that happen. Everything you wrote on this application and everything you share with us today is strictly confidential. If anyone talks about what happens today outside of this office, they're off the team." He rattled off a list of dos and don'ts and asked me to close my eyes.

"Imagine you're on the beach," he said. "What do you see?"

Immediately, a picture of the Pacific coast formed in my mind. I saw the dark-blue water, the brown sand. The waves crashed noisily on the shore. Gulls called to one another. Cool air ruffled my curls as sunlight warmed my skin. I described everything I was experiencing.

"Can you imagine God the Father there with you?" Tim asked.

To my right, a large being emanated light brighter than the sun, obscuring his features. He felt like a man and not like a man. Kind eyes looked at me through the blinding light. At first, they appeared to be brown and then not a color. At least not a color I knew.

I described the Father as I saw him, and Tim asked me to envision Jesus. This was easier. A man appeared, brown skinned and strong with dark shoulder-length hair, a full beard, and brown eyes. Next, I asked the Holy Spirit to join us. He appeared as a white dove enshrined in light. His wings fluttered above me, covering me in his shadow. I couldn't bring a single face into focus, but I recognized the comforting presence of the God I knew and loved.

"I'd like you to go back to the memory of the police officer who stopped you at night several years ago," Tim said.

Before he'd finished the sentence, I sat in my car on the side of a dark highway, my friend Madonna in the passenger seat. Red and blue lights flashed in my rearview mirror. All the fear came rushing back. The officer's disproportionate anger. My confusion about the reason he'd pulled me over.

"Now ask Jesus to show you where he was," Tim said.

"Jesus, show me where you were," I prayed aloud. At once, Jesus appeared at the front of the car on the passenger side. He followed me to the back of the car when the officer told me to get out. He stood with me as the officer gestured at his gun and threatened to take me to jail.

"Ask Jesus, 'What lie did I believe about this situation?'" Tim said.

I repeated the question.

That you were alone, and this man wanted to hurt you.

I reported the lie.

"Ask Jesus for the truth."

I have never left you, and I never will.

Aloud, I renounced the lie and declared the truth.

Tim said, "Ask Jesus what you need to do."

"Jesus, what do I need to do here?"

Pray for him to be saved.

In the memory, I reached out and touched the man's shoulder and prayed he would come to Jesus for salvation.

"Good," Tim said. "Now repeat this prayer of forgiveness after me."

Phrase by phrase, I repeated a prayer of forgiveness and release.

A loud clap startled me, and I nearly jumped out of my chair.

Tim grinned. "I'm sorry. I meant to warn you before the session. I'll clap after something happens. It helps the brain process the memory differently."

"Oh. Okay," I said, my heart still racing.

"Close your eyes again," he said gently.

Next, Tim directed me to forgive several of the doctors I'd seen. After each prayer of forgiveness and release, Tim clapped, at which point the memory disappeared and the scene changed.

Tim asked, "Where do you go when I clap?"

"My bathtub. It's where I like to pray," I said.

"That's your safe place. If you ever feel afraid in any of your memories, you can go there. Okay?"

"Okay."

When it was time to forgive Dr. Hall, Jesus revealed that I wasn't nearly as upset with her as I was with him. The lie I believed about her treatment was that God had led me to her to betray me. And so, I had to renounce the lie and forgive him. It had never before occurred to me that I was angry with God. I'd actually believed he was angry with me, a lie he refuted after I had released him from my judgments.

From there, Jesus brought me to the kitchen of the house where Brandon and I had lived before moving to Bear Creek, where the trouble had multiplied so rapidly. Brandon and I were arguing, as we often did back then. He wanted to move; I didn't. I felt it was a mistake. But then Jesus showed up and told me to allow Brandon to make the mistake. I forgave Brandon and found myself in our bedroom the night of the demonic visitation at our house on Bear Creek Road.

Fear snaked around my chest and throat as I watched the demon walk over to my side of the bed and touch me.

"What's happening?" Tim asked.

I described the scene.

"Ask Jesus for the lie you believed about the situation that night."

"I'm alone." The words, which had so often felt true, stung.

"What is the truth?"

Stand still, and let me fight for you.

I reported what I heard in my spirit. Tim said, "Repeat after me—I release authority over to Jesus to defend me and to take dominion over me and my family."

In the memory, Brandon muttered at my side. The evil spirit disappeared, and Jesus took its place. He touched my leg where the spirit had touched me. In place of a deathly chill, a warm energy passed through my body. Jesus took another step toward me and touched my left forearm. A warm tingling sensation passed through my fingertips, up my arm to my elbow and across my lower back.

"What's happening?" Tim asked.

"Jesus touched me," I whispered in awe.

"What does it feel like?" he asked.

"It feels like...life."

A soft laugh rumbled in Tim's chest. "It's a transfusion from death to life."

Of course it was. I'd asked him to heal my blood.

"Sit back, and enjoy it," Tim said.

And for a few moments, I was left alone to experience something so completely outside of my theological context or experience that all I *could* do was enjoy it.

More forgiveness followed. I released the pastor who had betrayed and accused me so harshly along with others. At Tim's clap, I returned to the bathtub. I gasped at the sight of an infant Sara in my arms.

"Are you back in your safe place?" Tim asked.

"Yes."

"Who's with you?"

"My baby. Sara."

"Good. Why don't you forgive her too?"

Of all the people who had appeared in my session that night, she surprised me the most. With hot tears soaking into my mask, I gazed into the face of my baby girl. She was as lovely in my imagination as she had been in reality. "I forgive you. I forgive you for how my pregnancy made me so sick and for your delivery that was so hard. I forgive you for being so sick when I was falling apart and couldn't take care of myself because I had to take care of you. It's so easy to forgive, baby girl. I would've done it already had I known. I release you from every judgment I ever made. I love you so much I would do it again and again and again."

I smiled—the first genuine smile I'd ever smiled when I thought about her babyhood. The memories of that season had always made me cringe in the past. Now, I could think about my precious baby girl and smile.

Finally, we addressed the memories I dreaded most, beginning in my kindergarten classroom. I forgave the boys who touched me and the teacher who let them. Jesus told me it wasn't my fault. We prayed for soul ties to be broken and for the return of my dignity and purity. I repeated these steps with the girls who later entered my life and pulled me into sexual experimentation while I was still a young child.

"Ask Jesus if he was ashamed of you," Tim said.

No. Never.

I renounced my shame and handed over my sexual sins to my Savior. In exchange, Jesus gave me a white bathrobe to clothe me and a crown for my head, symbols of righteousness I did not deserve and could never earn.

Jesus took me by the hand and led me into the throne room, which was so bright with white light that I couldn't make out anything except the large throne my Father sat upon. Father scooped me up and set me on his lap, where I rested with my head against his chest. His heart beat like thunder, and he smelled like rain. He closed the doors to fear, anger, and sexual sin in my life. One by one, I heard them slam in the distance.

"Ask him if you can return here anytime you want."

Father answered before I finished asking the question. *Yes.*

Tim then led me to forgive myself for everything I'd done and to receive the Father's love without conditions. When I opened my eyes, Tim said, "From this point forward, let everything past, present, and future lead you to the Father. He will teach you to change the judgment on your life, your sin, and your illness."

I nodded though I wasn't certain I understood.

Pamela and Erica laid hands on me and prayed for complete healing and for what the Holy Spirit had accomplished that night to be sealed. When we finished, I looked at my phone. The time read 8:30 p.m. We'd been in prayer for over three hours!

Brandon and David were chatting in the foyer. They looked up when we entered the room.

"Well?" Brandon said.

"It was powerful. Lots to process," I said.

David grinned. "Good to hear."

I looked at Tim. "I'm tired."

His dimple deepened. "That's normal. Rest tomorrow if you can."

"Okay. Thank you. All of you. That was amazing."

After we said our goodbyes, Brandon guided me into the cold. No reaction prevented me from recounting all that God had done on the ride home.

39

Unmasked

The morning after the session, I felt different. The difference wasn't physical as I'd expected. Physically, I felt quite tired. I spent the day resting, as Tim had recommended, and processing all that had happened. At times, a feeling of mortification overwhelmed me. A memory reel of my most shameful moments and embarrassing mistakes played through my mind on repeat until I wanted to hide my face in the bedsheets.

Shame had come to call. Lucky me.

The prayer tools used in the session had worked yesterday. There was no reason they couldn't work for me at home. I visualized David's office and my new friends sitting around me as they witnessed an account of my sins.

"Jesus, show me where you are," I prayed.

Jesus appeared at the center of the room.

"What is the lie I believe?"

That you are disgusting and shameful.

I renounced the lie. "Jesus, please rebuke the spirit of shame attacking me."

The compulsion to cover my face vanished. I intentionally recalled several cringe-worthy moments and was able to smile. God loved me even when I felt like an embarrassment.

That afternoon, I crawled out of bed, groggy from a long nap. The kids were already awake. Loosed from their rooms, they requested a snack and a movie. I obliged. Dinner prep would require lots of chopping, and it would take a while. Once the kids were settled, I snapped on a pair of nitrile gloves, pushed in my earbuds, and set my iPod to play a worship mix.

Roasted parsnips had become a favorite. It was difficult to make enough to satisfy both Brandon and me and have a little left over for his lunch the next day. I pulled out four from the refrigerator to peel and slice into fries. The task complete, I frowned.

My hands didn't itch. I tugged off the blue gloves to inspect my palms. The skin was a mottled pink but free of welts. I wasn't ready to celebrate just yet. It could be a fluke event.

The next night, I chopped without gloves. The carrots, which had been stored at the back of the refrigerator, were covered in a thin layer of ice. Again, my hands turned pink, but they didn't itch. No welts!

Was this really happening?

I threw open the freezer and grabbed a bag of frozen vegetables, pressing my palms into the cold bulk. My hands went numb, but no welts formed. "Look, Sara! Look, Micah! Mama can touch frozen vegetables!"

They scurried into the kitchen. Micah stared at my pink palms, wide eyed. "Wow, Mama!"

"Yay!" Sara cheered. She might not understand the significance, but she liked my excitement.

I handed Micah my iPod. "Hey bud, would you film a video for me? I think everyone who has been praying for me would like to know that my hands are healed."

"Yeah!" His dimple came out of hiding. It only appeared for extra-delighted grins.

"Okay! Here we go!"

Laughing, we recorded a video to announce the demise of this extraordinarily irritating symptom.

"Mama!" Micah said. "God's healing you!"

"Yes, bud. He is." And my children, who had born the weight of this illness as much as anyone, were witnessing it. Hallelujah!

I posted the video to Facebook so that my friends, family, and the world would know. Jesus still heals.

* * *

To have my hands healed the week of Thanksgiving compounded the gratitude and joy I always felt around the holiday. Thanksgiving morning, I shouted, danced, clapped, and sang along to my favorite worship choruses while I cooked. Brandon and I laughed remembering how Sara had prayed the night before the session that I would be able to "handle da cold," and here I was literally handling the cold less than a week later.

Though this particular symptom wasn't life threatening or terribly debilitating, in the healing of it, I felt God say, "I see you, and I care about your discomfort as you serve your family and go about your daily work."

I told everyone I saw what God had done for me and couldn't wait for the temperatures to drop below forty degrees again so that I could test my tolerance to the cold outside. Unfortunately, we lived in Louisiana, which meant we could be wearing shorts through Christmas. In the waiting, I rejoiced in the fact that I no longer suffered from chronic fever, interstitial cystitis, or insomnia—even after sex, a very real miracle I didn't feel inclined to share on Facebook.

The morning of December 3, Brandon poked me in the ribs. "Hey," he whispered.

I opened one eye. It was still dark outside. Groaning, I rolled onto my other side.

"Hey," he whispered again. "The forecast was right."

Why was he talking to me about the forecast before the sun was awake?

"It's thirty-seven degrees right now, but it won't stay that way for long."

My eyes popped open. This was my chance!

Within a few minutes, I stood outside in the predawn cold without a coat. Shivers racked my body, but my mind remained clear. Ten minutes passed. Nothing happened. Again, I pulled out my iPod and filmed a video to document the moment.

A sharp pang stabbed my chest. Jenny would have loved this.

Had things worked out as we'd hoped, I would have called her. Right then. She would have been as over the moon as I was. We would've planned that celebration we'd talked about.

Many rejoiced with me. Some remained silent. Brandon fell somewhere in between. He shared my happiness but held back, as if he expected the healing to be taken away. I didn't blame him. It had happened before, and he hadn't been there when Jesus touched me. Only I knew the power of that touch.

Time alone would tell, and I had the feeling God wasn't finished yet.

* * *

Brandon parked across the street from the Thomases' home as the clock rolled to 3:00 p.m., right on time for the celebration. Another car stopped behind us. "I've been waiting six years for this!" I said, clapping my hands.

Six years ago, my friend Audrey Thomas had asked me to attend a Beth Moore event with her. During worship, I was filled with a knowing she would one day be a mother and that God wanted me to tell her so. The message scared me. I'd never shared anything of that nature with anyone. If I was wrong, I could hurt my friend. She'd been praying to be a mother for years. My heart almost leaped from my chest before I obeyed.

I'd grabbed her shoulder, locked eyes with her, and said, "I don't know when, and I don't know how, but you're going to be a mother."

Months ago, she and her husband had adopted a newborn baby girl. Today, we celebrated a long-awaited answer to prayer. The healing I'd experienced, however small, had given Brandon enough confidence to escort me to the come-and-go event.

"We'll go at the beginning before the crowds arrive," he'd said.

Halfway across the empty street, I stopped. Brandon cocked his brow at me in question.

"Would you be okay if I tried this without my mask?" It was only fair to ask. If I reacted, he'd be the one taking care of me.

He worked his jaw, considering. "Yeah. But the minute you feel a reaction coming, you put it on."

"Deal," I said.

Audrey greeted us at the door with a wide smile and a beautiful baby girl on her hip. "No mask?" she asked, her eyes wide.

"Since there's just a few of us, I think I'd like to try it." I grinned at the baby. "Hello there. You don't know this, but I've been waiting six years to meet you. I'm so glad you're here."

Audrey wrapped her arm around my shoulders. "Thank you for coming. I put the dog in my bedroom, so that will be one less thing you need to worry about."

Her perfume didn't bother me, even when it soaked into my shirt. Inside, two fragrant candles burned. An attractive array of snacks spread across the bar. I muscle tested the air to be safe. No peanuts.

Others joined the party as the afternoon progressed. Brandon checked on me occasionally. Each time, I whispered, "Still good." Even when the house filled up, I felt fine. Several friends we hadn't seen in a while stared in awe of my maskless face. I answered their expressions with a sly wink.

A sense of déjà vu prodded my mind. I was at a party, a celebration of a promise fulfilled. Children weaved between bodies, furniture, and legs. People ate and laughed. Fragrances abounded. But this wasn't my memory.

Friends had dreamed this scene more than two years ago. Those two years had stretched into two lifetimes, and I'd almost forgotten. The days had seemed so monotonous, yet so much had happened—big decisions, near-death experiences, Jenny's passing, a diagnosis, hardship, loss, joy, waiting, exquisite suffering, a novel, a perilous search for community, a touch from Jesus—and here we were.

Gratitude sprang hot into my eyes and trickled down my

face. For once, I didn't care who saw. There would be no hiding anymore. God had been too good to me.

In the car, I said, "So can I try church tomorrow without my mask?"

Brandon clutched his breast. When he didn't say no, I heard yes.

* * *

You have not because you ask not.

The words whispered through my spirit as I read the email confirming my tickets to a gala benefiting a local sex-trafficking ministry. As the new intercessory team leader of the ministry, I wanted to attend now that I was well enough to do so. Brandon and I had decided to purchase a table with our moms although we knew we couldn't eat the catered meal, which was sure to be chock full of dairy, gluten, soy, and God only knew what else.

You have not because you ask not, the voice repeated.

If God was saying what I thought he was saying, the reason I hadn't been able to expand my diet was that I hadn't asked him to heal my food allergies. One thing I was learning about the Lord was that he wanted more for me than I wanted for myself, and he wanted me to want it too.

Staring at the screen, I drew in a long, slow breath. "Okay, God. May I please eat the food served at the gala?"

A sense of approval washed over me.

Mom took me shopping at a local boutique to find a white dress. We purchased a fitted above-the-knee number with a white blazer. Hannah cut my "I give up" veil of thick dark waves and styled it into a short and sassy new do. The night of the gala, I wore heels and red lipstick and felt beautiful for the first time in five years. When the food was served, I ate everything on my plate and even enjoyed a cup of coffee with my cheesecake, though I avoided the crust.

The food wasn't anything to shout about. The meals I cooked at home tasted far better. But I ate without an immediate reaction. That was the wonder. The expected stomachache didn't follow.

As he helped me hobble back to the truck in my ridiculous heels, Brandon shook his head. "A month ago, I could eat twice as much as you. Now I'm watching you eat cheesecake in front of me. It's like you're bulletproof."

He opened the door for me. I climbed into the truck and immediately pulled off the expensive little instruments of torture. "You sound mad," I said, rubbing my feet.

"More like jealous," he admitted.

"Who knows? God may have given me a free pass for the night. Either way, why not just be happy for me?"

He didn't answer and remained silent for the rest of the night.

A few weeks ago, Tim had told me that God wouldn't heal me all at once because everyone around me had to adjust as I improved. "Brandon has the biggest adjustment ahead," he'd said. "Be patient with him."

It hurt that Brandon couldn't fully rejoice with me, but I gave the situation to God and looked toward the next thing.

The following Saturday, the women in Dad's family would throw a bridal luncheon to celebrate our cousin's bride-to-be. When I first received the invitation, I hadn't considered going. Healing hadn't yet begun. But I'd done so well at the gala that I decided to attend. I hadn't seen most of Dad's side of the family for years.

On the drive to the luncheon, I felt a gentle pressure in my spirit.

You haven't asked to eat the food.

A failed experiment with oatmeal that week had led me to believe my experience at the gala had been a one-time event. "Okay. May I eat the food today?"

No answer or assurance came. I didn't know what to make of it.

When I arrived, everyone was crowded in the dining room of a local chef and caterer who had a reputation for excellent fresh cuisine. I introduced myself to my cousin's fiancé, thankful there was no mask to hide my smile, and hugged cousins I hadn't seen since before Sara was born. Their quirky humor and quick laughter reminded me of all I'd missed.

We all took our seats, and a gorgeous green salad was placed before me. "Why not?" I asked the salad.

The bright flavor of tomatoes burst on my palate. The nuts and onion perfectly balanced the sweetness of the vinaigrette. If it was the only thing I ate that meal, I would be satisfied.

But the roasted chicken smothered in a tomato-cream sauce, served over what looked like rice, was too enticing to resist. One bite bespoke my mistake. The grain was too chewy to be rice. I took another bite and asked my cousin across the table, "What is this that looks like rice?"

"Orzo, I think. It's pasta," she said.

I glanced at Mom wide eyed. Not even at the gala had I attempted wheat. My tongue didn't tingle or itch, though, so I ate as much of the dish as I wanted. When the lunch dishes were cleared away, a waiter placed a slice of cheesecake topped with caramel sauce in front of me.

I took a hesitant bite and giggled. The cheesecake was the best thing I'd tasted in over a decade. I took another bite and laughed out loud. "Oh my gosh," I whispered, covering my mouth. "That is so good."

Mom chuckled at my side. Soon, we were both overcome, laughing and crying over that decadent dessert. I tried to reel myself in—I really did. We were at a bridal shower, for heaven's sake, and I was having my own little moment. But it was for heaven's sake that I laughed.

And laughed and laughed and laughed.

40

Cake

Afternoon sun poured through the window, warming and brightening our white cotton sheets. After an intense week of managing my responsibilities at home, meetings, and prayer ministry training, my body was struggling to keep up with my new schedule. Though I could go anywhere and eat almost anything I wanted, I had physical limits. Fatigue and discomfort often reminded me I was still healing. After church, Brandon had suggested we cuddle and nap.

Lacing my fingers through his, I looked into his soft brown eyes. "Why did you stay?"

He blinked at me.

"Be honest," I said. "Was it for the kids? Because divorce is expensive? Because it was the right thing to do?"

He tucked a wayward lock of hair behind my ear and looked past me, lost in thought. "Leaving never crossed my mind. Preparing for your death—that was the hard part."

A shadow passed through his eyes. "There was this one Sunday. You weren't doing well. I remember sitting in church looking around and wondering if there was a single woman there willing to help me raise kids who weren't theirs."

"But why?" I pressed to know the reason.

His gaze locked with mine. "Well, I made promises in front of a room full of people. To you. To God. That's kind of a big deal. And besides"—the corner of his mouth twitched—"I like you a little bit."

I rolled over onto my back. "I don't think you realize how amazing you are."

"How do you mean?"

"Any other man would have left," I said. "That's all."

"I'm not like any other man you've met."

"Apparently."

He propped himself on his elbow. "Besides, if I'd left, I would've missed this part." He kissed me deeply.

Most people didn't know what to do with this part. While several friends had said they were ecstatic for me, others were clearly uncomfortable with how my healing had happened. Some cited individuals in the Ruston prayer group as the problem. Others took issue with the loose association between our ministry and Bethel Church's Sozo ministry. My church was completely silent about my healing, though I knew they knew about it. Many in the mast cell disease groups on Facebook had become seriously angry when I posted a link to my healing story on the page. I was attacked and blocked from the group when I posted their comments to my blog and answered each one as kindly and biblically as I knew how.

At a Sunday night meeting, someone mentioned to Tim what had happened to me. A wry smile unveiled his dimple. He turned to me and said, "Remember, the Pharisees wanted to kill Lazarus after Jesus resurrected him. Don't be surprised when your healing messes with people's demons and wounds."

Only my inner circle could fully rejoice with me. Only they knew the depths of Sheol to which I'd descended. My friend Melissa rejoiced with me and reported how a local doctor had discovered she had Lyme disease. Now that she was receiving the proper treatment, her physical and mental health had improved tremendously. Sara celebrated each improvement and adventure out of the house. My parents grinned at every experiment that tested the limits of my healing. Debbie laughed a lot. Carolyne just shook her head in wonder.

"God has finally heard our prayers!" Micah exclaimed one day. When I told him I could pick him up from school again, a wide gap-toothed smile spread across his face, and a fat tear trailed down the side of his freckled nose. "You made me cry happy, Mama," he said.

I cried happy too.

My children were witnesses of God's goodness and healing power. As far as they were concerned, there was nothing God couldn't do.

* * *

One Saturday afternoon in May, a woman drove half an hour to my home to receive prayer, an increasingly regular occurrence that was no longer a hassle for anyone as I didn't have to ask them to leave off perfume and hairspray and air out their clothes beforehand. Micah and Sara, having become used to these visits, each scattered to a preferred location and activity—Micah to his room to play with his extensive Hot Wheels collection and Sara to the kitchen table to color, listen in on the conversation, and join the prayer when she wanted.

After prayer, I shared the story of how God had healed me. "I can go anywhere I want now and eat just about everything," I said.

"Wow," the woman said. "That's amazing!"

A qualification was needed. "Except peanuts. I'm still a little scared of peanuts."

Four-year-old Sara dropped her crayon and spun on the bench to face me. "Why are you scared of peanuts, Mama? Dey're just peanuts, and Jesus healed you. You should go over to Gramma and Pops' house and eat some. I don't understand why you're scared. You're not scared of anything."

The woman turned to me with wide eyes and a dropped jaw. My expression likely mirrored hers. "Well, maybe I will," I heard myself say.

But first, I needed to address the trauma of almost dying from a peanut exposure—twice.

As I lay in bed that night, I recalled the first reaction. For me, it had been the more frightening of the two. "Where were you?" I whispered to Jesus.

He appeared in the memory, kneeling at Brandon's side, his hand on Brandon's shoulder. I smiled. I knew he'd been there.

"What lie do I believe about this situation?"

Jesus said nothing.

"What truth do I need to know?"

Jesus remained quiet, but a friendly smirk shifted his expression. He handed me a jar of peanut butter.

The next day the kids weren't home, which was good. I preferred they not be present for this experiment in case anything went wrong, mostly for Sara's sake. Leaving my Acute Rescue homeopathic at home, I crossed the yard, my iPod in hand. Without knocking, I pushed open Mom and Dad's front door. Mom stood at the kitchen island chopping vegetables.

"Got any peanut butter?" I asked.

The knife went still in her hand. I explained myself, and she pointed the tip of the blade toward the pantry. Her brow lifted as high as I'd ever seen it when I handed her my iPod and said, "Be ready to push the record button."

I dug a spoon out of the drawer and opened the pantry door. Inside was the exact jar of peanut butter Jesus had offered me during prayer last night. Scraping the bottom and the sides, I gathered enough peanut butter for a single spoonful. I sniffed. Nothing happened.

"Let's do this."

"Okay," she said and pressed the record button.

Looking into the camera, I said, "Sara, this is for you. Do the thing that scares you, right?"

I shoved the entire spoonful into my mouth, scraping the spoon clean with my lips.

Mom smiled. "Is it still good?"

"It's still very good," I mumbled through a mouthful of sticky, salty sweetness. A moment passed. "Well," I said. "I'm not reacting or dying. I think I'm gonna be okay."

Mom laughed.

* * *

Everyone standing at ground zero of the miracle was changed. Brandon was the first to have a prayer session after me. My sister and parents followed. Their sessions marked them as much as mine had marked me. None of us would ever be the same.

By June 3, 2016, almost all of my mast cell symptoms had disappeared. For my birthday, Mom made me a childhood favorite—honeybun cake. Brandon, Micah, Sara, and my parents gathered around the table with full bellies and glad hearts. I took in Sara's bright eyes and Micah's expectant smile. Mom and Dad laughed at something Sara said. Brandon's gaze smoldered into mine with the remnants of the fire we'd just walked through together.

Truly, God had been too good to us.

Everyone sang "Happy Birthday." My heart overflowing with gratitude, I blew out the candles. Then, surrounded by those who had witnessed it all, I realized God and Erica had been right. I had my cake—and ate it too.

Afterword

Almost six years have passed since I experienced the prayer session that changed my life, and there is still no trace of mast cell activation disease at work in my body. Seasonal allergies continue to plague me, and I've been seeing a rheumatologist from Dr. Broadwell's practice for three years for joint stiffness and discomfort. She tells me I have some kind of autoimmune arthritis. She recently discovered joint erosion in my left hand, advancing my state of disease from mild to moderate. There has been no diagnosis, but I imagine one is forthcoming. Fortunately, I know the God who heals me and the God who sustains me. I will wait upon him.

Micah and Sara are now twelve and nine, respectively, and are as thick as thieves, though as far as I know the only thing they've stolen is a few hearts. When a soul is tried by fire with another, they are welded together in a permanent way. Their relationship is one of the many good things that came out of that difficult season. I've been able to homeschool them for the last four years, and it's been one of the most fulfilling things I've ever done. Micah returned to Geneva Academy in August 2021, where he began his education. Sara will likely follow after another year at home.

Brandon and I will adopt Abigail, a baby girl we have fostered since she was born, as soon as we receive a court date. She is sweet and spicy, powerful, and always on a mission—the zesty firebrand we didn't know we needed. Experiencing her toddlerhood as a healthy mom tastes like redemption. Brandon and I plan to maintain our certification as foster parents until God releases us from that assignment. Our family may not be complete yet.

I've served as a prayer minister for over five years, ministering to countless individuals in private prayer sessions like mine. Mom and Dad minister with me and sometimes without me. From time to time, we call upon friends who helped to train me or who I've trained myself to partner with us. Brandon prefers a supportive role. Sometimes he keeps the kids, but he never fails to send me off with a kiss and a "Have fun storming the castle!" We've seen God deliver and heal time and again. It never gets old. People come from all over—from out of state and from all over the world—to encounter Jesus out here on Jubilee Farm.

We are still in relationship with our friends from the Ruston prayer group. Bruce and Pamela Siegmund remain our closest friends. That group revolutionized my family's walk with the Lord. We owe them all a debt we can never repay, particularly to Tim Everding.

Caroline Lunger's health journey had only begun in 2014, but she has significantly improved after surgery and proper treatment. She is now a happily married young woman.

The discovery of Lyme disease was pivotal for my friend Melissa. She is now back in the classroom at the school her children attend and serves as an ambassador for The Voice of the Martyrs. Her husband Michael took the rough plans Brandon drew for our home and turned them into blueprints. The foundation was poured in January 2020. We moved out of our little trailer in October of that year. The living area was designed with the Toledo Bend lake house in mind. As Jenny said, the space is perfect for hanging out, and it reminds me of her often.

Brandon and I are doing well. Our marriage isn't perfect, especially when we're building a house, when no one sleeps because the baby cries all night, or when I wait too long to start taking an antidepressant, but we are both committed to the end, whenever that might be. We aim, in some limited way, to reflect the glorious relationship between Christ and his Church and to point others to the ultimate Bridegroom.

Though I was fully healed of mast cell disease by May 2016, God has continued healing me from the inside out. During my prayer session, God delivered me from my lifelong struggle with sexual sin. Thank God—that battle is finished. Anger no longer swallows me whole. These days, I'm fully aware of the choice of whether to give in. In 2017, he radically healed the wounds of childhood sexual abuse. A year later, he delivered me from my addiction to people pleasing. Life is full and sometimes my load is heavy, but I am now secure in God's love. Whatever situation I find myself in, I know that God loves me, he is with me, and he is working things together for good.

I no longer fear death. Part of me looks forward to it. I know now that death isn't scary, and on the other side lies everything I've lived for in this life. But I still have a few things to do before I head home. Until then, I want as much of God as I can have on this side of eternity. I intend to lay up as much treasure in heaven as possible and bring in a harvest so formidable that the enemy will regret ever laying a finger on me. I will conquer by the blood of the Lamb and the word of my testimony. I pray you will too.

If this book has led you to hunger for a relationship with

Christ, that is the Holy Spirit's work in you. Confess and forsake your sin. Declare your need for Jesus. Follow and obey him. Join his family—the Church—by committing yourself to a group of believers. Be baptized. Pray for grace, and ask the Holy Spirit to fill you and to teach you to walk in step with him. Here is a prayer you can speak aloud:

Heavenly Father, thank you for loving me and sending Jesus into the world to die on the cross and rise again to save me from my sins. I confess that I am a sinner, that I've fallen short of your standard, and that the only way to have a relationship with you is through the work and person of Jesus Christ, your Son. I am guilty of sin, and I have broken all of your laws. Please forgive me and cleanse me from all my sins with the blood of Jesus. I give myself over to his authority and leadership. I declare that he is Lord of my life. Please fill me with your Holy Spirit that I may be able to walk in your ways. Lead me to the church you want me to join. I love you. Thank you for making a way home to you. Amen.

If you are in need of healing of any kind, pray this prayer:

Heavenly Father, you have revealed yourself as the God who heals. Jesus himself is healing. He never turned away anyone who came to him for healing. Fill me with the Spirit of your Son until there is no room for self, sin, brokenness, darkness, or disease. Have your perfect way in me. Make me whole and holy. I receive every good thing you want to give me. Reveal any sin or hindrance to healing in my life. I entrust my health, my heart, my wounds, my sin, and everything I am to you. Thank you for your atoning work on the cross. I am yours, body and soul. May your will be done in me as it is in heaven. I trust your heart and surrender to your process and timing. Amen.

"May the God of hope fill you with all joy and peace in believing, so that by the power of the Holy Spirit you may abound in hope" (Romans 15:13).

Acknowledgments

Before *The Road to Jubilee* is my story, it's God's story. He is the master author of every story of hope, faith, and redemption. God crafted the plot, characters, and themes. He delivered the miracle. I simply kept a record through journals, photos, and blog posts and finally typed out a consumable version. To God be the glory.

I don't claim to understand how prayer works, but I am convinced that this story would have had a different ending if not for the intercession of the saints. My deepest gratitude goes to my army of prayer warriors, too numerous to count. You co-labored with the Spirit for this outcome. May God richly bless each and every one of you, especially my sweet Micah and precious Sara.

This book wouldn't have been possible without my husband's support. Brandon encouraged me to keep writing when life was crazy, cared for the kids several times so I could work during the day, invested his time and money in the project, and lived the entire adventure with me. A simple "thank you" doesn't seem enough, but all the same—thanks, Babe. Thanks also to Micah, Sara, Abigail, and our exchange student / Italian daughter, Aurora, who bore my absences so patiently during the months of May and June.

My editor, Stephanie Chou, is a gift, not only to me and this book but to the body of Christ. During her own season of loss and trial, she has clung to the Resurrection and the Life. The light inside her shines in the darkness, bright and true, and gives her eyes of faith to embrace all that God has for her today as she hopes for what he's promised tomorrow. She caught the vision of the story, entered into suffering that wasn't her own, and has prepared this manuscript to be released into the world. Her insight and expertise have removed the stumbling blocks and doubled the impact. I love and admire you, Steph. You are amazing.

Thanks to my incredible team of beta readers—Brandon, Mom, Nona, Carolyne, Bruce, Eddie, Ashley, Meghan, Sherri, Renee, and Jennifer—who helped me trim the fat and clarify the details. Thanks also to Heather Trim, my award-winning author friend, who took time out of her busy schedule to read the manuscript and provide feedback and a quote that let me know I had accomplished my mission.

My beautiful cover was designed by my friend and fellow Classical Conversations homeschool mom, Rachel Rosales. Not only can she design a stunning cover, she's wonderful to work with too. I'm blessed to be in community with such a godly, gifted woman who also bakes the most slammin' chocolate chip cookies I've tasted to date. You can check out more of her work and find out how to hire her at www.orangepealdesign.com.

This book was formatted by Rajeswari Bevara, who formatted the e-book for my fantasy novel, *Eleora*. She is both skilled and efficient, which are qualities I appreciate. Thank you, Rajeswari, for another beautiful job.

Finally, I would be remiss if I failed to mention my spiritual father, Steve Wilson, who delivered a word to me in

April 2021 that mysteriously gave me the necessary umph to make the final push to complete this project. I wasn't doing all that great physically or emotionally at the time. I was worn out from much serving and hadn't touched the book in a year and a half. But after that word, I was somehow able to finish. Thank you, Papa Steve. I love you and Sally so much and rejoice in your recent victory in the Lord.